RUSSIA
after
the
FALL

Russian and Eurasian Books
from the Carnegie Endowment for International Peace

Belarus at the Crossroads
Sherman W. Garnett and Robert Legvold, Editors

The End of Eurasia: Russia on the Border between
Geopolitics and Globalization
Dmitri Trenin

Gorbachev, Yeltsin, and Putin: Political Leadership in Russia's Transition
Archie Brown and Lilia Shevtsova, Editors

Kazakhstan: Unfulfilled Promise
Martha Brill Olcott

Rapprochement or Rivalry? Russia-China Relations in a Changing Asia
Sherman W. Garnett, Editor

Russia after Communism
Anders Åslund and Martha Brill Olcott, Editors

Russia's Decline and Uncertain Recovery
Thomas E. Graham, Jr.

U.S.-Russian Relations at the Turn of the Century
*Reports of the Working Groups organized by the Carnegie Endowment for
International Peace and the Council on Foreign and Defense Policy*

Yeltsin's Russia: Myths and Reality
Lilia Shevtsova

To read excerpts and find more information on these and other publications visit
www.ceip.org/pubs

RUSSIA
after
the
FALL

Andrew C. Kuchins, Editor

CARNEGIE ENDOWMENT FOR INTERNATIONAL PEACE
Washington, D.C.

Carnegie Endowment for International Peace
1779 Massachusetts Avenue, N.W., Washington, D.C. 20036
202-483-7600   www.ceip.org

The Carnegie Endowment normally does not take institutional positions on public policy issues; the views and recommendations presented in this publication do not necessarily represent the views of the Carnegie Endowment, its officers, staff, or trustees.

To order, contact Carnegie's distributor:
The Brookings Institution Press
Department 029, Washington, D.C. 20042-0029, USA
1-800-275-1447 or 1-202-797-6258

Composition by Oakland Street Publishing. Text set in ITC Berkeley.
Printed by Jarboe Printing, Washington, D.C., on acid-free paper (20% recycled) with soy inks.

Library of Congress Cataloging-in-Publication Data

Russia after the fall / Andrew C. Kuchins, editor.
    p. cm.
Includes bibliographical references and index.
   ISBN 0-87003-197-X (cloth : alk. paper) -- ISBN 0-87003-198-8 (pbk. : alk. paper)
   1. Russia (Federation)--Politics and government--1991- 2. Russia (Federation)--Foreign relations--1991- I. Kuchins, Andrew.
  DK510.763 .R8573 2002
   947.086--dc21
                                                                    2002011905

9 8 7 6 5 4 3 2 1

Contents

Part Three. Russian Society

Part Four. Foreign and Security Policy Challenges

Conclusion

Foreword

Almost immediately after the collapse of the Soviet Union, Western analysts plunged into debates over the progress of Russia's transition away from communism. These arguments continued and intensified across the 1990s. Optimists hailed Russia's advances toward democracy and market economics, arguing that the basics were falling into place. Skeptics bemoaned what they saw as a chaotic disintegration of Russian society, charging the optimists with self-delusion or worse. The contending views permeated both U.S. policy and academic circles, provoking not just spirited exchanges but angry divisions.

Throughout these years and up to the present day, Russian realities fueled those debates by lingering in a halfway state between success and failure. Russia has achieved substantial features of liberal democracy and well-functioning capitalism, yet remains saddled in both the political and economic domains with substantial shortcomings. Russian foreign policy, too, has often hesitated between a true embrace of the West and the desire to continue with Russian exceptionalism. At every moment when it seemed a definitive judgment could finally be made, a surprise turned out to be in store, whether it was the financial collapse of 1998, the sudden rise to power of Vladimir Putin, or the huge effects of September 11 on U.S.–Russian relations.

Although the past decade was only the beginning of a long-term historic transformation of Russian society, enough time has passed since 1991 to merit a searching assessment. This volume is a collection of such essays, by an all-star group of American, Russian, and West European experts. Rather than seeking consensus, the editor, Carnegie's Andrew Kuchins, purposely sought out strong views that represent a wide spectrum of opinion. He asked each contributor to put his or her conclusions forward in a direct, accessible way and to put past events in a broad perspective.

The result is a captivating account of what Russia is today, as well as where it has been and where it is going. The quality, diversity, and insight of the chapters, as well as the remarkable range of subjects covered, embody the approach that Carnegie's Russian and Eurasian Program has brought to the subject ever since the collapse of the Soviet Union. We do not expect this book to end the debate over Russia's transition, but we do believe that it sheds considerable light on one of the most important turning points of our time. It will prove of great value to all those who care about Russia today and to tomorrow's historians.

Jessica T. Mathews
President
Carnegie Endowment for International Peace

Acknowledgments

The book in your hands results from the contributions and hard work of many people. It was part of a larger project of the Russian and Eurasian Program of the Carnegie Endowment to broadly assess the first post-Soviet decade of the Russian Federation. The Endowment organized and hosted on June 7–9, 2001, a major international conference entitled "Russia Ten Years After," held in Washington, D.C. The conference provided an excellent opportunity for the authors to present their arguments before an extraordinary group of experts, policy makers, and media.

My thanks go to Carnegie Russian and Eurasian Program staff Ann Stecker and Vilija Teel and Junior Fellows Victoria Levin, Erik Scott, and Elina Treyger for their assistance at the conference. Thanks also go to Dan Conway, Carmen MacDougall, Julie Shaw, and Rhonda Vandeworp for their support on the logistical and public relations efforts. I extend deep gratitude to Toula Papanicolas and especially Natalia Udalova Zwart, who led the planning and organizational efforts for what we aspired to make the best meeting marking the ten-year anniversary of the collapse of the Soviet Union. But the success of our efforts depended on the intellectual contributions of the conference participants, which were "off the charts," and I deeply thank all those who participated. Lest I be accused of idle hyperbole, a full account of the conference discussions can be found at www.ceip.org/russia10years.

The Carnegie publications team of Trish Reynolds and Sherry Pettie did a terrific job in professionally and expeditiously moving the manuscript from draft form to book. I am deeply appreciative to internal and external reviewers who provided a number of very useful substantive and organizational suggestions. Russian and Eurasian Program Associate Marc Fellman deserves special recognition for his tremendous support during all phases of production.

I would also like to thank my colleagues in the Russian and Eurasian Program in Washington—Anders Åslund, Rose Gottemoeller, Thomas Graham, Anatol Lieven, Michael McFaul, and Martha Brill Olcott—as well as Robert Nurick, Lilia Shevtsova, and Dmitri Trenin of the Carnegie Moscow Center for their advice and support in designing the conference and book project. My gratitude also goes to Carnegie Director of Development Cindy Sadler for her support in fundraising for the project. Special thanks go to the Endowment's remarkable senior management team of Executive Vice President Paul Balaran, Vice President for Studies Thomas Carothers, and President Jessica Mathews for their belief in the importance of the conference and the book and their advice and support all along the way.

Finally, and very importantly, I would like to take this opportunity to acknowledge the vision and the generosity of the funders whose support made the conference and this book possible. Thanks go the Boeing Corporation for its direct support of the conference and the book and to the Carnegie Corporation of New York, the Charles Stewart Mott Foundation, and the Starr Foundation for their general support to the Carnegie Moscow Center and the Russian and Eurasian Program.

Andrew C. Kuchins
Director
Russian and Eurasian Program

Introduction

Andrew C. Kuchins

For students of international relations, the collapse of the Soviet Union marked the most significant event of the second half of the twentieth century. The Cold War definitively ended, and the bipolar conflict between the United States and the Soviet Union no longer framed international politics as it had for more than forty years. The "long twilight struggle," as George Kennan termed the Cold War at its outset, was over, and although it has become politically incorrect to say so, one cannot deny that the West won. The Soviet edifice, including the East Central European allies, unraveled so quickly, however, that any euphoria felt by the West with the disappearance of its longtime adversary was mixed with feelings of shock and tinges of foreboding about possible anarchy in a vast territory armed with tens of thousands of nuclear weapons.

But for Russia there was no euphoria as 1991 drew to a close and the Soviet flag went down on the Kremlin for the last time. Democrats who had supported newly elected President Boris Yeltsin in his moment of historic and heroic defiance against the August 1991 coup plotters at the Russian parliament building had rightfully exulted, but the exultation was not widely shared outside Moscow and St. Petersburg. Most Russians were preoccupied with securing food and other goods as the Soviet economy collapsed, leaving shops perhaps more empty than at any time since World War II. Life would only get more difficult for the vast majority of Russians as price liberalization implemented in January 1992 eliminated the lifetime savings of millions of citizens virtually overnight. Goods returned shortly to stores, but ravaging inflation left prices beyond the means of most.

The Russian Federation embarked on the daunting path of simultaneously building a market democracy almost from scratch and developing a national identity and foreign policy for a country that, while still massive, was reduced to borders close to those of the Russian Empire of the seventeenth century. Russia, which for centuries in the Tsarist era was regarded as a great power and for the second half of the twentieth century as a superpower, found itself the recipient of humanitarian aid and a supplicant for large-scale economic and financial assistance. Violent conflicts flared along its periphery in Moldova, the Caucasus, and Central Asia (many of which Russia instigated and/or supported), and then in 1994 the Yeltsin administration disastrously attacked rebellious Chechnya, resulting in a civil war on Russian territory that it did not win. The central government's control over the Russian Federation dissipated to such an extent that many questioned the future viability of Russia.

In perhaps the most surreal moment of the last ten years in Russia, the Yeltsin government ordered the bombing of the parliament building, the Russian White House, in October 1993 to oust rebel legislators, many of whom had been former allies of Yeltsin, including Speaker Ruslan Khasbulatov. Russia teetered on the brink of civil war as the army carefully deliberated whether to follow the order of the president, which it did with much trepidation. The bombed-out, smoking hulk of the parliament, which only two years earlier had symbolized the victory of Russian democracy, tragically testified to the enormous difficulties of transforming Russia into a "normal" country. The subsequent victory of the fascist buffoon Vladimir Zhirinovsky and his misnamed Liberal Democratic Party in the December 1993 parliamentary elections marked a low point in a decade littered with low points for beleaguered Russians.

On the evening of those parliamentary elections, I recall being at the headquarters of a truly liberal democratic party, Russia's Choice—which was led by former acting prime minister Yegor Gaidar—as the early returns came in from the Russian Far East showing the strong performance of Zhirinovsky as well as the Communists. The festive atmosphere of the early evening dissolved into despondence as the scale of the electoral defeat for Russia's Choice became clear. The planned television broadcast of a huge party for Russia's Choice was cancelled when it was evident there was nothing to celebrate. Oddly, it seemed as though many that night did not see the electoral defeat coming, but I wondered how they could not, given the social, economic, and political trauma of the previous two years.

After the elections of 1993, the first shots were fired in the United States and the West of a "Who Lost Russia?" debate, echoing the vituperative "Who Lost China?" debate after the victory of the Chinese communists in 1949. The Clinton administration and the International Monetary Fund received most of the criticism either for not doing enough to support the Russian transformation or for intervening too much with advice supposedly inappropriate for Russia. The voices of doubters about the eventual success of Russia's efforts to become a market democracy became louder, and some of the optimists more carefully calibrated their positions. It was not entirely coincidental that the idea for expanding the North Atlantic Treaty Organization (NATO) began to generate more momentum within the Clinton administration and in some Western European quarters in 1994 as Russian realities darkened. The Clinton team, led by then national security advisor Anthony Lake, couched NATO expansion in the broader policy framework of enlargement of the community of market democratic nations in Europe, but the policy also conveniently served for many as a hedge against things going badly in Russia.

Perceptions of Russia hit rock bottom with the financial crisis of August 1998 when Russian economic progress was seemingly exposed as a chimera (in 1997 the Russian stock market had outperformed all other emerging markets). The prevailing discourse about Russia in both scholarly as well as media commentary increasingly emphasized the weakness and endemic corruption of the Russian state as a different kind of threat than the powerful Soviet Union of Cold War days. Official statistics indicated that the country had lost half of its GDP in less than a decade—a staggering collapse, if true, that made the Great Depression in the United States look like a pinprick. A demographic crisis of epic proportions loomed as the death rate, especially for working-age Russian men, far outstripped the birthrate. Another nasty war in Chechnya erupted in the fall of 1999, and the Russian military distinguished itself primarily for human rights violations. Legendary bluesman Albert King lamented in his song "Born Under a Bad Sign": "If it weren't for bad luck, I wouldn't have any luck at all"; for Russia it seemed that the only kind of news was bad news during the 1990s. When at the end of the millennium Boris Yeltsin unexpectedly resigned as president, his popularity ratings were in the single digits and his image badly damaged internationally.

The decade of the 1990s will likely be regarded historically as another *smutnoe vremya*, a "Time of Troubles," for Russia, akin to the original Time of Troubles at the end of the seventeenth century when Russia experienced extreme disorder after the long reign of Ivan the Terrible. The calamitous period of civil war and economic depression after the 1917 Bolshevik Revolution may also be regarded as such a dark moment in Russian history. But was it really unexpected that efforts to reform Russia and overcome the enormously debilitating legacy of more than seventy years of Soviet rule would involve massive dislocations and difficulties? Did anyone really think that achieving the goals of transforming Russia into a market democracy and integrating Russia more deeply into a rapidly globalizing international system would be easy? Was it not self-evident that life would initially become more difficult for the great majority of Russians and citizens of the Soviet Union before there would be a chance for improvement?

The answers to these questions are that nobody truly thought that Russia's transition, transformation, or whatever you want to call it would be easy, and it was implicitly assumed that things would get worse before they got better. Naturally the economic and social trauma of adjustment would bring serious and unfortunate political consequences for those in power and deemed responsible: the Yeltsin administration and, by guilt of association, the Western countries, leaders, and institutions perceived to be supporting Russia's policy course. Given the ponderous weight of the decades of bad policy decisions by the Soviet leadership, perhaps the more appropriate question is the one asked by Stephen Kotkin in his recent book *Armageddon Averted*: "Why weren't things worse?" Maybe we should be relieved that the most apocalyptic scenarios imagined and even predicted by many for Russia did not come to pass. There has been no nuclear conflict resulting from the disarray of the Soviet nuclear weapons complex. Russia did not break down into large-scale civil war. The Russian leadership did not seek to reestablish the Soviet empire by force.

Still, while avoiding the worst-case scenarios is obviously good, it is only a start in evaluating and reaching judgments, tentative as they may be, about what has happened in Russia in its first post-Soviet decade. Analyzing the political, economic, social, and foreign and security policy challenges for Russia of the past decade as well as charting the path ahead was the task for the authors of this volume. Reaching balanced conclusions on issues that have generated so much controversy both within and outside of Russia is particularly challenging because expectations of what was possible varied for many participants and observers of Russia's transformation. Analytical challenges are further complicated because the study of Russia has been deeply politicized. For example, although the future of Russia does not attract the same level of interest that the Soviet Union did during the Cold War, U.S. policy toward Russia was one of the only foreign policy issues that generated some debate during the 2000 U.S. presidential campaign as the Republicans sought to tar Al Gore for his association with Clinton administration Russia policy and his relationship with former Russian prime minister Viktor Chernomyrdin in particular.

It is not possible to cover the entire waterfront of the past ten years in Russia in a single volume. We have tried to describe the core features and some of the central debates of the past decade of Russian trials and transformation. The authors were not asked to write in an academic, heavily footnoted, monograph style; rather, we have requested thoughtful essays that will be both compelling to the specialist community and accessible to a broader audience. The volume is somewhat arbitrarily divided into four parts: (1) leadership; (2) economic development; (3) Russian society; and (4) foreign and security policy challenges. (The placement of Anatol Lieven's chapter on Chechnya into the final section of the book does not reflect any political statement on our part. Rather, it was placed there because Lieven's essay primarily addresses the foreign and security implications for Russia of these tragic wars.)

Leadership

The extraordinarily important role of leadership, from tsars to general secretaries to presidents, has long preoccupied students of historical and contemporary Russia. President Putin in effect acknowledged the validity of this preoccupation when he commented, "From the very beginning, Russia was created as a supercentralized state. That's practically laid down in its genetic code, its traditions, and the mentality of its people."[1] Although Russian presidents are now democratically elected—and democratically elected national and regional political figures as well as the judiciary provide some checks and balances to executive power—Russian political institutions such as political parties remain weak and underdeveloped. The 1993 constitution further strengthened presidential power in Russia. The focus on presidential power immediately brings us to two of the most controversial questions of the past ten years: What is the legacy of Boris Yeltsin, and what are the intentions of Vladimir Putin? And the second question may be appended by addressing what capacity Putin has to implement his intentions.

Boris Yeltsin was an oversized political personality during revolutionary times. Undoubtedly he had tremendous deficiencies as a political leader. He sporadically engaged in the day-to-day management of Russia, and his attention and behavior grew more erratic as his health declined during his tenure. While Yeltsin himself may not have personally benefited, his administration was thoroughly corrupt, and this damaged Russia's image. The decision to go to war in Chechnya was a colossal mistake. In his assessment in this volume, Michael McFaul argues that other key mistakes by Yeltsin included his failure to adopt a new constitution and call for new parliamentary elections immediately after the thwarted coup in 1991 and his failure to push economic reform more aggressively. Nevertheless, as McFaul notes, Yeltsin can point to some major achievements that include destroying the Communist Party of the Soviet Union, relatively peacefully dismantling the largest empire on earth, and introducing electoral democracy in a country with a thousand-year history of autocratic rule. He did not cancel presidential elections in the spring of 1996 even when his prospects looked very bleak and his closest advisors advised him to do so. At the end of his second term, he willfully stepped down and was succeeded according to the provisions of the Russian constitution.

It is nearly impossible to overestimate the degree of difficulty of the task Yeltsin faced. He inherited a devastated economy, a political system in total disarray, and a state with brand new borders. He needed to undertake a trifecta transformation: build a market economy where almost no market institutions existed, establish a democratic polity in a country with a thousand-year autocratic tradition, and develop a foreign policy identity and orientation for a nation that had only existed in modern history as an empire. There was no elite consensus on how to proceed on any of these tasks. To further complicate matters, as McFaul notes, while the Soviet regime collapsed in 1991, many constituent elements of the old system remained in place to block reform efforts. It is perhaps understandable that the leader facing these Herculean tasks would often disappear from the public for long stretches since the job was so overwhelming.

Thomas Graham assesses the Yeltsin period far more critically than McFaul by arguing that the fragmentation, degeneration, and erosion of state power during the 1990s brought Russia to the verge of state failure, and that these "processes had their roots in the late Soviet period, but they accelerated in the post-Soviet period as a consequence of Yeltsin's policies and Western advice." Part of the problem stems from the emergence of an independent Russia as a historical accident, a by-product of the power struggle between Yeltsin and Gorbachev. The denouement of this power struggle was accompanied by a massive extortion of state property by greedy insiders. The Yeltsin regime became closely tied to, even dependent on, a few oligarchs who controlled massive and in many cases ill-begotten assets. They were most noteworthy for corruption, asset stripping as opposed to wealth creation, and their cavalier disregard for social welfare. In cahoots with the Yeltsin regime, these "clans" drove Russia spiraling into socioeconomic decline. The Russian military was, of course, not exempted as conditions and morale were allowed to deteriorate to appalling conditions.

Not only was the authority of the central government tremendously weakened, but its ties with regional governments eroded. The regional governments of Russia suffered from many of the same maladies as the central government because corruption was endemic throughout. While the Soviet regime was characterized by a strong central government, the nascent Russian regime was noteworthy for its weak center and weak regions. Political power had fragmented to such an extent that on taking power Putin acknowledged that the future viability of the Russian state was threatened.

On the domestic front, at least two goals of Vladimir Putin seem clear: to restore the authority of the Russian state and to set the Russian economy on a path of long-term, sustainable growth. Both of these goals are central to Putin's efforts to restore Russia's power and influence in the world. Pursuant to the first goal, to restore the "vertical of power," as the Russians put it, Putin has taken a variety of measures to reduce the influence of all sources of power outside the presidency, including regional governors, oligarchs, political parties, the Duma, independent media, and civil society. Lilia Shevtsova asserts that the Russian president has succeeded to the extent that politics have nearly vanished and quotes a Kremlin insider who states his satisfaction that politics have "become rather boring." The ideological struggles that colored the 1990s have been replaced with a steely-eyed pragmatism that suggests that Deng Xiaoping's famous maxim—that it does not matter whether a cat is black or white but whether it catches mice—may be quite apt for Putin as well.

Putin has benefited from Russia's stronger economic performance in the past two years as well as by his image as a vigorous, take-charge, and capable leader, a sharp contrast to his feeble and less engaged predecessor. Consequently his popularity ratings have been consistently high, and by one poll he was even named the sexiest man in Russia. Certainly his allure in this regard is enhanced by his background as an espionage agent. As Shevtsova argues, Putin has carefully husbanded this resource but will need to risk his popularity to undertake further, more painful reforms ultimately required. In addition, if he continues to rule in a patrimonial style relying on cadres and personal relations, he will become increasingly liable to fall back into Yeltsin's style of rule that depended on a narrow circle of favorites and oligarchs. Indeed, his adherence to "imitation democracy" may ironically result not in a strong presidency but rather in merely the appearance of power.

Stephen Holmes accepts the premise that power has been deeply fragmented in Russia but suggests that this phenomenon has deep structural roots that cannot be explained only by Yeltsin's ineffective leadership. The greatest problem for Russia now is the huge gap between the massive challenges Russia faces and the state's resources to address them. This structural mismatch will not go away soon, and it raises serious questions about the ultimate effectiveness of Putin's consolidation of power. Power to do what? It is one thing for him to conduct a successful assault on Vladimir Gusinsky's media empire. Gusinsky was perhaps the easiest target of the so-called oligarchs because of his financial indebtedness, so this may not be a terrific test of presidential power. If Putin were able to cut down the arbitrary power of a much more deeply rooted and powerful institution like the Office of the Procuracy, that would be a convincing demonstration of power.

While what Holmes dubs the "school of hope" alleges that Putin is a liberal in authoritarian clothing and the "school of fear" believes the opposite, Holmes is firmly entrenched in the "school of doubt" about Putin's capacity to bring any fundamental change to how Russia is governed. The state resources at his disposal are too meager, and Russian society lacks adequate constituencies to support a rule-of-law system that protects property rights and brings greater predictability to state–society relations. If Putin continues to rely on security services as the key institution for the restoration of order in Russian society, this will obviously have a detrimental impact in establishing the rule of law and fostering confidence in the business community. Security services typically manipulate an atmosphere of uncertainty for purposes of intimidation and control. The rash of spy cases, political use of the tax inspectorate, and other extralegal methods of control have effectively intimidated Russian civil society to such an extent that in the view of many civil society leaders, a Brezhnev-like atmosphere is returning.

Neither Graham, Shevtsova, nor Holmes are particularly optimistic about where Putin's leadership is taking Russia. Holmes' assessment of Putin, however, is somewhat more forgiving because he places greater emphasis on the deep structural constraints facing the Russian president.

Economic Development

Russian economic policy has been hotly debated over the last ten years, as one would expect of an economy that according to official statistics has contracted by over 40 percent. Some of these debates are reflected in the three contributions in this section by Joel Hellman, Anders Åslund, and Clifford Gaddy. The most fundamental difference concerns the question of whether Russia is now on a path toward sustainable economic growth. Joel Hellman remains concerned that a weak legal system and enduring doubts about property rights and the propriety of privatization will constrain robust and equitable growth. Clifford Gaddy doubts Russia can maintain the high growth rates averaging about 5 percent since 1999 because structural reforms remain inadequate. Anders Åslund is most bullish on Russia and is confident that continuing reform efforts will fuel high growth rates in the years ahead.

The privatization of state property has been one of the most controversial issues in Russia for the last decade. Hellman suggests that the reformers may have been mistaken in their belief that once assets were privatized, the new owners would become a powerful constituency for a legal system that effectively guaranteed property rights. Another alternative exists, and it more aptly describes the unfolding economic conditions in Russia. As long as there is valuable property available for redistribution, the existing powerful owners may prefer to perpetuate the conditions that provide them advantages in the redistributive process, despite the adverse impact this may have on the value of their previously acquired property rights. Borrowing from Leon Trotsky's notion of "permanent revolution," Russia seems to be perpetuating a climate of "permanent redistribution."

This logic argues that powerful businesspeople and entrepreneurs will oppose the development of any institutions that may prevent them from being able to acquire valuable assets at below market prices. Rather than allocating resources to enhance the value of existing properties, the most successful and dynamic entrepreneurs make considerable investments in "capturing" politicians and bureaucrats who can assist in the acquisition of additional assets. The environment of permanent distribution in the Russian economy has encouraged asset stripping, theft, capital flight, low investment rates, barriers to market entry, and deterioration of Russian physical and human capital. It also helps explain the emergence of staggering differences in wealth distribution that make Russia one of the most unequal countries in the world in terms of the gap between the rich and the poor.

Anders Åslund challenges the conventional wisdom that the Russian economy contracted by nearly 50 percent during the 1990s, but even here it is a "good news, bad news" phenomenon. The good news is that the Russian economy has not declined that much; the bad news is that this is primarily due to a huge overestimation of the size of the Russian economy (and the Soviet economy before it) at the start of the decade. The overestimation of the size of the Soviet and Russian economies has many causes, but much of it boils down to deeply wasteful production of shoddy goods for which there was little demand in the first place. Regardless of your intellectual or ideological persuasions, anyone who traveled to the Soviet Union in the 1980s and spent time perusing the shops and department stores where normal citizens shopped knows there is validity to Åslund's argument. The Soviet economy was value detracting rather than value adding. His conclusion is that in 1991 Russia's economy was about the size of Brazil's, and ten years later it is still about the size of Brazil's.

Clifford Gaddy concurs that misallocation of resources was a monumental problem for the Soviet economy, but unfortunately it remains a hallmark of the Russian economy today. The Soviet Union simply built too many inefficient enterprises in places that made little or no economic sense. An innovative measurement of this misallocation may be measured in "thermal space," or people living and working in very cold places. In contrast to other industrial nations in cold climates, the Soviet Union's "per capita temperature" significantly declined over sixty years, and it has changed very little in the last ten, suggesting that Putin's assertions in the fall of 2001 that the Russian economy is "very dynamic" are spurious.

In his state of the union message for 2001, Putin established the goal of 7 to 8 percent annual growth for fifteen years for the Russian economy, a rate that would bring it to the per capita level of Portugal, one of the least well-off members of the European Union. This would, of course, be a tremendous achievement for Russia, especially if this wealth is more evenly distributed to a growing middle class. Gaddy is quite skeptical, however, about maintaining these growth rates in the near term. In his view, most of Russia's impressive economic growth beginning in 1999 can be almost entirely explained by high oil prices and the short-term effect of the 1998 devaluation. This is not to say that fundamentally more sound economic policies have not been implemented in the last two years. Some have, and they have resulted in greater technical efficiency, but they are inadequate to address the more fundamentally debilitating legacies of decades of misallocation or to support more than modest growth.

Russian Society

While one can debate the merits of Russia's efforts to reform its economy and the prospects for sustainable growth, there is no doubt that the last ten years have been traumatic for tens of millions of Russians as the Soviet socioeconomic safety net that guaranteed employment, health care, subsidized housing, and more has shredded under the stress of market reforms. As Judyth Twigg argues, the Soviet state's role in guaranteeing a basic level of material comfort and survival was an important source of legitimacy for the regime. The unprecedented poverty, material inequities, and pervasive insecurity have unanchored Russian society and damaged national identity.

Not surprisingly, women and children have been most deeply impoverished by changes that have resulted in many more broken families. The most powerful indicators of poverty during the last decade have been the birth of an extra child and the growing numbers of homeless children and social orphans. Low Russian birthrates reflect both financial insecurity and lack of confidence among many that their social and economic circumstances will improve. Alarming growth in alcoholism and drug addiction also reflects psychological despair and contributes to a public health crisis of catastrophic proportions. Rapid growth of infectious diseases, especially HIV/AIDS, poses further threats to an already shrinking and sickly Russian population. In his 2001 state of the union address, Putin rightly identified the demographic crisis as a major threat to Russia, but there is no indication that the Russian government and society have the vigor required to address some of these monumental problems. Twigg does point to a growing middle class that now comprises about 15 percent of the population. This would number the Russian middle class between 20 and 25 million, or the size of a medium European country.

In his chapter that addresses the impact of these human capital trends on Russian security, Harley Balzer notes not only that the current crisis results from imperial deconstruction and economic transition, but that its roots are deep and not easily reversible. But if current trends are not reversed, the human capital of Russia will be quantitatively and qualitatively less capable of securing Russia's place in the global economy. Migration has been looked on as one means of alleviating adverse demographic trends (including "brain drain"), but this policy will have to be managed very carefully to avoid explosive social tensions. Already it is probable that the two most rapidly rising populations in Russia in the coming decades will be Muslims and Asians (most likely Chinese).

Two of the Soviet Union's greatest achievements are the development of an educational system that brought high levels of literacy to nearly the entire population and the promotion of science and mathematics that were truly world class. The fate of the Soviet educational system and its strengths in science and technology reflect both the broader changes in Russian society of recent years and the Soviet legacy of a militarized society. As the Russian population has become increasingly differentiated, high education levels have been maintained and in some ways improved for a very narrow elite, but the drop-off from elite institutions has become steeper. Russian science has suffered major blows from brain drain with many of the best and brightest having left their impoverished laboratories for the West. Still, pockets of excellence remain that provide a foundation for the future, and traditional Russian excellence in science and mathematics does bode well for Russians and Russian firms playing a greater role in the global information economy.

Russian Foreign and Security Policy Challenges: From Superpower to Embittered Role Player

After World War II, former Soviet foreign ministers Molotov and Gromyko were fond of saying that no major international issue could be resolved without the participation of the Soviet Union. Of course, this was a bit of an exaggeration since the Soviet Union was not a major player on international economic issues, but on security issues their contention was no idle boasting. In the security realm it was a bipolar world, and the Soviet Union allocated tremendous resources to match the U.S. nuclear arsenal and to develop power projection capabilities to compete with the United States for influence in developing countries from Asia to Africa to Latin America. For much of the Cold War, many regarded Soviet conventional capabilities as superior to those of NATO. But this awesome military might was oddly juxtaposed with the Soviet Union's virtual abstention from the rapidly globalizing economy.

Mikhail Gorbachev concluded that Soviet power was ultimately not sustainable in conditions of domestic economic decline—a decline that was exacerbated by isolation from the world economy and excessive military expenditures. Gorbachev's motivations for reforming Soviet socialism also stemmed from concern about the decline of national morale in an overly repressive society. His perestroika strategy involved reforming the Soviet economic and political system, and this required support from the West as well as economic resources reallocated from military spending to the civilian economy. Requirements of reduced military spending and goodwill and support from the West led Gorbachev and Foreign Minister Eduard Shevardnadze to initiate a remarkable geostrategic retrenchment involving the dissolution of the Warsaw Pact, the unification of Germany, and a series of arms control agreements. In effect Gorbachev wanted to trade ending the Cold War for joining the world economy and fostering prosperity at home. To his great credit he succeeded beautifully on the first goal, and to his great disappointment failed miserably on the second task. Rather than reviving Soviet socialism, Gorbachev unleashed a process that got out of his control and resulted in the demise of the Soviet Union.

The goals set forth by Gorbachev have for the most part continued to guide Yeltsin and now Putin. And all three leaders have also come to understand that giving up geopolitical power is much easier than restructuring the economy and building prosperity. As a consequence of the policies of Gorbachev and his successors in the Kremlin, Russian power and influence in world affairs dropped more precipitously and rapidly than that of any major power in peacetime in modern world history. The most fundamental challenge for Russians in the last decade has been to fashion a foreign and security policy that matches the country's limited means. The ends and means problem has been complicated by the psychological residue of centuries of great-power and superpower status. Stephen Sestanovich suggested in 1996 that Russia needed to go into "geotherapy" to help ease the transition to its diminished international status.[2]

Dmitri Trenin argues that Russian security policy continues to struggle with both an elite mind-set mired in Cold War thinking and a force structure designed for the Cold War that is neither affordable nor capable of addressing Russia's most pressing threats. Although the Marxist-Leninist ideological framework has been dropped, much of the Russian security elite has adopted anachronistic geopolitical concepts that instinctively identify, for example, NATO expansion as a threat to Russia. Expansion of the alliance followed by the military campaign against Serbia confirmed for them the dangers presented by the West and informed the most recent iteration of a national security doctrine that describes the West in threatening terms for Russia. Unless and until Russia definitively concludes that the United States is not a potential enemy, reconfiguring the inherited Soviet defense structures to confront effectively what Trenin believes should be Russia's real defense concerns will not be feasible. It appears that President Putin has made his strategic choice to integrate with a nonthreatening West, and the September 11 attacks on the United States and the subsequent war on terrorism afford him an opportunity to consolidate this position.

Russia's most pressing real-time and near-term threats exist to its south. What Winston Churchill famously described as Russia's "soft underbelly" now consists of a set of weak and unstable states in the Caucasus and Central Asia that for the past ten years have been prone to conflict, religious (most often Islamic) extremism, terrorism, and drug trafficking. Trenin argues that Moscow's challenge will be to stabilize the region, but this is a task well beyond the capacity of Russia by itself. It will require that Russia and other states with interests and influence in the region abandon a competitive, zero-sum approach to work cooperatively to address regional security threats that pose dangers to all. Trenin believes that Russia's main security problem in the future will be the vulnerability of the Far East and Siberia, but here the principal challenge will be to develop and implement a coherent development strategy for a region that has experienced this transition decade even more traumatically than the rest of the country.

Through the vicissitudes of Russia's relations with the United States and the West during the 1990s, Russia steadily improved relations with China in the East. Often the triangular dynamics among Washington, Moscow, and Beijing have been interpreted by analysts and political elites in traditional geostrategic terms of balancing through alternative alliance and quasi-alliance relationships. Andrew Kuchins argues that this kind of interpretation of the Sino–Russian relationship is fundamentally flawed and that the likelihood of the emergence of a Sino–Russian alliance directed against the United States or a U.S.–Russian alliance directed against China is extremely small.

For Russia, constructive ties with China are naturally an important component of its overall foreign policy because the two countries share a very long and historically contentious border. But for economic, political, and cultural reasons, Russia's ties with Europe and the United States will remain the most important foreign policy orientations for any foreseeable future.

In the 1990s Russian sales of military technology and weapons to China were the most visible and controversial sector of an overall disappointing economic and trade relationship. Even though there are plans for this relationship to deepen to include collaboration on research and development of new systems, Russian supplies of energy, principally oil and natural gas, will be increasingly important in a far more robust economic relationship. This will be part of the broader development of the growing role of Russian and Central Asian energy in Northeast Asia, and it will be a means of more deeply integrating Russia into a region where historically military and security issues have dominated Russia's engagement.

The security threats for Russia to its south result primarily from the failures and difficulties in state building in the former Soviet republics of the Caucasus and Central Asia. Martha Brill Olcott's chapter explores many of the faulty assumptions about the nature of the challenges these states face and how regional policies based on these assumptions are increasing rather than alleviating the risks of regional instability. Although the Central Asian political elites were among the least desirous of independence, many assumed that independence could help them in addressing some of the maladies developed during the Soviet Union and even be a source for a better life. Ten years later, however, state institutions, with the exception of the security services, remain as weak or weaker, and the already meager quality of life has diminished. The weakness of the individual states has pushed them to establish regional organizations, but weak states make for weak partners.

In particular the assumption that Islam is inherently dangerous and needs to be contained has fueled authoritarianism and repression throughout the region. The repression of Islamic groups and civil society at large has been most pronounced in Uzbekistan under President Islam Karimov. The blanket repression there of Islamic groups—fundamentalist, modernist, conservative, and otherwise—has significantly contributed to the radicalization of those groups. This vicious circle of government repression and societal radicalization is self-perpetuating, and it is exacerbated by inadequate economic development strategies resulting in pervasive poverty. Despite Uzbekistan being the most "natural" state and the logical aspirant for regional hegemony, misguided state policies may render it the most fragile.

The most pressing security challenge for Russia from the south has been and, of course, remains Chechnya. Chechnya is a domestic problem for Russia, but the two military efforts there since 1994 have been the greatest preoccupations for the Russian military as well as their greatest shames. As Anatol Lieven writes, the causes of the war are not that unusual in a world where many national groups seek to remove their territories from the control of larger states. And like many civil wars or wars of national liberation (depending on your perspective), this fight has been ferocious, with abundant atrocities committed by both sides. The brutal tactics of the Russian military, like many antipartisan campaigns, have strengthened the rebels' ability to recruit new soldiers who seek revenge for their relatives who have been killed and for their homes destroyed.

Lieven is not optimistic about the current conflict ending anytime soon, as the political and national risks and costs of withdrawal for the Russians outweigh the costs of current casualties and potential gains of peace. He compares Russia's conflict in Chechnya with that of Turkey in Kurdestan, India in Kashmir, and other conflicts that defy resolution. Because Putin's political rise was so tied to the terrorist attacks in Russia in the fall of 1999 and the onset of the second Chechen war, it may be harder for this president to reach a political agreement to halt hostilities than it was for the Yeltsin administration, even though more and more political and military figures will admit privately that the war is a mistake.

The challenges that Chechnya, the Caucasus, and Central Asia present for Russia reflect a broader post–Cold War security agenda in which civil and ethnic strife both contributing to and resulting from state failures has seemingly overshadowed Cold War fears of nuclear Armageddon and great-power, hegemonic wars common until the advent of nuclear weapons. The U.S.–Soviet nuclear standoff was the defining element of the Cold War, and ten years past the Soviet collapse, the United States and the Russian Federation remain locked in a deterrent relationship. Despite this apparent stasis in the bilateral nuclear relationship, Rose Gottemoeller argues that a quiet revolution has been under way in how the United States and Russia relate to each other on nuclear matters. A variety of efforts—such as formal verification measures from existing arms control agreements, joint programs to eliminate components of the former Soviet nuclear arsenal and to prevent proliferation, high technology cooperation like the international space station, and others—have fostered a great deal of collaboration and transparency between the U.S. and Russian nuclear and military security establishments.

This history of cooperation and the personal relationships developed can provide a much stronger foundation of trust to help the United States and Russia take steps to move their nuclear relationship further from its dangerous Cold War legacies. The Bush administration assumed office in 2001 intent on developing a new framework for strategic cooperation with Russia. Missile defense is a controversial aspect of the new framework envisioned by President Bush, but other aspects such as deep reductions in strategic nuclear forces and de-alerting strategic weapons that remain on operational deployment enjoy much broader consensus. Reaching consensus about the nature of the new offense-defense relationship poses a key challenge for U.S. and Russian leadership. But even in cases where high-level consensus has existed—such as the agreement in June 2000 between Presidents Clinton and Putin to establish a joint center in Moscow for sharing early warning data—legal and procedural problems can and have stymied implementation. Gottemoeller acknowledges that it is possible that legal and procedural issues around liability and access to Russian facilities may be used as proxies for internal Russian opposition to cooperation with the United States.

In his chapter on U.S.–Russian relations, James Goldgeier points out that three times in the twentieth century the United States and Russia have cooperated in significant ways: in the 1940s to defeat Germany and Japan; in the 1970s to curb the nuclear arms race; and in the early 1990s to promote a Soviet then Russian transition. In each case there were either powerful international or domestic forces pushing cooperation. In Goldgeier's view it is not clear that such forces exist now. September 11 was a shock that promoted extensive cooperation in the war to oust the Taliban from Afghanistan, but it is not certain if the broader terrorist threat will help consolidate the U.S.–Russian relationship. The emergence of an aggressive China hostile to the interests of the United States and Russia could bring Washington and Moscow together, but that is definitely not something for which to wish.

And after the disillusions and mutual suspicions at the end of the 1990s, neither a Bush nor a Putin administration curries favor with their political constituencies with promotion of strong U.S.–Russian ties.

Europe, however, is the place where the United States and Russia need each other to achieve the broader goals of their foreign policy agendas. The U.S. goal of enlarging the Western zone of peace and prosperity to a Europe "whole and free" requires that Russia be more thoroughly integrated. Because of their proximity to Russia, Europeans are particularly concerned about dangers that might spill westward from instability in Russia. These concerns drive traditional Western European states like Germany, France, and Great Britain to urge the United States to remain engaged with Russia despite difficulties and frustrations. As Goldgeier and Trenin argue, Russia must have good relations with Europe, and it appears that Putin understands that this is possible only if Russia has good relations with the United States as well. Simplistic and flawed notions of NATO as the "bad Europe" and the European Union as the "good Europe" that seemed to animate Putin's first year in power have been discarded.

Finally, we need to stay realistic about our expectations of what is possible. Excessive expectations for U.S.–Russian relations ten years ago only sharpened the sense of mutual disappointment as the inevitable difficulties ensued later in the decade. Even in the much more cooperative environment generated in the second half of 2001, differences remain in the relationship. This is to be expected—all countries, even allies, experience differences, sometimes quite acrimonious. Although the United States and Russia may never experience the brief euphoric high of 1991–1992, neither are they likely to descend again to a new cold war. Similarly, we can also hope that Russia has already endured the worst of times domestically as the glacial ice of the Soviet legacy slowly melts into history.

Notes

1. N. Gevorkyan, A. Kolesnikov, and N. Timakova, *Ot pervogo litsa: Razgovory s Vladimirom Putinym* (From the First Person: Conversations with Vladimir Putin) (Moscow: Vargius, 2000), pp. 167–8.

2. Stephen Sestanovich, "Geotherapy: Russia's Neurosis and Ours," *The National Interest* (September 1996).

Part One

Leadership

1

Evaluating Yeltsin and His Revolution

Michael McFaul

The defeat of the August 1991 coup attempt marked one of the most euphoric moments in Russian history. For centuries before, dictators had ruled Russia, using force when necessary to suppress and at times annihilate society. Emboldened by liberalization under Soviet leader Mikhail Gorbachev, Russian society organized to resist this use of force by Kremlin dictators. To be sure, all of Russia did not rise up against the coup plotters; only citizens in major cities mobilized. Yet the ripple effects of this brave stance against tyranny in Moscow and St. Petersburg proved pivotal in destroying communism, dismantling the Soviet empire, and ending the Cold War.

The end of the Soviet dictatorship, however, did not lead immediately or smoothly to the creation of Russian democracy. Tragically, the ten-year anniversary of the momentous August 1991 coup did not prompt national public celebration. On the contrary, in response to a survey conducted in December 1999, over 70 percent of Russian voters believed that the Soviet Union should not have been dissolved, while a paltry 12 percent expressed satisfaction with the way Russian democracy is developing.[1]

Boris Yeltsin ruled an independent Russia for close to a decade. He started the period on top of a tank defying the coup and on top of the world. Days after staring down the August 1991 coup attempt, Russian President Boris Yeltsin boasted a 90 percent approval rating at home, adorned the cover of every international weekly in the world, and was christened a democratic hero by world leaders from Washington to Tokyo. When he suddenly resigned as president on December 31, 1999, Yeltsin enjoyed a 3 percent approval rating at home with a margin of error of plus or minus 4 percent. On his resignation day, Yeltsin probably had only a few international calls to make; with the exception of President Bill Clinton and a few others, he had almost no world leader friends left. Even the Western media ignored the passing of this onetime hero. When Clinton appeared that morning to comment on Yeltsin's retirement, most American national networks chose instead to air live the fireworks display in Beijing.

Many would argue that Yeltsin's pathetic passing from power correctly reflected his pitiful performance as Russia's first democratically elected president. In part, it did. Yeltsin made some very bad decisions that had detrimental consequences for his people and his country. But the Yeltsin story and era are not that simple. Side by side the poor decisions, he also made progress on some Herculean tasks. If he ever wanted another job, he might put the following achievements on the top of his resume: destroyed the Communist Party of the Soviet Union, peacefully dismantled the largest empire on earth, and introduced electoral democracy in a country with a thousand-year history of autocratic rule.

To seriously evaluate Yeltsin's legacy, however, these lists of achievements and failures must be placed within the larger context of Yeltsin's time. The measure of great women and men—for good or for ill—usually corresponds directly to the magnitude of their historical moment. Yeltsin reached the apex of his career during revolutionary times, when the foundational structures of the Soviet regime were crumbling. The scale of change first launched by Soviet leader Mikhail Gorbachev created opportunities for Yeltsin to catapult to power and play his historic role. At the same time, the enormity of change also overwhelmed Yeltsin's ability to confront multiple challenges simultaneously. Initially, the revolution made Yeltsin great, but eventually it also undermined his greatness.

Unlikely Revolutionary: From Communist to Democrat

Three decades ago, it would have been hard to guess that Yeltsin would one day become a revolutionary. Whereas Mandela, Havel, and Walesa devoted their adult lives to challenging autocratic regimes, Yeltsin spent much of his political career trying to make dictatorship work. Mandela, Havel, and Walesa all paid for their political views; Yeltsin won promotion within the Communist Party of the Soviet Union (CPSU) for his. To be sure, Yeltsin had a reputation within the CPSU as a populist crusader who worked hard to fulfill the plan, improve the economic well-being of his people, and fight corruption. Yet Yeltsin was not a dissident. During his years as a rising star within the Soviet Communist Party, he did not advocate democratic reforms, market principles, or Soviet dissolution. His embrace of these ideas came only after his fall from grace within the Communist Party, when Gorbachev fired him unexpectedly from his post as first secretary of the Moscow Communist Party in 1987.

Ironically, Gorbachev changed the rules that eventually and inadvertently resuscitated Yeltsin's political prospects. After tinkering unsuccessfully with minor economic reforms, Gorbachev came to the conclusion that the conservative Communist Party nomenklatura was blocking his more ambitious plans for economic restructuring.[2] To dislodge these dinosaurs, Gorbachev introduced democratic reforms, including most importantly a semicompetitive electoral system for selecting deputies to the Soviet Congress of People's Deputies.

These elections, held in the spring of 1989, were only partially free and competitive. Nonetheless, they provided Yeltsin with an opportunity to resurrect his political career, and he took full advantage of the chance. Competing in Moscow, Yeltsin ran an essentially anti-establishment campaign, calling the party's leadership corrupt and vowing to roll back the privileges of the party's ruling elite. He won in a landslide.

At this stage in his new career, Yeltsin was a populist running against the grain of the Soviet ancien régime. If what he stood against was clear, what he stood for was less so. At the time, many considered him a Russian nationalist. Others cast him as an autocratic demagogue, less cultured, less liberal, less predictable than his chief rival, Mikhail Gorbachev. Western leaders in particular feared this rabble-rouser who might disrupt the "orderly" reforms being carried out by their favorite Communist Party general secretary, Gorbachev.[3]

It was through the 1989 elections that Yeltsin first came in contact with Russia's grassroots democratic leaders. In the 1989 election campaign Yeltsin aligned with leaders of the burgeoning democratic movement, a small proportion of whom were elected to the new Soviet parliament. They coalesced to form the Inter-Regional Group within the Soviet Congress of People's

Deputies. This alliance, however, was an uneasy one. Yeltsin after all was a former first secretary in the Communist Party, the very organization that other members of the Inter-Regional Group considered the enemy. At the same time, Yeltsin was too popular for Russia's democrats to ignore. They needed him more than he needed them.

Yeltsin and his colleagues in the democratic opposition quickly became marginalized in parliament. Frustrated by their lack of power and Gorbachev's unwillingness to cooperate, Yeltsin and his allies made a tactical decision to abandon Soviet-level politics and focus their efforts instead on upcoming elections for the Russian Congress of People's Deputies. This strategic decision produced dire consequences for the future of the Soviet Union. Yeltsin spearheaded the charge.

Because the Russian population was growing impatient with Gorbachev's reforms, Russia's anticommunist forces captured nearly a third of the seats in the Russian Congress during the 1990 elections. With additional votes from Russian nationalists, Yeltsin then won election as chairman of this Russian legislative body. The anticommunists had essentially seized power from below. As one of their first acts as the newly elected representatives of the Russian people, the Russian Congress declared Russia an independent state in the summer of 1990.

But the Russian Congress and the Russian state were located within the Soviet Union. The Kremlin, not the White House (the home of the Russian Congress), still controlled all the most important levers of power. Consequently, a protracted struggle for sovereignty between the Soviet state and the Russian government ensued. In a replay of Russian history circa 1917, Russia once again experienced dual power in 1990–1991.

From January to August 1991, the balance of power between radicals and reactionaries swayed back and forth several times. Large demonstrations throughout Russia to protest the invasion of the Baltic states reinvigorated the democratic movement. In the first part of 1991, Soviet conservative forces also scored victories, including major changes in the Soviet government and electoral victory in March 1991, when a solid majority of Russian voters (and Soviet voters in republics that participated) approved a referendum to preserve the Soviet Union. In June 1991, Yeltsin won a landslide victory to become Russia's first elected president, a vote that returned momentum to Russia's anticommunist forces.

Sensitive to the momentum swing, Soviet conservatives attempted to strike back. After a prolonged set of negotiations during the spring of 1991,

Yeltsin and most of the other republican leaders were prepared to join Gorbachev in signing a new Union Treaty, scheduled for August 20, 1991. Soviet conservatives saw this treaty as the first step toward total disintegration of the USSR and therefore preempted its signing by seizing power. While Gorbachev was on vacation, the State Committee for the State of Emergency (GKChP in Russian, the abbreviation used hereafter) announced on August 19, 1991, that they had assumed responsibility for governing the country. The GKChP justified their actions as a reaction against "extremist forces" and "political adventurers" who aimed to destroy the Soviet state and economy. Their announcements were flavored with heavy doses of Soviet nationalism. Had these forces prevailed, it is not unreasonable to presume that the Soviet Union, in some form, would still exist today.

But they did not prevail, because Yeltsin and his allies stopped them. Immediately after learning about the coup attempt, Yeltsin raced to the White House and began to organize a resistance effort. As the elected president of Russia, he called on Russian citizens—civilian and military alike—to obey his decrees and not those of the GKChP. In a classic revolutionary situation of dual sovereignty, Soviet tank commanders had to decide whether to obey orders from the Soviet regime, which came through their radio headsets, or orders from the Russian president that they received by hand on leaflets. At the end of the day, enough armed men obeyed the leaflets to thwart the coup attempt. By the third day, the coup plotters lost their resolve and began to negotiate a surrender.

August 1991–December 1991: Five Months That Shook the World

The outcome of the August 1991 putsch attempt dramatically and fundamentally changed the course of Soviet and Russian history. Even for a country blessed and cursed with a history of pivotal turning points, these three days rank as some of the most important for the first decade of postcommunist Russia. For the first time since the Bolsheviks seized power in 1917, Soviet authorities had moved to quell societal opposition in Russia and failed. The moment was euphoric. For many Russian citizens, perhaps no time is remembered with greater fondness than the initial days after the failed August 1991 coup. Even Gorbachev belatedly recognized that after the August events, there "occurred a cardinal break with the totalitarian system and a decisive move in favor of the democratic forces."[4] Western reactions were even more euphoric with headlines declaring "Serfdom's End: A Thousand Years of Autocracy Are Reversed."[5]

Immediately after the failed coup, Russia's revolutionaries took advantage of their windfall political power to arrest coup plotters, storm Communist Party headquarters, seize KGB (Committee for State Security) files, and tear down the statue of Felix Dzerzhinskii, the founder of the modern-day KGB. But what was to be done next? As in all revolutions, destruction of the ancien régime proved easier than construction of a new order. Although August 1991 may have signaled the end of communist rule, it remained unclear what kind of political regime, economic system, or society could or should fill the void. Even the borders of the state were uncertain. Especially for those in power, euphoria surrounding the closing of the Soviet past was quickly overshadowed by uncertainty haunting the beginning of Russia's future.

Yeltsin's defeat of the August 1991 coup attempt was his second greatest achievement as Russia's first elected president. His most important achievement—the peaceful dissolution of the Soviet regime—occurred five months later. Most of what Yeltsin accomplished as a political figure took place between these two momentous events.

The failed coup attempt and Yeltsin's victory rapidly accelerated the pace of change within the Soviet Union. Gorbachev, imprisoned in his vacation home in Crimea for the three days of Emergency Rule, returned to a different country when he flew back to Moscow. Believing that they had a new mandate for change, Yeltsin and the Russian Congress of People's Deputies seized power. They pressured the Soviet Congress of People's Deputies to dissolve, disbanded the Communist Party of the Soviet Union, assumed control of several Soviet ministries, and compelled Gorbachev to acquiesce to these changes. Most dramatically, Yeltsin then met with the leaders of Ukraine and Belarus in early December to dissolve the Soviet Union. On December 31, 1991, the Soviet empire disappeared. Buried with this empire were Soviet autarky, the Soviet command economy, and the Soviet totalitarian state.

The Soviet regime died peacefully. Remarkably, only three people lost their lives during the August putsch attempt. Even more remarkably, the pillar institutions of the Soviet regime—the KGB, the Red Army, the military-industrial complex, and the Communist Party—did not try to halt Yeltsin's disassembly of the ancien régime. Yeltsin's success in orchestrating this peaceful collapse is especially amazing when one remembers that only a very small minority of Russians actively resisted the coup attempt. The democratic movements in Moscow and St. Petersburg mobilized tens of thousands on the streets, but the rest of Russia and most of the other Soviet republics stood on the sidelines, awaiting a winner. Similar to revolutionary myths in Russia and elsewhere, the end of Soviet communism in 1991 now seems inevitable, the triumph of democracy certain. At the time, however, nothing seemed preordained. Perhaps Yeltsin's third greatest achievement was making the dissolution of the Soviet Union seem inevitable and easy.

1991–1992: The Year of Decision and Indecision

Like the storming of the Bastille in 1789 or the seizing of the Winter Palace in 1917, August 1991 marked the peak of Russia's Second Revolution. For many, this moment, coupled with Soviet dissolution a few months later, *was* the revolution. What happened after that was simply cleanup—a job for technocrats, not revolutionary heroes.

Revolutions, however, take years to complete. The years 1789, 1917, and 1991 marked the beginnings of revolutionary upheavals, not their ends.[6] The destruction of the ancien régime is a critical turning point in any revolution, but the construction of a new regime constitutes the real drama of revolutionary change. Often, the revolutionary masters of destruction do not make good evolutionary builders of new political and economic institutions. Yeltsin most certainly struggled with the transition.

The tasks confronting Yeltsin and his allies in the fall of 1991 were enormous. The economy was in shambles. Shortages of basic goods existed in all cities, inflation soared, trade stopped, and production declined. Many predicted massive starvation in the winter. Centrifugal forces that helped pull the Soviet Union apart had infected some of the republics within Russia's borders. Months before the Soviet Union dissolved, Chechnya had already declared its independence. At the same time, the political system was in disarray. Yeltsin enjoyed a honeymoon period of overwhelming support after his August 1991 performance. Yet the formal rules of the game for sharing power between the executive and legislative branches were still ambiguous. Yeltsin, after all, had only been elected president of Russia in June 1991. In the deal to allow this election to occur, the constitutional amendments delineating his power were scheduled for approval in December

1991 and thus were not in place when Yeltsin suddenly became head of state in the newly independent Russia.

In the fall of 1991, the Russian state did not really exist and Russia's "independence" was an abstract concept, not an empirical reality. It must be remembered that in August 1991 Russia had no sovereign borders, no sovereign currency, no sovereign army, and weak, ill-defined state institutions. Even after the December 1991 agreement to dissolve the Soviet Union and create the Commonwealth of Independent States, Russia's political, territorial, and existential location was still unresolved. Throughout the former Soviet Union, thirty million ethnic Russians became expatriates overnight at the same time that ethnic minorities within the Russian Federation pushed for their own independence.

In tackling this triple transition of defining borders, transforming the economy, and creating a new polity, Yeltsin and his allies had few relevant institutions to resurrect from the Soviet system. In many of the transitions to democracy in Latin America, Southern Europe, and East Central Europe, old democratic institutions, suspended under authoritarian rule, were often reactivated, a process that is much more efficient than creating new institutions from scratch. As O'Donnell and Schmitter conclude in their study, all case studies examined "had some of these rules and procedures [of democracy] in the past."[7]

Russian leaders had no such democratic institutions to resurrect. Likewise, even the most radical economic reform programs undertaken in the West, including even the Roosevelt New Deal in the 1930s, took place in countries with experience in markets, private property, and the rule of law. After seventy years of communism, none of the economic institutions of capitalism existed in Russia in 1991. In contrast to the transitions from communism in Eastern Europe, even the memory of these institutions had been extinguished within the collective mind-set of Russian citizens after a century of the command economy. The inheritance from the Soviet era was even worse than a clean slate.[8] Russian leaders had to tackle the problems of empire, economic reform, and political change with many of the practices and institutions of the Soviet system still in place. Yeltsin and Russia's revolutionaries, therefore, did not enjoy a tabula rasa in designing new market and democratic institutions in 1991. The Soviet regime as a whole imploded in 1991, but constituent elements of the old system remained in place.

The new regime also lacked a clear sense of what it was striving to create. Democracy and capitalism were buzzwords of Yeltsin's ideology of opposition, not concepts that he had struggled with over years and years of opposition. Yeltsin's meteoric rehabilitation occurred in only two years. Russia's democratic movement was even younger. Democratic Russia, the umbrella organization for Russia's grassroots democratic movement, held its founding congress in October 1990, only nine months before the coup attempt. In contrast, Solidarity remained in opposition for a decade before taking power in Poland; the African National Congress in South Africa spent most of the century preparing for power.

Finally, Yeltsin also had to deal with the ambiguous balance of power between political actors who favored reform and those who opposed it. In contrast to several East European countries, consensus did not exist in Russia in 1991 about the need for market and democratic reform. On the contrary, Russia's elite and society were divided and polarized.

In August 1991, those political forces that favored preservation of the old Soviet political and economic order were weak and disorganized, but they soon recovered and reorganized within the Russian Congress of People's Deputies, in regional governments, and on the streets to demonstrate their power. On the other side of the barricade, those in favor of reform looked invincible immediately after the August 1991 coup, but this anticommunist coalition quickly fell apart after the Soviet Union collapsed.

The simultaneity of change under way on every front must have over-whelmed Yeltsin. No wonder he vacated Moscow in October and hid out in Crimea for three weeks. Upon his return, he made a series of critical deci-sions that shaped the course of Russian political and economic reform for the rest of the decade, but he also avoided making a set of critical decisions that had long-term, path-dependent consequences for Russia's future.

After successfully dismantling the Soviet state, Yeltsin made his boldest moves on the economic front. He hired a small group of neoliberal econo-mists headed by Yegor Gaidar to oversee the introduction of radical reforms. Beginning with the freeing of most prices on January 1, 1992, Gaidar and his team initiated the most ambitious economic reform program ever attempted in modern history.[9] His plan aimed to liberalize prices and trade, achieve macroeconomic stabilization, and privatize property all within a minimum amount of time, earning this plan the unfortunate label of "shock therapy." Yeltsin did not understand the plan but initially embraced it as the only path to creating a "normal" market economy in Russia.

Yeltsin was less decisive regarding the creation of new political institu-tions. On the one hand, like many other revolutionary leaders during such moments of change, he could have used his windfall power generated by August 1991 to establish an authoritarian state: disbanding all political institutions not subordinate to the president's office, suspending individual political liberties, and deploying coercive police units to enforce executive policies. His opponents expected him to do so. Some of his allies encouraged him to take such a course, believing this strategy to be the only way to introduce radical economic reform. On the other hand, Yeltsin could have taken steps to consolidate a democratic polity. He could have disbanded old Soviet government institutions, adopted a new constitution codifying the division of power among executive, legislative, and judicial as well as federal and regional bodies, and called new elections to stimulate the development of a multiparty system. Many leaders in the democratic movement expected as much.[10]

Yeltsin, however, pursued neither strategy. While he did not attempt to erect a dictatorship, he did little to consolidate a new democratic polity. Importantly, he resisted calls for new national elections and actually postponed regional elections scheduled for December 1991. He also did not form a political party. He delayed the adoption of a new constitution, even though his own constitutional commission had completed a first new draft as early as October 1990. Finally, unlike most other successful revolutionary leaders, he did not initiate internal reform or major personnel changes within the Soviet state's coercive institutions such as the army and KGB. Toward these potential foes of his cause, Yeltsin's strategy was cooption not transformation.

His first priority was not the creation or consolidation of a new democratic political system (or a new authoritarian regime). Rather, Yeltsin decided that Russian independence and economic reform were of greater priority. Most of his initial energy for designing new institutions was focused on these two agendas. Yeltsin and his new government believed they could sequence reforms. First, they wanted to fill the vacuum of state power by codifying the new borders of the Commonwealth of Independent States, then begin economic reform, and finally reconstruct a democratic polity. Their decisions regarding institutional design reflected this ranking of priorities.

Yeltsin and his advisors also believed that they had achieved major political reforms before August 1991. Democracy seemed secure; it was now the development of capitalism that needed their attention. Western governments and assistance organizations also encouraged this sequence of reform, devoting nearly 90 percent of their budgets to economic reform.[11]

Consequences of Indecision

In retrospect, Yeltsin's series of nondecisions regarding political reform in 1991 and 1992 constitutes his greatest mistake as Russia's first president. The consequences of these nondecisions haunted his administration for the rest of the decade. The absence of well-defined political rules of the game fueled ambiguity, stalemate, and conflict between the federal and subnational units of the state. Both confrontations ended in armed conflict. Political instability and conflict in turn also impeded market reforms.

October 1993

The Russian Congress of People's Deputies was an odd foe for Boris Yeltsin. In 1990, this body elected Yeltsin as its chairman. After Yeltsin became president, this Congress then elected Yeltsin's deputy chairman, Ruslan Khasbulatov, to become speaker. In August 1991, Yeltsin, Khasbulatov, and their supporters huddled inside the Congress building—the White House— as their chief defensive strategy for thwarting the coup. In November 1991, the Congress voted overwhelmingly to give Yeltsin extraordinary powers to deal with economic reform. In December 1991, the Supreme Soviet of the Russian Congress ratified Yeltsin's agreement to dissolve the Soviet Union. Only six deputies voted against the agreement.

To argue in retrospect, therefore, that the Congress was a hotbed of communist conservatism is revisionist history. To be sure, communist deputies controlled roughly 40 percent of the seats in the Congress: the distribution of power of those for the revolution and against the revolution was relatively equal within this institution. Yet this balance did not prevent Yeltsin from being elected chairman. It should not have prevented him from reaching agreement with this Congress about the rules of the game that governed their interaction with each other.

Initially after the putsch attempt, the institutional ambiguity between the president and Congress did not have a direct impact on politics, because most deputies in the Congress at that time supported Yeltsin. After price liberalization and the beginning of radical economic reform in January 1992, however, the Congress began a campaign to reassert its superiority over the president. The disagreement over economic reform in turn spawned a constitutional crisis between the parliament and president. With no formal institutions to structure relations between the president and the Congress, polarization crystallized yet again, with both sides claiming to represent Russia's highest sovereign authority. During the summer of 1993, in preparing for the tenth Congress of People's Deputies, deputies drafted a series of constitutional amendments that would have liquidated Russia's presidential office altogether. Yeltsin preempted their plans by dissolving the Congress in September 1993. The Congress, in turn, declared Yeltsin's decree illegal and recognized Vice President Aleksandr Rutskoi as the new interim president. In a replay of the 1991 drama, Russia suddenly had two heads of state and two governments claiming sovereign authority over the other. Tragically, this standoff ended only after the military conquest of one side by the other. Rutskoi and his allies initiated the violent phase of this contest when they seized control of the mayor's building and then stormed Ostankino, the national television building. Yeltsin in turn responded with a tank assault on the White House, without question one of the lowest points in his political career.

Had Yeltsin called for new elections to the Russian parliament in the fall of 1991, this military standoff might have been avoided. Had Yeltsin pushed for the adoption of a new constitution earlier in the first Russian Republic, the rules of the game defining the division of power between the executive and legislative branches would have been clearer. Greater clarity of the rules also might have helped to diffuse polarization between the parliament and president.

Chechnya

The same constitutional ambiguity that fueled conflict between Yeltsin and the Congress also allowed federal conflicts to fester. Eventually, one of them—Chechnya—exploded into a full-scale war.

Federal problems actually arose before the 1993 executive-legislative standoff. Immediately after the August 1991 coup attempt, Chechnya declared its independence. In March of the following year, Tatarstan held a successful referendum for full independence. The first of several federal treaties was signed in March 1992, but negotiations over a new federal arrangement embedded within a constitution dragged on without resolution into the summer of 1993, prompting several other republics as well as oblasts to make their own declarations of independence, complete with their own flags, customs agents, and threats of minting new currencies.

For two years after independence, Yeltsin allowed these federal ambiguities to linger. Consumed with starting market reform and then distracted by the power struggle with the Congress, Yeltsin chose not to devote time or resources toward reconstructing the Russian federal order. After the October 1993 standoff, Yeltsin did put before the people a new constitution, ratified in December 1993, which formally spelled out a solution to Russia's federal ambiguities. The new constitution specified that all constituent elements were to enjoy equal rights vis-à-vis the center. Absent from the document was any mention of a mechanism for secession.

The formal rules of a new constitution did not resolve the conflicts between the center and the regions. Negotiation over the distribution of power between the central and subnational governments has continued and will continue as long as Russia maintains a federal structure. Nonetheless, all subnational governments except one—Chechnya—did acquiesce to a minimalist maintenance of a federal order. Ironically, the clarity of rules generally highlighted the specific problem of Chechnya's status. In December 1994, Yeltsin eventually decided to use force to deal with this single exception.

The results were disastrous. Almost two years later, during which time 100,000 Russian citizens lost their lives, Russian soldiers went home in defeat. In the summer of 1996, Yeltsin's envoy, Aleksandr Lebed, negotiated an end to the war but did not resolve Chechnya's sovereign status. After the peace accord, the Chechen government failed to establish a viable regime. Instead, warlords and Islamic revolutionaries established their own local jurisdictions. One of these groups, headed by Shamil Basayev, crossed the Chechen border into the Russian republic of Dagestan in the summer of 1999, with the stated intent of "liberating" Muslims in the Caucasus from the Russian empire. Russia's military response renewed the armed conflict within Chechnya, which has festered for more than two years with weak near-term prospects for resolution. Failure to deal with Chechnya effectively will tarnish Yeltsin's legacy forever.

Partial Economic Reform

Partial economic reform is a third lingering consequence of Yeltsin's indecision in fall 1991. Yeltsin initially embraced the big bang approach to market reform and appointed Gaidar as his chief architect of such a course.

Once the program began to meet public resistance—as everyone expected it would—Yeltsin began having doubts about his choice. Sustaining support for Gaidar's reforms was complicated by the institutional ambiguity between the president and the parliament. Who ultimately had responsibility for selecting the government or charting the course of economic reform? The constitutions in place at the time did not provide a definitive answer. Subsequently, Yeltsin felt compelled to negotiate with the Congress over the composition of his government, diluting the Gaidar team to include enterprise managers—the so-called red directors—whose aim was not real reform but the preservation of the incredible moneymaking opportunities offered to themselves and their allies by partial reform. By December 1992, these Soviet-era managers were back in control of the Russian government under the leadership of Prime Minister Viktor Chernomyrdin.

Shock reform in Russia was never really attempted. Well before his ouster in December 1992, Gaidar and his government had lost control of economic policy making, a loss of authority that produced partial reforms and contradictory policies. After December 1992, Yeltsin allowed Chernomyrdin and his government to creep along with even more watered down reforms— reforms that included big budget deficits, insider privatization, and partial price and trade liberalization, which in turn combined to create amazing opportunities for corruption and spawned a decade of oligarchic capitalism. The August 1998 financial collapse dealt a major blow to the economic oligarchs and may, in the long run, provide new opportunities for genuine structural reforms and economic growth.[12] The lost years of the earlier part of the decade could have been avoided, or at least shortened, had Yeltsin been more decisive in his support of the early Gaidar effort. The poor design of political institutions in the first years of the Russian Republic helped to impede the adoption of real reform measures.

Electoral Democracy

A final consequence of Yeltsin's decisions in 1991–1992 has been a mixed record on the consolidation of democracy. Yeltsin must be given credit for the fact that Russia today is an electoral democracy. Political leaders come to power through the ballot box and not through the Communist Party appointment process. They do not take office by seizing power through the use of force. Most elites in Russia and the vast majority of the Russian population now recognize elections as the only legitimate means to power. Leaders and parties that espouse authoritarian practices—be they fascists or neocommunists—have moved to the margins of Russia's political stage. Given Russia's thousand-year history of autocratic rule, the emergence of electoral democracy must be recognized as a revolutionary achievement of the last decade.

Even so, Russia is not a liberal democracy. The Russian political system lacks many of the supporting institutions that make democracy robust. Russia's party system, civil society, and the rule of law are weak and underdeveloped. Executives, at both the national and regional levels, have too much power. Crime and corruption, forces that corrode democracy, are still rampant. Russia's independent media, one of the real achievements of the 1990s, have become more controlled by the state, especially under President Putin. The Russian state still lacks the capacity to provide basic public goods. All of these attributes impede the deepening of democratic institutions.

Yeltsin deserves partial blame. Had he pushed for the adoption of a new constitution in the fall of 1991, the balance of power between executives and legislatures would have been more equally distributed. Ironically, Yeltsin compromised too much on economic reform but too little on political reform during the first years of independence. Imposed by Yeltsin in the wake of a military victory, the current Russian constitution is a direct consequence of failed compromise earlier in the decade. By failing to call elections in the fall of 1991, Yeltsin robbed Russia's democratic parties of their ripe opportunity for emergence and expansion. Instead, he convened the first postcommunist Russian election in December 1993. By this time, most parties created during the heyday of democratic mobilization in 1990–1991 had disappeared. Liberal parties were especially hurt by the postponement of new elections, as many voters associated the painful economic decline from 1991 to 1993 with their leaders and their policies. The development of civil society also suffered as a result of the weakness of legislative institutions and the underdevelopment of Russia's party system.

Who Is to Blame? Yeltsin Versus the Revolution

What if Yeltsin had pushed for the ratification of a new constitution in the fall of 1991, held new elections, and then had his new party compete in this vote? Would the October 1993 military confrontation have been avoided? Would the Chechen wars not have occurred? Would economic reform be farther along today?

We will never know the definitive answers to these questions. In comparing Russia to other more successful transitions from communism, we do know that those that adopted democracy the quickest are the same countries that have avoided internal conflicts and wars, while enjoying the fastest economic growth. Big bang democracy helps to support big bang economic growth.

Yet it is wrong to assume that one man could have the power or ideas to either guide or crash Russia's revolution, because the scale and scope of the revolution were bigger than any one person, including even a larger-than-life personality like Boris Yeltsin. Yeltsin did not make the same decisions that Walesa or Havel made, because Russia is not Poland or Czechoslovakia. Two factors in particular distinguish Russia's revolution from these more successful transformations in East Central Europe. First, the agenda of change was much larger in the Soviet Union and Russia. Yeltsin had to address the end of empire, the specter of Russian federal dissolution, the construction of a new polity, and the introduction of market principles all at once. Russia's enormous size and diversity exacerbated all of these problems. Seventy years of communism also had a more distorting effect on the Russian state, polity, and economy than the forty years of communism in Eastern Europe.

Even more important than the large agenda of change, however, was the balance of power within Russia between those who supported change and those who resisted it. In contrast to the democratic movements in Poland, Hungary, or Czechoslovakia, Russia's "democrats" did not have overwhelming support, either within the elite or among the population at large. In contrast to most East European transitions, Russian communist groups refused to recognize the democratic victory in August 1991 and considered the policies pursued by the democrats thereafter to be illegitimate and undemocratic. Russian leaders might have been able to manage the wide array of changes facing them had they all agreed on a common strategy of action, but they did not agree. This absence of consensus was the central cause of Russia's troubled transition. Had most major political actors in Russia agreed with Yeltsin's policies of Soviet dissolution, federal unity, market reform, and presidential democracy, partial reforms and their detrimental consequences might not have occurred.

Compared to What? The Nightmares That Did Not Occur

In leaving office on December 31, 1999, Yeltsin bequeathed to his successors several serious political and economic conundrums. Russian democratic institutions are weak, the economy is growing but still in need of further reforms, and corruption and crime remain rampant. Most tragically, the war in Chechnya continues with little prospect for genuine resolution. Yeltsin already has earned his place in history as one of Russia's most important leaders. What kind of adjectives will modify his legacy, however, will become clear only after the resolution of these lingering issues. He could be remembered as the father of Russian democracy and the initiator of Russia's market economy and sustained economic growth. Or he could be remembered as the first postcommunist leader who squandered Russia's chances of becoming a liberal democracy and a capitalist economy. Yeltsin's last important decision—his appointment of Vladimir Putin as prime minister and then as acting president—will have a profound effect on how the Yeltsin legacy is finally judged.

Yeltsin also created the foundation for his successors to succeed and secure for him the more positive modifiers to his legacy. The revolution is not over, but it also has not reversed. The Soviet Union is gone and will never be resurrected. Communism also will never return to Russia. Russia has not gone to war with Ukraine, Latvia, or Kazakhstan to defend Russians living there and is less likely to do so today than when Yeltsin first took office. Though they threatened with periodic electoral splashes, neither neofascists nor neocommunists ever succeeded in coming to power in the 1990s and do not seem poised to do so in the near future. Even the Russian Communist Party has lagged behind its counterparts in Eastern Europe in not being able to recapture the Kremlin. Individual freedoms in Russia have never been greater.

Finally, by avoiding the temptation of dictatorship, Yeltsin also established an important precedent of democratic behavior that will raise the costs for future authoritarian aspirants. In defiance of his critics, he did not cancel elections in 1996, he did not suspend the constitution after the August 1998 financial crisis, and he did not stay in power by any means necessary. On the contrary, he won reelection in 1996, abided by the constitution and even invited communists into his government in the fall of 1998, and then stepped down willingly, peacefully, and constitutionally. Although Putin has shown little proclivity for deepening democratization in Russia, his cautious approach to decision making will make it very difficult for him to break this precedent. If dissolving the Soviet Union was Yeltsin's most important destructive act, his seizure and surrender of power through democratic means may be his most important constructive act.

Notes

1. Timothy Colton and Michael McFaul, *Are Russians Undemocratic?* Working Paper (Washington, D.C.: Carnegie Endowment for International Peace, 2001), pp. 5–6.

2. Mikhail Gorbachev, *Memoirs* (New York: Doubleday, 1995).

3. Jack Matlock, *Autopsy on an Empire: The American Ambassador's Account of the Collapse of the Soviet Union* (New York: Random House, 1995).

4. Gorbachev, as quoted in *Sovetskaya Rossiya*, October 22, 1991, p. 1. Implicitly, Gorbachev's comments suggest that his own attempts at political reform had not yet dismantled the Soviet totalitarian system.

5. This title is from *Time*, September 2, 1991, p. 3.

6. On the several stages of the first two revolutions, see Crane Brinton, *Anatomy of Revolution* (New York: Vintage Press, 1938). On the stages of the third revolution, see Vladimir Mau and Irina Staradubrovskaya, *The Challenge of Revolution: Contemporary Russia in Historical Perspective* (Oxford, U.K.: Oxford University Press, 2001).

7. Guillermo O'Donnell and Philippe Schmitter, *Transitions from Authoritarian Rule* (Baltimore, Md.: Johns Hopkins University Press, 1986), p. 8.

8. Clifford Gaddy, *The Price of the Past: Russia's Struggle with the Legacy of a Militarized Economy* (Washington, D.C.: Brookings Institution Press, 1996).

9. The best account of these reformers and these early reforms is Anders Åslund, *How Russia Became a Market Economy* (Washington, D.C.: Brookings Institution Press, 1995).

10. For details on these debates, see Michael McFaul, *Russia's Unfinished Revolution* (Ithaca, NY: Cornell University Press, 2001), ch. 4.

11. Michael McFaul and Sarah Mendelson, "Russian Democracy—A U.S. National Security Interest," *Demokratizatsiya*, vol. 8, no. 3 (Summer 2000), pp. 330–53.

12. Åslund forcefully advances this argument in Anders Åslund, *Building Capitalism: The Transformation of the Former Soviet Bloc* (Cambridge, U.K.: Cambridge University Press, 2001). See also Åslund's chapter in this volume.

2

Fragmentation of Russia

Thomas E. Graham, Jr.

For much of the first decade after the collapse of the Soviet Union, the issue of reform—of transition to free market democracy—dominated discussions of Russia in Russia itself and in the West. Russian President Yeltsin advocated reform, Western governments declared their support and offered their assistance, and Russian and Western leaders declared publicly that despite inevitable setbacks and difficulties, Russia was making steady progress. The financial collapse of August 1998 belied those assertions; it marked the failure of the grand project of quickly transforming Russia into a vibrant, prosperous free market democracy integrated into the Western world.

It was only against the background of that failure that attention began to focus on the real drama of the first decade of the new Russia: the fragmentation, degeneration, and erosion of state power. These processes had their roots in the late Soviet period, but they accelerated in the post-Soviet period as a consequence of Yeltsin's policies and Western advice. By the end of Yeltsin's presidency, the central debate was whether Russia was a "failed state" or on the road to becoming one, whether Russia would disintegrate much as the Soviet Union had nearly a decade earlier. Yeltsin's successor,

Mr. Graham is the director for Russian Affairs on the National Security Council. This essay was written while he was a senior associate at the Carnegie Endowment; it reflects his own views and not necessarily those of the National Security Council or the U.S. government.

Vladimir Putin, admitted those dangers implicitly in a document released shortly before he became acting president.

How Russia came to that juncture, after the high hopes of the immediate post-Soviet period, is a story of political shortsightedness, unprincipled political struggle, ill health, greed, and bad fortune. The fundamental question for the first decade of the new millennium is whether Russia can reverse the trend of its first post-Soviet decade and rebuild an effective state or whether it will move further along the path to collapse, with all the far-reaching consequences that would entail in both human suffering and geopolitical dynamics.

Uneasy Birth of the Russian Federation

In 1991, Russia emerged out of the ruins of the Soviet Union, not as the ultimate goal of a detailed strategy successfully pursued, but as a historical accident, the unintended by-product of the struggle for power and property within the Soviet state. Throughout the Soviet period, Russia occupied a unique position among the Soviet Union's fifteen constituent republics because of its enormous political and economic weight. It harbored the overwhelming share of the country's vast natural resources, including 90 percent of oil and gas production. Toward the end of the Soviet period, it accounted for three-quarters of the country's territory, 60 percent of its economy, and half of its population. For that reason, throughout most of Soviet history, Russia was never granted, as the other constituent republics were, the full trappings of formal sovereignty or, most important, its own subdivision of the Communist Party of the Soviet Union (CPSU). Had it been, it would have provided a formidable base for challenging the Soviet leadership.

The situation changed only in the Soviet Union's final years, as the opponents of Soviet leader Gorbachev moved to bolster their own positions by enhancing Russia's status. Hardline conservatives pressed for the creation of a Russian Federation Communist Party, which they hoped to turn into a nationalist organization dedicated to preserving the Soviet empire.[1] The radical democrats, allied with Yeltsin, focused their attention on the Russian Congress of Peoples' Deputies (or parliament) in the belief that they could use it to drive reform forward across the Soviet Union. No one was talking of Russia's independence. Indeed, that was so far from Yeltsin's mind, according to one of his advisers, that he originally turned against Gorbachev in part because he thought Gorbachev's policies would lead to the disintegration of the Soviet Union.[2]

Yeltsin did, however, aggressively use his base in Russian institutions to challenge Gorbachev for preeminence in the Soviet Union. One of his first acts upon being elected to the then-highest office in Russia, chairman of the Russian Supreme Soviet, in spring 1990 was to push through a declaration of Russian sovereignty, which, among other things, asserted the primacy of the Russian constitution and laws over their all-union counterparts on Russian territory.[3] The following spring, Yeltsin succeeded in establishing—and being popularly elected to—the post of Russian president to parallel Gorbachev's naming to the newly created office of USSR president by the Soviet Congress of People's Deputies a year earlier. That step was clearly intended to transform Yeltsin into a co-leader of the Soviet Union with massive popular support, not simply into the sole leader of Russia.[4]

Even after the failed putsch in August 1991, Yeltsin wavered over whether to push for the dissolution of the Soviet Union.[5] In the fall, he participated, along with Gorbachev and the leaders of six other constituent republics, in discussions over a new Union Treaty. There was intense debate over whether to create a new federal state or simply a confederation of sovereign states. The talks finally reached a dead end in November. The decision to disband the Soviet Union in December—agreed to first by Yeltsin and the heads of Ukraine and Belarus—in many ways only marked the recognition that the Soviet Union as such was beyond saving.

Nevertheless, a close look at the record indicates that Yeltsin and his allies remained committed to Russian domination of the Soviet space, however it might be organized politically, and that the preferred outcome was some form of a Russian-led federation or confederation. For that to happen, the Russian leaders believed, Russia would have to undertake radical economic reform to rebuild its strength. And that reform, they were convinced, would never be pursued if Russia tried to harmonize its program with the other, more conservative Soviet republics or had to rely on the disintegrating institutions of the Soviet government.[6]

Moreover, rather than celebrate Russia's independence at the end of 1991, Yeltsin chose to stress that the accords dissolving the Soviet Union and creating the Commonwealth of Independent States (CIS) were the only alternative to "further uncontrolled decay of the Union."[7] They had been necessary, he later argued, "to strengthen sharply centripetal tendencies in the decaying Union, to stimulate a treaty process." The CIS, he added, "offered at the time the only chance of preserving a unified geopolitical space," particularly after Ukrainians had overwhelmingly supported independence in a referendum at the beginning of December.[8]

Finally, concrete actions underscored the determination of Yeltsin and his allies to dominate the former Soviet Union and their hope of rebuilding a Russian-dominated entity. As the Soviet Union decayed in fall 1991, Russia worked to establish itself as the sole legitimate successor state. Russia was the only republic that did not formally declare its independence from the Soviet Union. With widespread international support and the concurrence of the republics, it received the Soviet Union's seat in various international organizations, including, most importantly, the permanent seat on the UN Security Council. It assumed the entire Soviet debt in exchange for title to all Soviet assets abroad.

More important, the Russian leadership initially tried to maintain key structures that would have bolstered Russia's presence and influence across the former Soviet Union. Although he said he supported the formation of a Russian Defense Ministry in December 1991, Yeltsin only set one up several months later in May 1992. In the interim, he explored whether the Russian-dominated CIS Armed Forces could be used as a way to retard the breakup of the former Soviet space. Russian troops remained stationed in several other former Soviet republics. At the same time, the Russian leadership supported the maintenance of a ruble zone, which it hoped to control by establishing a single monetary authority in charge of issuing money throughout the zone (an idea the other former Soviet republics rejected). That the CIS did not live up to Russian expectations as a unifying structure was not for the lack of effort on Russia's part. Rather, that failure was primarily due to the resistance of other former Soviet republics, with Ukraine in the lead, to anything that smacked of Russian hegemony over them.

As a consequence of the struggle with the Soviet center, the attitudes and goals of the Russian leadership, and Gorbachev's policies, Russia emerged at the end of 1991 as a state of uncertain legitimacy in institutional disarray confronted by mounting centrifugal forces. Although the radical democrats and Yeltsin had spoken eloquently of "the rebirth of Russia," they paid scant attention to legitimizing Russia as a sovereign republic or independent state. Indeed, they consciously cut the ties to the past that would have given the new Russia a modicum of historical legitimacy. As Yeltsin stressed in his inaugural address as the first Russian president, the new Russia represented a radical break not only with seventy years of Soviet totalitarianism, but also with a thousand years of Russian authoritarianism. He spoke of altering the relationship between state and society that had existed "for centuries," of building democracy "for the first time," while devoting one short paragraph to Russia's "most rich and original" culture.[9]

Further underscoring this break with the past, the new Russia bore little geographic resemblance to any historical Russian state, nor did it follow the pattern of ethnic Russian settlement. Some twenty-five million ethnic Russians found themselves living outside Russia in former Soviet republics. Most Russians believed that Russia encompassed more territory than the Russian Federation. As if reaffirming the illegitimacy of the new Russia, Yeltsin's government sought to prevent the foreclosure of the border issue, while casting itself as the protector of the rights of Russians living outside Russia in the former Soviet Union.[10]

The weak legitimacy of the Russian state was exacerbated by the institutional disarray in Moscow, in particular by the situation of "dual power" that pitted Yeltsin against the Russian Congress of People's Deputies. According to the Russian constitution, the president was "the highest official of the RSFSR (Russian Soviet Federative Socialist Republic) and the head of the executive branch of the RSFSR" (Article 121), whereas the Congress of People's Deputies was "the highest organ of state power" with the right to "review and decide any question relating to the jurisdiction of the Russian Federation" (Article 104).[11] Beginning in spring 1992, Yeltsin and the Congress were engaged in a political contest that escalated into a life-or-death struggle over the next year.

Regional elites exploited the state's weak legitimacy and the bitter conflict in Moscow to enhance their autonomy. The process had already begun in the late Soviet period, as Gorbachev and Yeltsin sought the support of Russia's regional leaders in their sharpening battle. Following a number of constituent republics, the North Ossetian Autonomous Republic in Russia declared sovereignty in July 1990. The "parade of sovereignties" within Russia gathered momentum after Yeltsin told audiences in Tatarstan and Bashkortostan to "take as much sovereignty as you can swallow." Autonomous oblasts unilaterally raised their status to that of republics and declared sovereignty, as did several autonomous districts such as Chukotia, Nenets, and Yamalo-Nenets. By the end of 1991, all the autonomous republics and oblasts and half the national districts had declared sovereignty, while Chechnya had gone even further by declaring independence (from Russia, while remaining in the Soviet Union).[12]

In a more threatening step to Russia's integrity and Yeltsin's position, Tatarstan, Bashkortostan, and Chechnya-Ingushetia all sought to raise themselves to the status of constituent republics within the Soviet Union. This was particularly important for Tatarstan, which was larger in territory and population—and potentially richer—than many of the constituent republics. Not surprisingly, prior to the fall of the USSR, Gorbachev encouraged these republics by inviting several of them to participate in the negotiation of a new Union Treaty. The new treaty finally agreed to would have given them the status of co-founders of the Union of Sovereign States (which was to replace the Soviet Union), casting into question Russia's territorial integrity without violating that of the Soviet Union.[13] The August putsch intervened, however, before the treaty could be signed.

Once the Soviet Union had been dissolved, Yeltsin moved quickly to arrest the centrifugal forces within Russia. On March 31, 1992, Moscow signed the Federation Treaty with all the ethnic-based republics, except Tatarstan and Chechnya, as well as separate agreements delineating rights and powers with the remaining subjects of the federation.[14] The treaty and agreements, however, fell short of reversing trends threatening Russia's territorial integrity for two reasons.

First, many ethnic Russian regions were disturbed that the republics had received a privileged position. Most important, Moscow acknowledged that the natural resources in the republics were regional government property; the same was not true of the natural resources in other regions. In addition, many of the republics signed separate protocols with Moscow that dramatically lessened their tax burden to the federal government. To right these perceived wrongs, several ethnic Russian regions contemplated declaring themselves to be republics.

Second, just as the Federation Treaty was signed, the conflict between Yeltsin and the Congress began to escalate. While most regional elites sought to stay out of that struggle, they did seek to exploit it to enhance their own autonomy. With the exception of Chechnya, Tatarstan went the farthest: In March 1992, over 60 percent of the voters supported independence in a referendum held in Tatarstan. In November, Tatarstan adopted a new constitution declaring Tatarstan to be "a sovereign state, a subject of international law ... associated with the Russian Federation on the basis of a Treaty on the mutual delegation of powers and spheres of authority" (Article 61).[15]

The conflicts in Moscow, between Moscow and the regions, and among regions reached their apogee in 1993. After a resounding victory in a popular referendum on his policies in April, Yeltsin convoked a constitutional conference to break the deadlock between him and the Congress. The conference made considerable progress in delineating the responsibilities of the executive and legislative branches, only to falter over the question of federal structure. The ethnically based republics were intent on maintaining their hard-won status as "sovereign states" with its corresponding privileges, whereas the ethnic Russian regions were determined to do away with this bias and create equal conditions for all Russia's regions.

With the conference stalled, Yeltsin sought to break his impasse with the Congress by unilaterally disbanding it and calling for new parliamentary elections. A two-week standoff ended in violence, as Yeltsin used force to put down a rebellion by supporters of the Congress. Yeltsin then had a new constitution drafted to provide for a strong presidency, which was adopted by popular referendum in December 1993. The period of "dual power" was brought to an end; recentralizing forces were in ascendancy. In February 1994, Moscow and Tatarstan signed a bilateral treaty, in which Tatarstan recognized itself to be part of Russia. There were widespread expectations that the period of conflict and drift was finally over.

Those expectations were to be greatly disappointed, however. In fact, within a year, Russia was in the midst of a chronic political and socioeconomic malaise that sapped Moscow's energy, further fragmented the state, and endangered the country's integrity. The reasons were multiple and reinforcing: Yeltsin's hands-off leadership style, lack of strategic vision, and increasingly fragile health; internecine elite struggles in Moscow; sharp socioeconomic decline; and drives for regional autonomy.

The new constitution had indeed provided a basis for getting beyond the conflicts of the first two years of the new Russia. It did away with the ambiguities of the old, leaving no doubt that the presidency was the center of power in the political system. The president was no longer simply the "highest official of the RSFSR"; he was now the head of state and guarantor of the constitution and the rights and freedoms of Russian citizens. He was to defend the sovereignty, independence, and territorial integrity of Russia; ensure the coordinated functioning of the organs of state power; and determine the main directions of foreign and domestic policy (Article 80). He was the commander-in-chief (Article 87). Unlike under the old constitution, he now had the right to dismiss the Duma (Article 84), and removing him from office was no longer a matter of majority vote by the parliament, but of a long process involving both the upper and lower houses of the Federal

Assembly, the Constitutional Court, and the Supreme Court (Article 93). Overriding his veto no longer required a simple majority, but a two-thirds majority in both houses of the parliament (Article 107). At the same time, the president retained his extensive power of appointment of executive and judicial branch officials.[16]

Yeltsin's Leadership and the Struggle for Power

For as long as Yeltsin was president the power of the presidency was much greater on paper than in practice, in part because of his leadership style. He affected policy—and expanded his room for maneuver—primarily through his power of appointment, not by clearly articulating detailed strategy.[17] According to one of his advisers, Yuri Baturin, Yeltsin's vision for Russia was vague to the extreme, amounting to little more than helping Russia become a prosperous country.[18] This Kremlin insider noted that "After each victory, he, as a rule, did not see clearly how to use its fruits, what to do next. Yeltsin's well-known, 'deeply meaningful' pauses are explained most often by the fact that in a series of cases and situations he did not know what to do concretely."[19] But Yeltsin could keep everyone off balance by shaking up the government, which he did frequently, particularly during his last two years in office as he sought a loyal successor who would both protect him from any political or legal retribution and continue, in broad terms, his policies.[20] He fired four prime ministers in the seventeen months before he appointed Putin as prime minister and designated him his successor in August 1999.

More important, however, in eroding Yeltsin's power and authority was his failing health. From the very beginning, his prolonged absences at critical moments were noted; for example, he was absent for a few weeks shortly after the failed August putsch when the structure of the new Russian government was being decided. The absences grew longer as his health deteriorated. After Yeltsin's reelection, a Kremlin insider wrote, "it was obvious to all who witnessed the official beginning of Yeltsin's second term that the leader's health had become one of the key factors in Russian politics."[21] By the time he resigned on December 31, 1999, he was largely an absentee president, and senior government officials paid less heed to his preferences. To put it bluntly, "The reasons for the contradictions in the White House [Russian government] were so deep and the risk of becoming the victim of the president's anger so small, that his words changed nothing in the relations among the members of the cabinet."[22]

Yeltsin's health had implications that went far beyond the erosion of his authority. His problems distracted attention from the urgent task of rebuilding Russia by thrusting the political elites into a prolonged succession struggle. The constitution did not provide for a vice president to serve out the term of a prematurely departing president. Rather, it stipulated that, should the president leave office prematurely for any reason, the prime minister would serve as acting president for three months, during which elections would be held for a permanent successor (Article 92). As a consequence, would-be successors had to be prepared to run at a moment's notice, while making preparations for elections in mid-2000, should Yeltsin serve out his term. More often than not, the exigencies of short- and long-term campaigns contradicted one another.

At the same time, the possibility of patronage, command over an executive apparatus with lines into every region, and the chance that its occupant would become acting president all made the prime ministership the central target in the succession struggle, with deleterious effects for the smooth functioning of the government. After Yeltsin's reelection, all successive prime ministers were viewed as successors—whether they were true heavyweights, such as Viktor Chernomyrdin or Yevgeny Primakov, or novices, such as Sergei Kirienko, brought to Moscow to serve in the government just a year before he was appointed prime minister at the age of thirty-five. The rapid turnover in prime ministers in Yeltsin's last two years was a reflection in large part of the sharpening succession struggle.

That turnover was also a reflection of the political instincts and insecurities of Yeltsin, who insisted—right up to his surprise resignation—that he would serve out his term. He was profoundly jealous of his prerogatives as president and deeply resented any suggestion of a campaign to succeed him. This made the job of the prime minister almost untenable. Because of Yeltsin's frailties, any prime minister was compelled to assume greater responsibility and authority, even to encroach on presidential prerogatives, if only to keep the government at a minimal level of efficiency and coherency and to represent Russia with dignity abroad. That inevitably enhanced his attractiveness as a presidential candidate, which in turn raised the risk that Yeltsin would come to see him as a rival.

Assuming the responsibility without provoking Yeltsin's ire was a line no prime minister (with the exception of Putin) was able to toe for long. Yeltsin fired both Chernomyrdin in March 1998 and Primakov in May 1999 in large part because they appeared too presidential. And he did this with a seeming lack of concern for the consequences for Russia's development. Chernomyrdin was fired at just the moment that the country needed governmental stability and strong leadership to deal with the mounting pressures of a global financial crisis, which finally overtook Russia five months later in August 1998. Likewise, Primakov was fired just as he was beginning to push through the Duma key legislation required by the much needed loan agreement with the International Monetary Fund.

The succession struggle, of course, was about more than individual politicians. Its outcome would have far-reaching consequences for the large political-economic coalitions, or oligarchic groups, that had come to dominate politics in Moscow after Yeltsin put an end to the period of "dual power" in 1993.[23] These groups had emerged as state assets were rapidly privatized after the breakup of the Soviet Union. The most powerful controlled key positions in government, financial and industrial capital, information-gathering agencies and media outlets, and instruments of coercion (both private and nominally state). They were engaged in a constant struggle for power and property, and the main battlefield was the government itself, because control of various parts of the government conferred great advantages in obtaining access to financial flows and lucrative enterprises.

The most infamous episode of suborning the state for private gain was the "loans-for-shares" program of late 1995 that put some of the country's leading oil companies and other strategic enterprises in the hands of a few well-placed financiers at cut-rate prices. Under this program, worked out by the financiers themselves and Anatoly Chubais, then first deputy prime minister, banks would lend the government money in exchange for the right to manage the state's shares for a specified term. If the state did not repay the loan by the end of the term (something that was almost a certainty at that time, given the government's financial straits), then the banks would have the right to sell the shares, splitting the profits between themselves and the state. The loans and any sales were supposed to be open to competitive bidding. Typically, the banks that organized the auctions (selected by the state) also won the bidding. According to one leading banker, the winners of the auctions were all known in advance: "Simply put, the matter concerned the 'appointment as millionaires' (or even billionaires) of a group of entrepreneurs, who, according to the plan, were to become the main supports of the regime."[24]

The leading oligarchic groups played a decisive role in masterminding Yeltsin's come-from-behind victory over his communist challenger in the election of 1996. Much of Yeltsin's second term was dominated by the struggle over the fruits of that victory by four groups in particular: (1) the Chubais coalition, built around control of the macroeconomic policy bloc in the government and the Oneksimbank financial-industrial group; (2) the Berezovsky/Gusinsky coalition, built around control of Russia's major television channels, key positions in the presidential administration, and a few leading financial-industrial groups; (3) the Chernomyrdin coalition, built primarily on Gazprom (the giant gas monopoly) that Chernomyrdin set up at the end of the Soviet period; and (4) the Luzhkov coalition, or Moscow group, built around the mayor's control of the city's politics and economic assets.

These groups played a central role in all the government shuffles during Yeltsin's second term, including the dismissals of four prime ministers. A number of them were instrumental in Yeltsin's final decision to select Putin as his successor. At the same time, as the circumstances of the struggle changed over time, the coalitions themselves shifted. In particular, Berezovsky was a master at shifting coalitions to maintain his own position near the center of power, at least as long as Yeltsin was in office.

One thing all of these coalitions had in common was a lack of interest in rebuilding the state, for they all prospered by preying on a weak state. The bureaucracy was manipulated to allow these coalitions to lay their hands on strategic industries. Standing as "authorized banks," private commercial banks granted the right to handle budgetary funds and allowed these coalitions to use those funds for private gain. Insider influence was used to obtain tax breaks or access to the financial accounts of government departments. The focus was on dividing up property, not on creating wealth. And for this reason, there was little interest in creating the commercial and legal conditions that would have produced incentives for productive enterprise because they would have complicated the stripping of assets and the seizure of state property.

Thus, throughout Yeltsin's second term, as was so often the case in Russian history, power took precedence over policy. The uncertainties about succession—and its far-reaching consequences for individuals, including the question of physical survival for some—only concentrated the focus on the question of power. The constant shuffling and battling for position eroded the government's coherence and discipline and thereby its capacity

to govern effectively and to translate Yeltsin's policy preferences into concrete actions. Not surprisingly, few ambitious leaders—and certainly no
would-be presidents—were prepared to risk the tough, unpopular measures needed to address the country's deepening ills.

Bitter elite struggles, widespread high-level corruption, massive asset
stripping, and an appalling lack of concern for social welfare all helped
accelerate the socioeconomic decline that had begun in the Soviet period.
The costs during the Yeltsin period were staggering, in both real and psychological terms, for the population as a whole and for the state in particular. Statistics do not begin to capture the full costs, but they provide a
sense of the scale. Between 1992 and 1999, inclusive, the Russian economy
collapsed in real terms by nearly 40 percent, according to official statistics.
Public health told a similar story of decline and decay. During the 1990s, life
expectancy fell for both men and women. For men, the decline was dramatic, from 64.2 years in 1989 to as low as 57.6 in 1994 before rebound-
ing to 61.3 in 1998.[25] Contagious diseases, such as tuberculosis and
diphtheria, made strong comebacks. As one demographer put it in the late
1990s, "Russia's health profile no longer remotely resemble[d] that of a
developed country; in fact, it [was] worse in a variety of respects than those
of many Third World countries."[26]

This socioeconomic decline, coupled with the disarray in Moscow, had
dire consequences for two key symbols of state power and authority: military and money.

According to a leading Duma expert, the military, once the pride of the
country, was on the verge of ruin in the late 1990s as a consequence of
slashed budgets, neglect, corruption, political infighting, and failed reform.[27]
Budget outlays for defense spending fell from some $130 billion in 1992 to
as little as $40 billion in 1998.[28] The overwhelming share of that money
went for salaries and provisions. Even then, military officers frequently
moonlighted to augment their pay; commanders used units to perform services for local officials and businessmen to earn money for provisions; and
enlisted men were frequently seen on the streets begging for money or other
items, even in the center of Moscow. Corruption among high-level officers
was rampant. The military's dismal performance in the first Chechen war in
1994–1996 graphically underscored the deep problems that beset it.

As for money, Moscow did not manage a reliable countrywide financial
and monetary system at any point during Yeltsin's presidency. While the
ruble remained the nominal currency, regions and enterprises issued quasi-

currencies in the form of promissory notes, while barter flourished as a means of exchange. In the late 1990s, the overwhelming share of commercial transactions, up to 75 percent by some estimates, took place outside the monetized sector in the form of barter or currency surrogates.[29] Moreover, a large share of economic activity—perhaps as much as 40 percent—took place in the "shadow economy," which, by definition, lies beyond state control. In August 1998, the financial system finally collapsed as a consequence of Moscow's inability to collect taxes and its effort to cover the budget deficit through foreign borrowing and the issuance of various domestic debt instruments that amounted to little more than a massive pyramid scheme.

This crumbling state, not surprisingly, commanded little respect and instilled little fear. The lack of fear was evident in the pervasive tax and draft evasion, as well as in such mundane matters as the widespread nonobservance of traffic regulations. The lack of respect was evident in the general disregard for national holidays and monuments and the profound public distrust of high-ranking government officials and central government institutions, repeatedly recorded in public opinion polls.[30] Kremlin intrigue fed cynicism about the state, while Yeltsin's deteriorating health, both physical and mental, reinforced pervasive doubts about the state's strength and will.

Fragmentation of Central Power

Regional leaders were quick to exploit the disarray and decay in Moscow to seize key regional economic assets and to consolidate their autonomy. Moscow elites only reinforced this trend through repeated concessions to regional elites to obtain their support in their own battles in Moscow. That was particularly true of the presidential campaign of 1996, when active support from regional leaders was critical to Yeltsin's victory. His most consequential concession at that time was to relinquish his power to appoint the heads of regional governments in favor of direct popular elections. The popular legitimacy that resulted vastly strengthened regional leaders' freedom of maneuver.

The extent of this regional autonomy was all the more remarkable because, with rare exception, the regions remained dependent on Moscow for budget support.[31] Part of the explanation lies in the incoherence of the central government. Regional leaders did not have to approach a unified government for money. Rather, they could deal with multiple sources of financing in Moscow, some technically state, some technically private, and play on their contradictions to obtain the best deal for themselves. Back home, political leaders and enterprise managers formed protection circles to advance their common interests against Moscow and to subvert many of its economic reform initiatives. Regional leaders also used their control over local resources to suborn local representatives of federal agencies, who, underfunded by Moscow, were at the mercy of local authorities for housing, conveniences, and other amenities. As already noted, even military commanders found it necessary to cut deals with the local authorities to ensure themselves continued flows of food, energy, and other provisions to their bases.

Moscow periodically made efforts to reassert its authority in the regions, but to little avail. For example, after signing the bilateral treaty with Tatarstan, Moscow concluded that it was more promising to deal with regions individually rather than as parts of collectives, such as ethnically based republics. By the middle of 1998, it had signed agreements with over half of the country's eighty-nine regions. Many of these agreements, however, contradicted the Russian constitution, and most gave the regions control over federal properties located on their territory. Thus, while this approach might have undermined cooperation among regions—something Moscow saw as positive—it had the added consequence of enhancing the regions' autonomy individually and eroding respect for the constitution. Another effort to raise Moscow's authority—a move in 1996 to enhance the power and authority of the presidential representatives in the region— came to naught for lack funds and attention (the move's chief author, Anatoly Chubais, then head of the presidential administration, was diverted by a stiff challenge to his position in Moscow from the Berezovsky/Gusinsky coalition).

By exposing the weakness of the central government, the financial meltdown of August 1998 further fueled centrifugal forces. Many regional leaders acted unilaterally in setting price controls and forbidding the export of certain products, primarily foodstuffs, from their regions (although in both cases the implementation was not always effective). Some spoke of creating local currencies or gold reserves. Yevgeny Primakov, at the time of his confirmation as prime minister in September, warned that there was a growing danger of Russia's splitting up and vowed to take tough steps to avert it.[32] In particular, he advocated discontinuing the election of regional governors in favor of their appointment by the president. But little came of these efforts as Primakov became bogged down in a struggle with the Kremlin that ultimately led to his dismissal in May 1999.

Moscow's weakness did not, however, turn the regional leaders into unchallenged authorities. Governors and republic presidents may have been the most powerful figures at the regional level, but their power was limited by local elites, much as Yeltsin was constrained by national and regional ones. The mayors of administrative centers, especially if popularly elected, and the heads of major enterprises, particularly if they provided the bulk of funds to the regional budget, often acted as effective counterweights. Gubernatorial and republic presidential elections provided graphic evidence of these limits. In the electoral cycle from September 1996 through February 1997, incumbents won only twenty-four of fifty elections. In 1998, they won five of eleven contests.[33] Moreover, during the Yeltsin era, regional leaders did not capitalize on their newfound possibilities by developing joint positions vis-à-vis Moscow. The eight interregional associations were noteworthy primarily for their lack of concrete actions. The Federation Council, where the regional leaders sat ex officio beginning in 1996, never developed the corporate identity the State Duma did. It met infrequently— once or twice a month for two to three days. Regional leaders preferred to spend their few days in Moscow each month not debating legislation but individually lobbying government officials for funds. Although dozens of agreements were signed between regions, the preferred channel of communication was the vertical one with Moscow. Regional leaders focused on signing bilateral treaties with Moscow delineating powers suited to their own situations, rather than on developing a uniform set of rules governing federal relations.

Finally, the regions grew increasingly isolated from one another during the 1990s. The breakdown of the countrywide production processes of the Soviet period and the accompanying sharp economic decline gave regions less reason and capacity to deal with one another. At the same time, the liberalization of the economy opened up greater possibilities for foreign trade. Imports surged by over 70 percent between 1992 and 1997 (the last year before the financial crisis sharply reduced imports).[34] On average, only a quarter of a region's product was sent to other Russian regions, slightly less was exported abroad, and the rest was consumed locally.[35] Housing shortages, the close link between the workplace and social services, and other constraints on labor mobility tied most workers to their place of employment and impeded the development of national labor markets.[36] Sharp increases in fares, declining income, and the general deterioration of infra-structure sharply reduced interregional travel.[37]

Thus, the crumbling of the central state apparatus and disarray in Moscow did not create strong regions or promote a powerful group of regions that could impose its designs on Moscow. Regions suffered from the same range of disabilities as the country as a whole, and the overall economic decline deprived them of the resources they needed to address those ills. Although there were a few strong regional leaders, in general they remained weak and ineffective: "Weak center–weak regions" provided an apt description of the situation. The striking feature of the Russian political and economic system at the end of the Yeltsin era was the near total absence of concentrations of power anywhere in the country capable alone of control-ling the situation or of creating a coalition for that purpose. Effective gov-ernment, to the extent it existed, was found at the local level, built around tight relations between political authorities and industrial, agricultural, and construction enterprises. In this diffusion and fragmentation of power, Russia resembled more feudal Europe than a modern state.

Putin Comes to Power

Putin came to power determined to stop the rot, to rebuild the Russian state, and to regain Russia's standing in the world. "I am absolutely con-vinced," he said in an interview shortly after he became acting president, "that we will not solve any problems, any economic or social problems, while the state is disintegrating."[38] Moreover, he made it clear that rebuild-ing the state required a recentralization of power in Moscow, or, more pre-cisely, in the Kremlin. "From the very beginning," he said, "Russia was created as a supercentralized state. That's practically laid down in its genetic code, its traditions, and the mentality of its people."[39] While he has laced his remarks with talk about democracy, his views on the state reflect tradi-tional Russian attitudes toward power and the state with their stress on its being strong, centralized, and paternalistic.

In his first months in office, Putin moved aggressively in reining in the competing power centers and reasserting the Kremlin's power and prerog-atives. First, he took aim at the regional governors by establishing seven "superregions" headed by personal representatives charged with coordi-nating the activity of all federal agents in their regions and monitoring compliance of local laws with the constitution and federal laws. He pushed through two laws that enhanced his leverage over regional elites. The first restructured the Federation Council, the upper house of parliament, to deprive governors of their seats (held ex officio) and, thereby, their immunity from criminal prosecution; the second gave the president the right to dismiss regional leaders and legislatures for actions contradicting federal law. Shortly thereafter, Putin established the State Council, a purely consultative body composed of the regional governors and led by the president—a reliable mechanism for keeping abreast of the mood of key regional leaders.

Then Putin moved to rein in the free-wheeling press. The effort began with the raid on headquarters of Russia's major independent media holding company, Media-Most, and the arrest of its head, Vladimir Gusinsky, shortly after Putin's inauguration. These actions were clearly intended to intimidate the journalists—at least many journalists saw that as their intent—and to limit, but not eliminate, public criticism of Putin and his policies.[40] Self-censorship spread as editors and journalists feared the Kremlin had the capacity and will to destroy them if it so wished, a fear given greater credence by the Kremlin's destruction of Media-Most in spring 2001.

Finally, Putin dealt with the oligarchs. A well-publicized series of attacks on business leaders—including the opening of some criminal cases for tax evasion—was intended to put them on notice that they would no longer be allowed to ride roughshod over the government.[41] When Putin met with eighteen oligarchs shortly thereafter, he assured them that there would be no general review of the privatization process, although he left open the possibility of reviewing specific cases (presumably involving his critics). His goal, he indicated, was not to renationalize any property but, more simply, to ensure that big business worked in the interests of the state.[42]

While taking on these various power centers, Putin also revived the historical symbols of statehood to legitimize the Russia that emerged from the wreckage of the Soviet Union. He catered to the interests of the military and increased its public prominence, not only because it had been instrumental in his rise to power, but also because historically it was a potent symbol of the Russian state. He sought to restore the continuity of Russian statehood by reaching back to both Soviet and Tsarist traditions. That effort was best illustrated by his decision to restore the old Soviet anthem (with new words) as the national anthem, while retaining the prerevolutionary tricolor and Tsarist double-headed eagle as the national flag and herald.

As he moved to consolidate power at home, Putin launched—to the surprise of most observers—an activist foreign policy, with high-profile visits to several European capitals, as well as to North Korea, China, Japan, and India in the first months after his inauguration. He reenergized relations with a number of former Soviet client states, including Iraq, Libya, and Cuba. In this way, he underscored Russia's interests around the globe and its intent to act—and its demand to be treated—as a great power.

Throughout his first year in power, Putin was blessed by a strong economic upswing and broad popular support. In 1999, the Russian economy recovered from the financial collapse of August 1998, growing by over 5 percent; in 2000, the growth accelerated to over 8 percent. By most accounts, optimism within the business community grew exponentially after Putin took over from Yeltsin (although the continued high level of capital flight raises questions about the depth of that optimism). In large part because of this economic success, Putin's popularity remained remarkably high, hovering over 60 percent for most of his first year in office.

Despite this impressive start, a year after his inauguration, Putin still faced numerous challenges to his authority and to his effort to build a reliable "presidential vertical," which would ensure that his policies and government programs were implemented faithfully across Russia.

First, Putin had not yet mastered the Kremlin, where three groups remained locked in a struggle for power and influence: "the Family" (Yeltsin cronies who were responsible for naming Putin as Yeltsin's successor), the security services (drawn from Putin's colleagues from his St. Petersburg KGB days), and the liberal economists (many of whom also hail from St. Petersburg). According to well-informed circles in Moscow, Putin would like to distance himself from the Family to demonstrate his own independence and free himself of any obligations he may have undertaken in exchange for Yeltsin's decision to designate him his successor. But Putin had difficulty in doing this because the Family continued to control financial flows and key cadres and because Putin did not have a sufficiently deep team of loyalists to staff all the key positions in the government. As long as the Family remained ensconced in the Kremlin, Putin would not have free rein there.

Second, the oligarchs and governors were far from tamed, even if their autonomy had been trimmed. The Family was just one of the oligarchic groups that still exercised extensive economic and political influence. What had changed was that the oligarchs had become much less public in the way they exercised power and influence in the Kremlin and government. As for the governors, they displayed less of an inclination to become involved in national-level politics, and most demonstrated a willingness to bring regional laws and constitutions in line with national statutes and the constitution. But they were tenacious in their efforts to retain control over local economic and political resources. The Kremlin's poor record in getting its candidates elected in the cycle of regional elections at the end of 2000 underscored the limits of its authority.[43]

And, third, Russia's financial straits put strict limits on what Putin can do. With a federal budget of some $40 billion (at current exchange rates), Putin simply does not have sufficient resources to rebuild the military and security services, pay off pension and wage arrears, rebuild the educational and health systems, fight corruption, and so on.[44] He will have to make difficult choices and trade-offs, something that will almost certainly provoke greater resistance to his policies and retard his consolidation of power.

Moreover, the economic recovery that has yielded a spike in government revenue remains fragile. It was built primarily on high oil prices and a sharp devaluation of the ruble. Little, if any, of the growth was due to greater efficiencies in the economy. While there has been much talk of reform and a few important steps such as reform of the tax system and the passage of a balanced budget for 2001, much remains to be done. Only in the summer of 2001 did the government begin to move, for example, to regulate the natural monopolies, end domestic subsidies for energy and transportation costs, and build a reliable independent court system. Little, however, has been done to relieve the crises in health care and public education, which will have severe negative consequences for the quality of the workforce, and therefore the quality of economic development, well into the future. As a result, it is far from certain that the current recovery is sustainable.

Two years after Putin took over from Yeltsin, the outlines of his Russia are slowly taking shape. Developments suggest that the extreme scenarios for the Russian state are improbable. Putin is not likely to succeed in building the supercentralized state of which he once dreamed. As a consequence of the breakdown of the state in the Yeltsin period, there are simply too many countervailing forces in Russian society today and too few resources at Putin's disposal. But neither is the country in danger of disintegration, as many in the Russian elite feared just a few years ago. The system, for all the turmoil of the past decade, has demonstrated a considerable amount of stability at the macro level. Nor is Russia likely to witness a breakthrough toward Western liberal democracy. There is simply too little support within the elites for that variation.

Rather, the most likely scenario is the slow consolidation of the regime that emerged under Yeltsin, that is, the slow ordering of the elements of an oligarchic regime, in which Putin will be a key figure, simply because of the position he occupies, but not necessarily the dominant one. He will be surrounded by others who control critical elements of the political and economic system at the national and regional levels. What Putin, or better the Kremlin, will demand of the oligarchs and governors is political loyalty and a payment of tribute (called taxes), in exchange for which they will be able to run their enterprises or regions much as they please. The struggle among the oligarchic groups will lose—indeed, it has already lost—much of the unruly character it had under Yeltsin. There will be a greater semblance of order. If there is an analogy to this regime, perhaps it is the Mexican regime for most of the twentieth century.

Such a regime would mark a rebuilding of the state. But the question is whether that rebuilt state could generate a sustained socioeconomic recovery that could slowly regain Russia's standing in the world. It is far from clear that it could. Mexico offers some hope; it took two to three generations for the Mexican regime to produce robust growth, and Putin is looking for major results much sooner. Economic booms, such as the one Russia is now experiencing, are possible, but as the Mexican experience suggests, busts are inevitable. Over the near and medium terms—and that means for the duration of Putin's presidency—Russia is unlikely to experience a sustained, robust recovery. In other words, Putin may have halted the erosion of the state only to find that real socioeconomic progress has eluded him. He may have halted the decline only to replace it with stagnation.

Notes

1. See Yitzhak M. Brudny, *Reinventing Russia: Russian Nationalism and the Soviet State, 1953–1991* (Cambridge, Mass.: Harvard University Press, 1998), pp. 250–6.

2. See Yuri Baturin et al., *Epokha Yel'tsina: Ocherki politicheskoy istorii* (The Yeltsin Epoch: Essays in Political History) (Moscow: Vargius, 2001), pp. 104–8.

3. See "O gosudarstvennom suverenitete Rossiyskoy Sovetskoy Federativnoy Sotsialistich-eskoy Respubliki" (On State Sovereignty of the Russian Soviet Federative Socialist Republic), in *Khrestomatiya po konstitutsionnomu pravu Rossiyskoy Federatsii*, ed. Yury L. Shul'zhenko (Moscow: Yurist, 1997), pp. 748–50.

4. See Archie Brown, *The Gorbachev Factor* (Oxford, U.K.: Oxford University Press, 1997), pp. 285–305; Baturin, *Epokha Yel'tsina*, pp. 112–3.

5. On Yeltsin's wavering, see Lilia Shevtsova, *Rezhim Borisa Yel'tsina* (The Regime of Boris Yeltsin) (Moscow: ROSSPEN, 1999), pp. 7–39.

6. See Yegor Gaidar, *Dni porazhenii i pobed* (Days of Defeats and Victories) (Moscow: Vargius, 1997), pp. 71–87.

7. See "Yeltsin Addresses Russian Parliament on 25th December," BBC, SU/1264/C3/1, December 28, 1991.

8. Boris Yeltsin, *Zapiski prezidenta* (The President's Notes) (Moscow: Ogonek, 1994), pp. 150–3. The quotations can be found on p. 152.

9. See "Speech by Yeltsin at His Inauguration as RSFSR President," BBC, SU/1121/C2/1, July 11, 1991. See also Aleksey Salmin, "Poka ne..." (Until ...), *NG-Stsenarii*, April 12, 2000.

10. In the Minsk Agreement Establishing a Commonwealth of Independent States, December 8, 1991, the parties recognized one another's territorial integrity "with the Commonwealth," not in general. They also guaranteed the "openness of borders and freedom of movement for citizens and of transmission of information within the Commonwealth" (Article 5). The text of the agreement can be found in *SIPRI Yearbook 1992* (Oxford, U.K.: Oxford University Press, 1992), pp. 558–9.

11. See "Konstitutsiya (osnovnoi zakon) Rossiyskoy Federatsii—Rossii" (Constitution [Fundamental Law] of the Russian Federation), in Shul'zhenko, *Khrestomatiya*, p. 758.

12. For more detailed treatment of developments between the Russian leadership and Russia's regions, see Gail W. Lapidus and Edward W. Walker, "Nationalism, Regionalism, and Federalism: Center-Periphery Relations in Post-Communist Russia," in *The New Russia: Troubled Transformation*, ed. Gail W. Lapidus (Boulder, Colo.: Westview Press, 1995), pp. 79–113.

13. For Gorbachev's views on the new Union Treaty, see Mikhail Gorbachev, *Zhizn' i reformy* (Life and Reforms), vol. 2 (Moscow: Novosti, 1995), pp. 513–54.

14. The text of the treaty can be found in Shul'zhenko, *Khrestomatiya*, pp. 73–95.

15. On events in Tatarstan, see Mary McAuley, *Russia's Politics of Uncertainty* (Cambridge, U.K.: Cambridge University Press, 1997), pp. 54–64. The text of the Tatarstan constitution is available at http://www.tatar.ru.

16. The text of the constitution can be found in Shul'zhenko, *Khrestomatiya*, pp. 34–72.

17. As Yeltsin, or his ghostwriter, put it, "Any victim, any resignation, any change in the political configuration could not be accidental or only tactical. In each of my moves, I was obliged to bear in mind the general strategy, the main task." See Boris Yeltsin, *Prezidentskiy marafon* (Presidential Marathon) (Moscow: AST, 2000), p. 115.

18. Baturin, *Epokha Yel'tsina*, p. 795.

19. Baturin, *Epokha Yel'tsina*, p. 802.

20. Baturin, *Epokha Yel'tsina*, pp. 778–91.

21. Baturin, *Epokha Yel'tsina*, p. 575.

22. Baturin, *Epokha Yel'tsina*, p. 729.

23. On the structure and development of the oligarchy, see Thomas E. Graham, "From Oligarchy to Oligarchy: The Structure of Russia's Ruling Elite," *Demokratizatsiya*, vol. 7, no. 3 (Summer 1999), pp. 325–40. See also Lilia Shevtsova, *Politicheskie zigzagi postkommunisticheskoy Rossii* (Political Zigzags of Post-Communist Russia) (Moscow: Moscow Carnegie Center, 1997),

pp. 25–38; and Vladimir Shlapentokh, "Russia: Privatization and Illegalization of Social and Political Life," *The Washington Quarterly*, vol. 19, no. 1 (Winter 1996), pp. 65–85.

24. Petr Aven, "Ekonomika torga" (The Bargaining Economy), *Kommersaint-Daily*, January 27, 1999.

25. Judyth L. Twigg and Kate Schecter, "The Russia Initiative: Social Cohesion," in *The Russia Initiative: Reports of the Four Task Forces* (New York: Carnegie Corporation of New York, 2001), p. 73.

26. For details on Russia's health crisis, see Nicholas Eberstadt, "Russia: Too Sick to Matter?" *Policy Review*, vol. 95 (June/July 1999); also available at http://www.policyreview.com/jun99/eberstadt.html. The quotation is found on p. 4 of the Internet version. See also Murray Feshbach, "Russia's Population Meltdown," *The Wilson Quarterly*, vol. 15 (Winter 2001).

27. Alexei G. Arbatov, "Military Reform in Russia: Dilemmas, Obstacles, and Prospects," *International Security*, vol. 22, no. 4 (Spring 1998), pp. 83–5.

28. See Christopher Hill, "How Much Does Russia Spend on Defense?" summary of remarks at the Center for Strategic and International Studies, Washington, D.C., January 31, 2001. Hill notes correctly that "conversion of Russian defense budget data into dollars using market exchange rates, though frequently undertaken, is hopelessly misleading. For 1999, for example, it implies that Russia spent under $4 billion on defense compared to US outlays approaching $300 billion."

29. According to a study of over 200 enterprises by the Interdepartmental Commission on Balances of the Federal Bankruptcy Service, nearly three-quarters of their earnings are in the form of barter or promissory notes, that is, they lie outside of the monetized sector. See "Zhizn' vzaimy" (Life on Credit), *Ekspert*, no. 8 (March 2, 1998), p. 13. For a study of the rise of barter in the Russian economy, see David Woodruff, *Money Unmade: Barter and the Fate of Russian Capitalism* (Ithaca, N.Y.: Cornell University Press, 1999).

30. Yu. A. Levada, "Vlast' i obshchestvo v Rossii glazami obshchestvennogo mneniya" (Power and Society through the Eyes of Russian Public Opinion), in *"Vlast' i obshchestvo": Resul'taty reprezentativnogo oprosa zhiteley Rossii: Analiz i materialy* (Power and Society: Results of a Representative Survey of People Living in Russia: Analysis and Materials), ed. N. A. Zorkaya (Moscow: Moscow School for Political Studies, 1998), pp. 11–25.

31. In 1997, for example, only eight regions did not receive money from the federal Fund for the Financial Support of Subjects of the Federation, and even these received funds for federal programs carried out on their territory. See A. Lavrov, V. Shuvalov, A. Neshchadin, and E. Vasilishen, eds., *Predprinimatel'skiy klimat regionov Rossii: Geografiya Rossii dlya investorov i predprinimateley* (Entrepreneurial Climate in Russia's Regions: Geography of Russia for Investors and Entrepreneurs) (Moscow: Nachala-Press, 1997), p. 126.

32. See *RFE/RL Newsline*, September 14, 1998.

33. See Michael McFaul and Nikolay Petrov, eds., *Politicheskiy al'manakh Rossii 1997* (Political Almanac of Russia 1997), vol. 1 (Moscow: Moscow Carnegie Center, 1998), pp. 117–8, 271, 279–81; and Aleksey Titkov, "Izmeneniya v sostave organov vlasti i deputatov Gosudarstvennoy dumy po regionam s dekabrya 1997g po mart 1999g" (Changes in the Composition of State Organs and State Duma Deputies by Region from December 1997 to March 1999), in *Regiony Rossii v 1998g. Yezhegodnoe prilozhenie k 'Politicheskomu al'manakhu Rossii'* (Russia's Regions in 1998: Annual Supplement to the Political Almanac of Russia), ed. Nikolai Petrov (Moscow: Gendal'f, 1999), pp. 41–8.

34. See S. B. Avdahseva et al., *Obzor ekonomicheskoy politike v Rossii za 1998 god* (Overview of Economic Policy in Russia in 1998) (Moscow: ROSSPEN, 1999), p. 626.

35. A. Lavrov, L. Polishchuk, and A. Treyvish, "Ekonomicheskie problemy stanovleniya federalizma v Rossii" (Economic Problems in the Formation of Federalism in Russia), paper prepared for the Conference on Contemporary Russian Federalism: Problems and Prospects, Moscow Carnegie Center, Moscow, December 10, 1997, p. 4 and attached map.

36. See Simon Clarke and Inna Donova, "Internal Mobility and Labour Market Flexibility in Russia," *Europe-Asia Studies*, vol. 51, no. 2 (1999), pp. 213–43; Mikhail Dmitriev, "Roossiyskiy rynok truda silen neispolneniyem zakonov" (Russian Labor Market Strength Is in Nonenforcement of Laws), *Ekspert*, vol. 5 (February 5, 1998), pp. 14-6.

37. Passenger traffic by all modes of transportation in 1996 was less than two-thirds of the 1990 level, while increasingly fewer of those trips were between cities. See D. S. L'vov et al., *Put' v XXI vek: strategicheskie problemy i perspektivy rossiyskoy ekonomiki* (Path to the Twenty-First Century: Strategic Problems and Prospects of the Russian Economy) (Moscow: Ekonomika, 1999), pp. 628–9. See also Gavriil Popov, "Transport," *Nezavisimaya gazeta*, March 15, 2000, Internet version.

38. Interview with Acting President Vladimir Putin, ORT (Russian media/news organization), January 4, 2000; transcript available in the Kremlin Package, Federal News Service, January 5, 2000.

39. N. Gevorkyan, A. Kolesnikov, and N. Timakova, *Ot pervogo litsa: Razgovory s Vladimirom Putinym* (From the First Person: Conversations with Vladimir Putin) (Moscow: Vargius, 2000), pp. 167–8.

40. See, for example, Aleksandr Gol'ts, "Sinie ushi Kremlya" (The Kremlin's Blue Ears), *Itogi*, vol. 25, no. 211 (June 20, 2000), pp. 16–7; see Afanasiy Sborov, "Pervyy sredi ravnoudalennykh" (First among Equals), *Kommersant-vlast'*, vol. 24, no. 375 (June 20, 2000), pp. 5–9, who describes Putin's logic as follows: "He is criticizing us: we are trying to build the state: therefore, he is an enemy of the state and has to be rendered harmless." See also Vitaliy Tret'yakov, "Pochemu 'Media-MOST'" (Why Media-Most), *Nezavisimaya gazeta*, May 16, 2000 (Internet version), who argues that the issue is not freedom of the press but Gusinsky's political and commercial activities.

41. See Natal'ya Arkhangel'skaya et al., "Provokatsiya" (Provocation), *Ekspert* (July 17, 2000), Internet version.

42. See "Oligarkhov v Kremle sovsem obnulili" (Oligarchs in the Kremlin Completely Zerod Out), *Kommersant-Daily*, July 29, 2000, Internet version.

43. Of thirty-two contests between Putin's inauguration and the end of 2000, Kremlin-backed challengers won only five, while eleven candidates opposed by the Kremlin won. See Julie A. Corwin, "The Incumbency Advantage," *The Russian Federation Report* (Radio Free Europe/Radio Liberty), vol. 3, no. 1 (January 3, 2001).

44. The budget is larger when expressed in terms of purchasing power parity (PPP). It should be stressed, however, that for the next few years Russia faces a substantial foreign debt burden of several billion dollars. That debt is paid in dollars at the current exchange rate, not in PPP dollars.

3

Power and Leadership in Putin's Russia

Lilia Shevtsova

In many ways Yeltsin's legacy determined the course of Russia's newest stage of political development that began with Vladimir Putin's meteoric ascendancy to power. Society's disillusionment with the post-Soviet transition of the 1990s, the increasing nostalgia on the part of various social groups for the Soviet past, the longing for order and a strong state, and the degradation of what had previously been the country's main political forces have all had a substantial impact on the priorities, style, and methods of the new rule. Political development under Vladimir Putin and the character of his leadership reflect his ability and that of the ruling elite to consolidate society on the basis of order; they also show Russian society's readiness to resume its path toward liberal democracy.

Yeltsin's Successor Becomes Yeltsin's Terminator

President Vladimir Putin and his team have succeeded in bringing the country out of the revolutionary cycle that Boris Yeltsin kept in place throughout his rule. For Yeltsin, permanent revolution, with its constant shake-ups, became the major instrument of his continued rule and the tool that he used to stabilize Russian society. This stabilization occurred not by strengthening the state (defined as the totality of independent political institutions and the complicated structure of their interdependencies within society) but rather through increasing the power of the political regime and, above all, a single element of it—the presidency. While Yeltsin allowed for the disintegration of power and its distribution among various groups of influence, Putin has demonstrated a more conscious desire to return to a paradigm, characteristic of Tsarist and Soviet Russia, of monolithic power. He refuses to recognize even limited authority for the State Duma, the Federation Council, or the government.

Throughout 2000, the Kremlin tried to change the decision-making mechanism that characterized Russian politics from 1992 to 1999. Yeltsin's policy of give-and-take and mutual tolerance and compromises was dismantled step by step to create in its place a "transmission belt" mechanism, based on the principles of subordination, hierarchical dependence, and unification. Instead of Yeltsin's system of relying on a "web" of various groups that balanced off one another—liberals, technocrats, great-power advocates, bureaucrats, oligarchs, regional elites, representatives of the raw-materials industries, among others—the new regime began to rely predominantly on the central bureaucracy with the support of the security structures and the office of the prosecutor.[1]

In 2000, federal reforms initiated by the presidential administration strengthened the unitary character of the Russian state.[2] Under Yeltsin, the parliament—even given its limited constitutional powers—still had the possibility of influencing the president's course of action and could limit the appetite of the executive branch. The Duma's tools of influence included threatening the president with impeachment, refusing to approve the president's candidate for prime minister, and voting on the budget. Now the ability of both chambers of parliament to affect executive branch policy is significantly reduced. The number of powerful propresidential factions in the Duma has virtually eliminated the possibility for opposition groups to overturn presidential decisions. As for the Federation Council, the new principle of its formation (through appointees of regional powers) practically precludes it from playing an independent role.

Looking at Putin's rise to power, we can observe a clear movement toward limiting political pluralism and forming a manageable multiparty system through the adoption of a law on parties that increased the role of the executive authorities in their formation and functioning. The institution of the party lost even the limited importance that it had under Yeltsin's rule. Rising through the ranks of power no longer occurs through party channels, but rather on the basis of bureaucratic rules or through specific loyalty and subservience to the president. Party differences play a decreased role in current Russian politics, and the bureaucratization of politics is more evident.

The centralization of power through a vertical chain of authority (known as the "presidential vertical" in Russia) was something Yeltsin tried to create without much success. Putin's policy has weakened Russia's nascent system of local self-government. The central authorities began with a deliberate policy of taking control over the independent news media. The takeover of NTV—an independent television station that broadcasts nationally—and a crackdown on other independent media outlets lead to the unambiguous conclusion that the ruling team's understanding of politics is one that views any critical gestures toward the Kremlin as an antistate activity. The existence of independent media is perceived as a threat to stability.

Nature of the Putin Regime: Continuity and Change

It is remarkable that after almost ten years of rather broad freedoms and openness, all major groups of influence have agreed to Putin's new rules of the game and voluntarily given up their autonomy and opposition activities.[3] No one is left on Russia's political scene who could oppose the central authorities and offer a serious challenge, much less a threat, to Putin. Even former rivals of the Kremlin and of Putin personally, such as Moscow Mayor Yury Luzhkov, have been forced to take an oath of loyalty to the president.[4] This unexpected servility and readiness to forsake independence, limit political ambitions, and obey the center is telling. The Russian political class still does not see pluralism, freedom of opposition and expression, or political autonomy as necessary elements of a political system. Alternatives to liberal democratic governances are not out of the question, and the political class is willing to return to the old, Soviet forms of governance based on compliance and subordination if its survival is guaranteed in return.

The complex political structure that arose under Yeltsin—characterized by a high level of political struggle, decentralization, and the emergence of complicated horizontal interdependence—has been gradually replaced by a process of unification and the formation of administrative teams along strict hierarchical lines. The central executive authorities, with the help of security structures and prosecutors, control the regions, oligarchs, and other business groups. By 2000, one could already observe the emergence of a political desert: Putin has no rivals and no opponents. No serious forces that might endanger Putin's position or have any impact on the political process exist. The parliament has been tamed, the regional barons have been politically neutralized, and the oligarchs, while not yet extinct, are expecting to be rewarded for their loyalty. A member of the Kremlin team proudly admitted, "We have achieved all our goals. Politics has become so boring." In fact, politics in its traditional meaning as the plurality of methods and institutions fighting for power and resources has nearly vanished since Putin's rise to power.

Russian politics is also losing its ideological character. Previous conflicts over ideas and paradigms no longer have meaning. It is unimportant whether one is a communist, a democrat, or a nationalist. What matters now is how one views the central authorities' campaign to strengthen the state and the submission of the political establishment to the center and its leader. Many observers conclude that an authoritarian regime has arisen in Russia. However, while political development during the first stage of Vladimir Putin's rule was hardly in the direction of liberal democracy, it is still too early to form any final conclusions about the regime. The political situation in the country is far from defined, and trends beneath the surface bear watching.

By the beginning of 2001, it was clear that the ruling team had failed to govern purely on the basis of subordination and had been forced to return, at least in part, to haggling and political barter. In essence, this barter is compliance on the part of various interest groups in exchange for a limited degree of freedom in actions. After a brief period of scare tactics, the Kremlin was forced to reverse some of its pressure and instead trade with the oligarchs, regional bosses, and other key political forces (liberals and communists, to name a few). True, Putin's policy of compromising and bargaining is limited. Unlike Yeltsin, who was often hostage to the arrangements he made, Putin controls the situation; in all his compromises, he maintains a dominant role. He wants to create "slots" for every influential political group with which to control their activity and at the same time leave them limited autonomy so long as they follow the established rules of the game. One could see the beginnings of an attempt by the Kremlin to create a quasicorporate state where all its units follow strictly defined rules and functions; they would be controlled by presidential appointees in a vertically built system structured to serve the will of its chief manager—the president. However, it gradually became apparent that the ruling team allowed interest groups substantial autonomy in implementing their own agendas so long as they followed the rules of the "presidential vertical" and rejected their own political ambitions.

The easing of the "transmission belt" mechanism of authority during 2000–2001 could be explained by the fact that the ruling team concluded that the center's resources are limited and that it is impossible to carry out the policy of subordination without resorting to direct pressure and coercion. So far, though, Putin is not prepared to turn to severe and explicit force. In short, the ruling team drew the conclusion that either a straightforward policy of pressure is not sufficiently effective or the center lacks sufficient resources to implement such a policy. The result was a return to Yeltsin's tried and true policy of providing limited autonomy for limited submission. This combination of intimidation and pressure on one hand and bargaining on the other does not exclude totalitarian manifestations should the Kremlin feel threatened or need to defend its position.

From the evolution of Yeltsin's legacy under Putin, we can identify the formation in Russia of a quasi-authoritarian bureaucratic regime.[5] It generally fits within the framework of Yeltsin's "elected monarchy."[6] The very nature and substance of the Yeltsin regime remain intact: a personal style of rule, the levers of power concentrated in the hands of the president, and a weak role reserved for other institutions. Still, as long as the other sources of legitimate power in Russia—including the armed forces, parties, and ideology—remain weak, the need for using democratic institutions, above all elections, to legitimize power will continue. Thus, one can observe in Russia an extraordinary mix of continuity and change; power is still undivided, but the relations between power and society have changed.

Unlike Yeltsin, Putin openly relies on the bureaucratic instruments of consolidating power, limiting both democratic and oligarchic tendencies simultaneously. The new president has been flexible in applying intimidation techniques and in using the power ministries. Putin stubbornly proceeded to demolish Gusinsky's media empire and nationalize the only nationwide private television channel, while bargaining and striking deals with other interest groups, allowing them a rather wide field for maneuver to keep them from influencing federal politics or threatening his power. Defying expectations, Putin has avoided becoming hostage to the power structures and security services.

To immunize himself from challenge, Putin simultaneously began to do away with an overly monarchical style of rule, and he rationalized the system of power, making it more technological. He renounced favoritism and the oligarchs who were necessary elements of Yeltsin's entourage. He finally proposed a renewed model of the presidency, with the president appearing only as the highest government official rather than an arbiter of power, ruling like a monarch. Putin made an important step toward overcoming the monarchical atmosphere that prevailed during the Yeltsin era and moving toward a more pragmatic and rationalized system of power.

In the final analysis, however, Putin has only partially been able to carry out the task of rationalizing the old system of "elected monarchy." Elements of Yeltsin's court still orbit Putin, and the decision-making process continues to rely on personal networking and behind the scenes "sweet deals." Old interest groups continue to enjoy freedom to pursue their own interests, and new shadow groups of influence are emerging to associate themselves with members of the current Kremlin team. Thus, by forming the new rules of the game with the oligarchs, the Kremlin once again, as under Yeltsin, stressed a system of cooptation rather than a system of law.

As for the other powerful political force—the regional barons—the Kremlin first tried to deprive them of levers of influence on federal policies and weaken their position in the regions. But having afforded some regional leaders the opportunity to be elected a third (and in some cases a fourth) time, a violation of the Russian constitution, Putin gave the regional clans a chance to preserve their power.[7]

Putin's style of ruling, his rhetoric, and his sources of support indicate his intention to substantially change the Yeltsin system of monarchical patrimonialism. Yeltsin not only ruled, but also lorded over his close circle in the Kremlin court and his favorite oligarchs. He permitted society to enjoy elements of democracy not because he understood their value but because, probably, he could not rule without legitimizing his power through democracy. Yeltsin was not stubborn in persecuting his opponents and hardly ever showed feelings of political revenge. After the 1993 crackdown on the parliament, Yeltsin did not dare to limit the activities of the opposition and independent media, two groups that annoyed him greatly. Likely, he did not see them as threats. Perhaps he felt that a certain degree of spontaneity and political pluralism would even help his regime survive, which was true.

Outwardly, Putin demonstrates an entirely different pattern of ruling. He is rational and cold. He tries not to show any preferences for one political force over another. Publicity still makes him uncomfortable, although he makes progress in dealing with the issue. He has less tolerance than Yeltsin when he encounters resistance. He does not leave as many options for his opponents, tries to control political developments more intimately, and interferes more actively in all spheres of day-to-day governing. For all his harsh manners, his dynamism, and his attempts to control everything, we do see times when Putin lacks confidence, is indecisive, and tries to avoid responsibility for controversial decisions. It is increasingly clear that this outwardly dynamic style does not always reflect his vigilance and reserve but rather is a consequence of his lack of vision for Russia's future path of development, an inability to prioritize, and a tendency to postpone strategic choices. By relying on all groups, attempting to be everybody's man, Putin displays his unreadiness to pursue a definite course of action. There is still a great deal of continuity with the Yeltsin era, and this continuity is a result of the new leadership's failure to choose clearly defined goals or the direction in which to lead society. The attempt to strengthen monolithic power and to return to early twentieth century understandings of the state is another sign of continuity with the previous regime.

Pitfalls of the New Regime

Making politics and power more pragmatic, Putin and his team nevertheless have been unable to cope with a series of problems engendered by the Yeltsin system of power. The first is the problem of responsibility, which Yeltsin solved by consistently making the prime minister and shadowy gray cardinals from his inner circle accountable for all failures and thus preserving his position above the fray. By renouncing the court and favorites and announcing that he would be "responsible for everything," Putin gave up his political cover, making it necessary that he alone take responsibility in the case of failures and mistakes. This means that his legitimacy might be seriously endangered in a crisis situation.

The Kremlin's policy of maintaining Putin's popularity ratings is based on public relations spin, manipulation of the social mentality, and stirring up the dark sides of societal consciousness by playing on fears, nostalgia for the past, insecurities, illusions, and a longing for order. During the first year of Putin's rule, the inclination to move backward to the Soviet past sharply increased. The belief in a "special path for Russia" received new life, which increased suspicion toward the West. Disillusion with liberal democracy is increasing across some sections of society that see it as a way of life alien to Russian traditions and mentality.[8]

As a result of the present uncertainty, part of Russian society searches for various foundations and returns to traditional values and mechanisms that promoted stability in Soviet times; a kind of neoconservatism or Russian Gaullism has begun. The restoration of the Soviet hymn reflects the Kremlin's efforts to find a place for the generation of Soviet people who found themselves lost after the fall of the Soviet Union. The return of the Soviet hymn shows that both the authorities and some groups within society are trying to find a way out of the Yeltsin period, aiming backward and seeking refuge in the past.

Furthermore, the democratic and market mechanisms that arose in the Yeltsin period fit in with the new system of stabilizing society only to the extent that they do not contradict the spirit of neoconservatism. Of course, this movement backward began even before Putin. The retrenchment is the reaction by part of society to the collapse of the old state and former way of life, as well as the inability of many ordinary people to adapt to new conditions. Putin and his team came to power on a wave of this neoconservatism, and they have only increased it.

A future problem that Putin must face is developing a new class capable of replacing the current ruling team. Yeltsin solved this problem by supporting a loyal clan, creating a complex system of mutual dependence, and searching for a successor who would guarantee his safety and allow his court to retain influence, after giving up power. The "reproduction of power" is an integral part of the logic of elected monarchy. Putin was forced to submit to this logic even before the presidential elections took place. He was required to preserve part of the Yeltsin ruling team. But most important, once he began to follow the logic of Yeltsin's path, Putin deprived himself of the necessary freedom to make decisions that could de-privatize the state and bring order to Yeltsin's legacy. Paradoxically, within the framework of an elected monarchy, Putin's renunciation of certain groups and oligarchs and failure to actively seek replacements could make him more vulnerable than Yeltsin was in his time. In the end, Putin's efforts at making the regime more rational while preserving its old core of monolithic power may weaken his position; pragmatism and the kind of monolithic power that Putin seeks to wield are in essence incompatible.

The question arises: Could the turn toward bureaucratic neoconservatism have been avoided, or was it inevitable? Given that in Russian society 30 to 40 percent of people support liberal democratic values and about 40 percent of the population follows the leader and supports him under any circumstances, movement toward institutional democracy was feasible. But realizing such an option required a strong political will and agenda, along with support of society and interest groups, in creating a mechanism for reform.

Society needed a clear-cut evaluation of its problems and possibilities as well as the risks and threats that a new breakthrough in reform could bring. By addressing himself to the people and offering a clear-cut reformist goal, the new leader, of course, would be taking a risk. He would have to not only go against the former ruling elite but also virtually renounce the system of elected monarchy, which guaranteed him his personal power. Besides, to move more radically in the direction of liberal democracy, Putin would have to change his base of support and be willing to alienate parts of society and rely on other forces such as small and medium-size businesses interested in transparent relations with power, intellectuals, the younger generation, and the pragmatic part of the modern bureaucracy. To build institutions, he would have to reform a complicated structure of personal networking that serves as a base for stability. There is no guarantee that he could have succeeded in this endeavor. However, Putin might have risked even more by preserving the rules of elected monarchy and its structural inadequacies.

The optimistic belief expressed by some Russian observers that economic modernization is made easier by the quasi-authoritarian bureaucratic regime has no basis. It is true that in spring 2001, Putin used his power to push through a long-overdue economic package—the new tax bill, pension reform, land code, and judicial reform. This demonstrated that power for President Putin is not an end in itself, and he is apparently sincere in his attempts to modernize Russia. It is also true that the economic reform package serves the interests of the executive power, natural resources monopolies, and the central bureaucracy. The Kremlin has yet to risk crossing the threshold where reforms endanger the position of groups that compromise the current regime's base. The example of judicial reform is quite significant: This reform takes away the prerogatives of the prosecutor (a positive outcome), but at the same time it increases the influence of the federal executive branch and its leverage over the judges, making them even more vulnerable than before. The same can be said about the package of laws aimed at deregulating the economy. They do cut the number of licenses necessary for doing business in Russia. But the government still lacks the courage to begin true administrative reform, and the country has roughly

1.8 million federal and local bureaucrats who will still find ways to exert control. Before all is said and done, the bureaucrats may neutralize the positive impact of deregulation.

Current economic reforms in Russia are aimed at only limited modernization within the existing pattern of the system; the final result might only be to preserve Russia's character as an industrialized country without making the breakthrough to a postindustrial society. This type of economic modernization might create a more favorable situation for the development of an oil- and gas-driven economy and the presence of huge *chaebols* (the oligarchic families who dominated in South Korea) without doing what is necessary to stimulate small and medium-size businesses. There is no evidence that the government intends to dismantle the current fusion between power and big business. The Yeltsin period has already demonstrated that attempts to build a market in the framework of an elected monarchy will inevitably lead to an oligarchic, corrupt, shady model of capitalism. The politicization of the police and security structures might even make this form of capitalism repressive.

Hopes that a bureaucratic quasi-authoritarian regime could be stable are not well founded. Under relatively favorable economic conditions and the lack of any unexpected social and political shake-ups, this regime could truly provide stability, at least until the next presidential elections. However, the structural pitfalls inherited from the past will inevitably impair the regime and its structures, gradually undermining it from within.

A serious threat to the regime is the so-called pitfall of stability. On one hand, the president can avoid abrupt changes: relying on widespread popularity (being all things to all people), keeping the country calm, and winning election for another term. Putin could even prolong his current presidential term. In addition, he would continue to rely on his electoral "swamp"—those who have a low ceiling of expectations and are prepared to return to a Soviet atmosphere of survival. But such a policy, oriented to the conservative sector of society and the maintenance of the status quo, means preserving a stagnant stability. If the president ever chose to pursue further structural reforms, this policy would have to end.

On the other hand, if Putin succeeded with structural market breakthroughs and reform of the elected monarchy, he would truly disturb the current balance of power in society, bringing about the resistance of those who have contented themselves with the current rules of the game. Furthermore, any radical transformations in the economy or the establishment of independent institutions and parties would give positive results only after ten to fifteen years, beyond the scope of Putin's political life. In short, Putin is faced with a dilemma: stability today and guarantees of power in 2004, or reforms and an unpredictable future. But in fact, the current stability, which is based on previous rules of the game despite a superficial reordering, will not guarantee the authorities immunity from failures or a safe life, even in the immediate future. Moreover, any leader who relies on cadres and personal networking and not on institutions is doomed to dependence on the clans surrounding him and personal guarantees. The leader will fall victim to the next echelon of favorites, oligarchs, and perhaps even a new "family." This is the inevitable ending of any patrimonial rule, even if the leader himself has a public face of functionality and pragmatism and really means it.

The other threat to consider is Russian neoconservatism: for example, the organization and control of all aspects of social life, increasing centralization, the creation of a "party of power" under Kremlin control, and manipulation of the media and parliament. The Kremlin's fall 2001 effort to create a manufactured role for civil society and nongovernmental organizations (NGOs) reflects the transmission belt mechanism of government that Putin employs. This policy is meant to make society more manageable. With these efforts to limit initiative and spontaneity comes the danger that marginalized forces might spontaneously engage in destructive antiregime protest. A restructuring of power through spontaneous protest makes the state vulnerable; if one block of the system falls, it could create a domino effect that could spread throughout the vertical structure. This is the price that the regime must pay for the absence of independent institutions and a system of checks and balances. As the Soviet experience demonstrates, the stability of the pyramidal structure of power, burdened by an enormous bureaucratic ballast, makes the state unstable.

The regime's hope that it could maintain the current system of rational pragmatism is unwarranted. It is clear that President Putin is hostage to his own popularity ratings, and with future elections ever looming, he must follow the laws of populism. He is afraid to do anything that could cause serious dissatisfaction among his supporters. In 2001 Putin postponed housing reform because he understood that it could undercut his popularity. Putin has become more prone to cajoling certain groups and giving out small favors. Toying with society and relying on small deeds of appeasement in no way guarantees that society will remain loyal at a decisive movement. At present, populist politics forces Putin to rely on a team of manipulators and political technologists who have reduced the country's politics to an endless popularity campaign. The leader himself, without explicitly desiring it, has become a public relations president; his main resource is not ideology, or the party, or charisma, but his popularity ratings.

Putin's approval rating in 2001 never dropped below 70 percent and never more than 20 percent of respondents disapproved of his activities. However, if one digs deeper, the picture is not so optimistic. Only 35 percent of Russian society supports Putin's policies unequivocally; the rest—the swamp—is hesitant and is easily swayed in any direction, thus making the overall base of Putin's support unstable. Moreover, in 2001 only 28 percent of respondents were satisfied with the economic course of the government (with 64 percent unsatisfied). Thirty-seven percent of respondents thought that Kremlin policy was correct, and 42 percent believed it was leading to a dead end. At the beginning of 2002, 75 percent of respondents approved of President Putin's activity as president (19 percent disapproved), but only 48 percent trusted him.[9] These data demonstrate that Putin's approval rating is based not on his achievements but on the people's hopes and lack of alternatives. This does not inspire optimism for the future.

In a liberal democracy, elections optimize power and manage political competition in an atmosphere of uncertain outcomes, but in the conditions of an elected monarchy, elections are a decoration that conceals the lack of real choice. Putin, increasingly hostage to his populist campaign and his team, finds it harder to extract himself from a model of behavior geared toward creating the appearance of efficiency rather than solving real problems. Putin's imitation democracy is gradually spreading throughout all spheres of society. There is a semblance of order, a semblance of a multiparty system, and a semblance of a parliament and independent media.[10] If the process of favoring appearances over reality is not stopped, the strong presidency itself will be undermined and all that will remain will be the mere appearance of presidential power.

Russia's neoconservatism has acquired its own logic of development that may induce the center into mobilizing society's discontents (in a nonthreatening way) by playing on anti-Western feelings and reviving a great-power mind-set, especially if state policies turn out to look as if they have failed. But even if the situation in Russia becomes much worse, it is not certain that the current system of power would collapse. In this stagnant atmosphere, a clear alternative to the present powers—a strong opposition with ideological definition—is unlikely, because the regime skillfully balances various social forces off one another and avoids responding to the country's challenges in ways that might stir widespread anger. This situation existed under Yeltsin when he filled his circle of power with representatives of every interest group so that well-defined opposition could be bought off.

Under Putin, the unimportance of ideology and the lack of clear alternatives to the regime make the reemergence of political struggle very difficult. Consequently, the current regime is unlikely to be threatened in the near future by collapse or upheaval. There is another threat, however—the threat of rot and decay, loss of initiative and energy, demoralization, and the danger of sabotage by elements of the bureaucracy. This threat is especially clear when one considers the regime's reliance on the bureaucracy and security structures, which in Russian tradition have long been reactionary. The obscurity of the decision-making process is giving Russian politics a Brezhnev-like atmosphere.

When predicting Russia's future, another contingency gives rise to misgivings. Neither the president nor his regime is prepared to handle a crisis. Already during times of internal squabbling in the inner circle, Putin has shown himself to be indecisive. In crisis situations the president prefers to keep silent, wait, and not interfere, or he pretends not to notice problems.[11] In summer 2000, after the tragic sinking of the submarine *Kursk*, Putin tried to distance himself from the situation and diminish its importance. He resorted to typical Soviet-era ways of handling the crisis—blaming enemies and looking for scapegoats. The inability of the ruling team to choose the best option and control conflict situations speaks not only of the inexperience of Russian leaders and their indecisiveness but also of the structural inefficiency of the Russian political system that prevents open discussion so vital to facing the country's challenges. Moreover, the structure of an elected monarchy does not give the ruling team the opportunity to take responsibility for solving problems. The mechanism of power is built on the premise that everyone should avoid responsibility. Further, the mechanism of power itself produces irresponsibility.

Can Russia Avoid Harsh Authoritarianism?

During a period of relatively smooth and stable development and the lack of serious international challenges, both society and the authorities in Russia can avoid moving toward a pure authoritarian regime. It is a blessing that Putin belongs to the pragmatic school of Russian elites. But if the regime faces a crisis or any social collapse, the ruling team could turn to more harsh authoritarian means of governing to protect itself. Ironically this transformation can take the form of either an isolationist, nationalist course or a more pragmatic, even pro-Western policy.

During Yeltsin's rule, the threat of harsh authoritarianism was minimal—both because society still maintained a certain inertia of movement toward liberal democracy and because Yeltsin himself was not ready for dictatorship in any form. In the post-Yeltsin period, the limits and obstacles to the pure authoritarian scenario have weakened. The influence of the pro-reform minority in society has also weakened. The growing belief within the Russian political class that any pacts or compromises symbolize weakness might also lead to harsher policies and the use of coercion. Thus, one cannot exclude that part of the political establishment could once again unite to support an "iron hand" government in Russia.

In Russia today there are no instruments for transitioning to strict authoritarianism or totalitarianism. That Putin does not want to play the role of a Bonaparte should not calm or lull us. The center does not have even elementary means to establish an authoritarian regime. There is no effective and monolithic bureaucracy devoted to the center, nor does a well-paid army enjoying a high status exist. The power structures are not capable of becoming instruments of violence. Russia remains a very fragmented country, and it is unlikely that the center could reestablish the hold it once had over its regions where rather influential interest groups have already formed. It seems that ordinary Russian citizens, even those who greatly desire a strong leader and order, are accustomed to living in an atmosphere of freedom and unlikely to give it up easily. Moreover, even from a purely technological view, it is difficult to imagine in the age of globalization and the Internet how you could fence off the country from the rest of the modern world and keep it under lock and key.

However, we should not rule out the possibility that a wide mass of people could support a tougher regime with increased repression. The center in no way needs additional coercive factors—the existing ones are sufficient. Moreover, a desire for authoritarian order could arise from continuing degradation of the social, economic, and technological infrastructure. How much longer can people tolerate the constant energy crisis and freeze every winter? Catastrophes are already gripping entire regions, and they are beginning to effect chain reactions. Even if a move toward authoritarianism were merely reduced to an information vacuum, selective persecution of dissidents, the introduction of censorship, and redistribution of property to the regime's supporters, this alone could complicate Russia's move toward liberal democracy for a long time.

The current tendencies in Russian political life and the mixed nature of political leadership give an ambivalent picture of Putin. The president and his team are clearly not moving in a democratic direction at the moment. Yet society's lack of a real democratic and liberal paradigm may mean that Putin's pragmatism is the only obstacle keeping the pendulum from moving more sharply to the right in the direction of a truly harsh totalitarian regime. Besides, with its market and pro-Western orientation, this regime gives Russia options. Here, then, lies the next trap for Russia. The current ruling team is not yet ready to abandon traditional nondemocratic or even pseudodemocratic models of development. It cannot do so because the mechanisms associated with the elected monarchy system and their repressive and populist orientations are growing. It may well be that Russia cannot allow Putin to lose an election or leave office voluntarily because the lack of democratic alternatives to him could mean that a more aggressive and authoritarian leader with a more pronounced populist agenda could replace him.

Many centrists and government liberals hope the authorities will stop before crossing the line from the present hybrid regime to strong authoritarianism, but these hopes may be illusory. Can the use of the prosecutor general's office and the police and security structures for political ends be stopped? Can their political appetites be forcibly diminished? Will the president and his government avoid becoming hostage to the machinery of order that they set in motion? History has examples of times when the wheels of administrative pressure and coercion, once set in motion, could not be stopped. Russia after 1917 is only one example. Furthermore, we should remember that the particularities of Russian traditions would keep the wheels in motion, spinning toward authoritarianism.

Hopes for a New Pro-Western Realignment?

Putin's pro-Western shift in the wake of the September 11, 2001, attack on the United States and his support for the antiterrorist coalition created a new window of opportunity for Russia's movement toward the West. Unexpectedly the Russian president broke with his previous pattern of "wait and see" behavior and demonstrated a quick reaction with a good sense of history and intuition. Putin showed that he has learned and matured; he has acquired resourcefulness and become more comfortable with his own power. It is significant that Putin lined up with the West when Russian society was divided on the issue of what the antiterrorist response should be and when more cautious elites preferred a slow approach. Putin's actions immediately after September 11 and during the war against the Taliban clearly show he has decided in favor of a Western course. The September 11 events gave Putin the impetus to choose his geopolitical stance.

The terms for Russia's integration with the West are not yet clear. Putin, the Russian political class, and Russian society are not sure how great a break they are willing to make with their old mentality, stereotypes, ways of life, and understandings of national interests. The same can be said about the West, which so far has not decided what its new and more realistic strategy of integrating Russia will be. Whether the West will continue its "Faustian bargain" of keeping Russia onboard even at the price of softening its principles toward liberal democracy, or whether it can devise a more effective strategy is unclear. The new Western strategy should include conditions for Russia's cooperation with the West while also including pressure on Russia to adapt to Western rules of the game. In the end, whether this quid pro quo policy of the West toward Russia can convince the Russian establishment that Russia's national interests are tied to Western integration is an open question.

The great opportunity created in September 2001 for a renewed integration between Russia and the West will depend on how both sides address decades-old problems. True Russian integration into Western civilization demands that Russia fully accept the principles of liberal democracy. Either the current Russian leader or his successor must initiate a new political reform and restructure the "presidential vertical" to build viable institutions and allow for real self-governance to emerge. Much of what Putin has done will have to be undone in the process. Without these steps, the implications of Putin's pro-Western shift will remain murky. It is entirely possible that foreign policy pragmatism and alignment with the West might in the end help to preserve old, undemocratic rules of the game in Russia. Theoretically Putin still has a chance to make a break with the old Russian tradition of monolithic power. However, he has little time, and the steps he has taken to strengthen executive power will have unpleasant consequences. The results of the present system's experimentation with prolonging the life of autocracy are becoming clear. It is still uncertain where Russia will head when the autocratic forms of leadership, masked in pragmatic and more rational disguises, have been exhausted.

Notes

1. Lilia Shevtsova, "From Yeltsin to Putin: Evolution of Presidential Power," in *Gorbachev, Yeltsin, Putin: Political Leadership in Russia's Transition*, ed. Archie Brown and Lilia Shevtsova (Washington, D.C.: Carnegie Endowment for International Peace, 2001), pp. 67–113.

2. Eugene Huskey, "Political Leadership and the Center-Periphery Struggle: Putin's Administrative Reforms," in Brown and Shevtsova, *Gorbachev, Yeltsin, Putin*, pp. 113–43.

3. Those who continued resisting (such as Boris Berezovsky and Vladimir Gusinsky, two of Russia's most well-known oligarchs, both of whom had substantial media holdings) have been forced to leave Russia.

4. Luzhkov and Primakov's Fatherland party formed one party, "United Russia," with the Kremlin's Unity movement and thus became a part of Putin's political base.

5. This regime resembles the bureaucratic-authoritarian regimes described by Guillermo O'Donnell and Fernando Cardoso and is also an attempt to regulate power on the basis of the primacy of the executive branch. See David Collier, ed., *The New Authoritarianism in Latin America* (Princeton, N.J.: Princeton University Press, 1979). The difference between bureaucratic authoritarianism in Latin America and the quasi-authoritarian bureaucratic regime in Russia is that the Russian government refrains from using coercion and strives for illusory stability, which, for the most part, rests on hopes and expectations of society but still not on real accomplishments.

6. See Shevtsova, "From Yeltsin to Putin," pp. 67–111.

7. This compromise was perceived as nothing other than the beginning of a new system of mutual obligations between the center and the regions. By indulging such regional masters as Mintimir Shaimiev of Tatarstan and Yury Luzhkov of Moscow, the center could ask them for the same support before the presidential elections of 2004.

8. To the question "Which historical path should Russia take?" posed in 2000, 12 percent were in favor of following the path of European civilization, 18 percent supported a return to the Soviet past, and 60 percent were for a "special path" for Russia. See Lev Gudkov and Boris Dubin, "Bse edino. Rossiiskomu obshchevstu zhit' stalo khuzhe, zhit' stalo skuchnee" (All the same, for Russian society, life has become worse, life has become more boring), *Itogi*, November 23, 2001.

9. Lev Sedov, *Social-Political Situation in July 2001*, VTSIOM, July 8, 2001; see also VTSIOM, January 25–28, 2002. Both are online at http://www.polit.ru.

10. There are quite a few examples of imitation mechanisms that have sprung up recently in Russia: the new Media Union, the Kremlin alliance of the Unity and Fatherland parties, the emergence of the new youth movement called Walking Together, and even an attempt to create a civil society from above (that is, under the president).

11. For example, Putin vacillated for a long time over the choice of models for military reform and could not put an end to the conflict between the general staff and the defense ministry. He also delayed in finding a solution to the question of how to reform the United Energy Systems of Russia and pensions.

4

Simulations of Power in Putin's Russia

Stephen Holmes

Vladimir Putin's "consolidation of vertical power" bewilders observers even more than it impresses citizens. What tactics has Putin used to advance it? Who backs it and who defies it? How far has it gone? How much farther can it go? What does he intend to do with the power he is recompressing in the hands of central authorities? Which partial interests profit most from a reinvigorated central state? Which groups have suffered the gravest losses from such a renewed engrossing of power? These and related mysteries demand unraveling. But I wish to pose a slightly different, and perhaps prior, question: How can we distinguish a genuine from a merely apparent consolidation of power?

Putin's style of rule is outwardly unlike Yeltsin's. But has the underlying situation that led to the dispersal or fragmentation of political power from 1991 to 1999 radically changed? The political situation in Russia over the past ten years has been characterized by a mismatch between the meager tools of effective governance available to the center and the massive, intractable problems it faces. This disproportion generates two strong and mutually reinforcing tendencies in the Kremlin. First, the central government washes its hands of unsolvable problems by unloading them on hapless local officials. Second, the center purchases cooperation from lesser

An abridged version of this chapter appeared in the October 2002 issue of *Current History*, vol. 100, no. 648, in an article, "Simulations of Power in Putin's Russia."

power wielders by granting them unsupervised carte blanche within restricted local domains. This is a familiar tactic for overwhelmed and underequipped central authorities. If the fragmentation of power during the 1990s has such "objective" roots, it cannot be blamed on Yeltsin's ineffectiveness alone. If the disintegration of power before Putin's accession was not a failure of wit or nerve but the result of unmasterable forces, then Putin himself will not be able to reconsolidate power by "political will" or by appointing a handful of "super-governors," though he may be able to deceive careless observers by organizing Potemkin consolidations accompanied by the Soviet anthem.

Surveying the field, we can identify three rival schools of thought about Putin's presumed consolidation of power. These are the school of hope, the school of fear, and the school of doubt. Adherents of the school of hope allege that Putin is a liberal in authoritarian clothing. They see him as a "reformer" and "pragmatist" who is struggling to establish new rules of the game, stanch capital flight, knock sense into the predatory elite, introduce political stability and legal certainty, shield ordinary citizens from racketeers and bribe-taking officials, and encourage investments. And there is some evidence supporting this optimistic view.

Exponents of the school of fear, however, draw a diametrically opposite conclusion from more or less the same set of facts. They argue that Putin is an authoritarian in liberal clothing. They see him as a KGB strong-man and master of disguises. He may have rented a few liberal advisers as cabinet dressing, but he is obsessed with secrecy and bristles at the slightest criticism, however justified or constructive. He has restricted the independent monitoring of government agencies and chilled most critical voices in the media. He has even attempted to fill the space vacated by genuine civil society organizations with cardboard replicas that do the bidding of the state. There is evidence for this view as well.

This surface credibility of blatantly contradictory interpretations is a revealing fact. Perhaps Russia is now balanced on a razor's edge, ready to stumble in either a liberal or an authoritarian direction. Indeed, the country today does resemble an ambiguous halfway house. Some social voices have been repressed, while others still flourish; a number of civil society organizations have been rudely snuffed out, while many, especially when compared to Soviet times, remain vibrant. Putin's Russia, in other words, raises that classic question: Is the cemetery of civil society half empty or half full? And the answer, as usual, is that it all depends on how you look at it.

A third perspective, alongside the schools of hope and fear, is the school of doubt. Advocates of this warier approach allege that changing the man at the top does not really create change, because the underlying situation remains forbiddingly difficult. Fear and hope engender pessimistic and optimistic points of view, but if we look past the panic and the public relations, we will discover neither authoritarianism nor liberalism but rather an intermittently confused and often paralyzed Kremlin that continues to respond haphazardly to events outside its control, including centrifugal pressures that have not slackened over the past few years.

Before making a case for the school of doubt, I want to interject a word of caution. It is very difficult to estimate the power of a state in a situation where the irritants that it combats and occasionally eliminates are intrinsically weak and defenseless, where the plants that it plucks out have embarrassingly shallow roots. Forcing Vladimir Gusinsky into exile or taking over his television channel, NTV, is not especially difficult. Such coups de main, as a consequence, do not evince massive power. If Putin could discipline the Procuracy, by contrast, or if he could whip into shape another such well-organized and entrenched vested interest, then we would be on safer ground in acknowledging his consolidation of vertical power. In any case, to estimate Putin's success as a consolidator of power, we need to take the measure of the resistances over which he is rolling. If these resistances are noisy but essentially feeble and defenseless, we should hesitate to join the choruses of praise and blame for his recentralizing of formerly strewn powers.

To understand the basic political dynamic in Putin's Russia, it is essential to grasp that authoritarianism is just as difficult to set in motion as democracy. Putin's team may or may not have authoritarian ambitions, but does Putin's team have authoritarian resources and authoritarian skills? Adherents of the school of fear have warned of the worst, but they have not been able to demonstrate that the Kremlin is capable of imposing authoritarian discipline on Russian society. Ruling with an iron fist is not as easy as it sounds, especially when the iron is corroded and the arm has multiple fractures. Without an inspiring ideology to rally supporters or money to pay soldiers and policemen a living wage, the government's authoritarian options are modest. A genuine restoration of Soviet-style rule, moreover, would require a resealing of the borders or at least a drastic scaling back of currently unfettered contacts with the West. Such a reversion to autarky is unlikely, for many reasons. Not only would it strike directly at material interests of influential individuals in the Russian establishment, but it would also leave

Russia alone with problems (such as maintaining the country's territorial integrity despite a militarily exposed southern flank) that cannot be confronted without serious Western help over the long haul.

The problem facing would-be authoritarian factions in the Kremlin, assuming they exist, has nothing to do with a rebellious mobilization from below. An autocratic restoration in today's Russia is not blocked by the stubborn resistance of democratic forces who remain poorly organized and basically ineffective. It is difficult to create an authoritarian regime in Russia for a very different reason. The fundamental obstacle is the disproportion between the Kremlin's tools and Russia's daunting problems. The problems include a massive crisis of deferred maintenance in eleven times zones—the crisis of demodernization that ranges from a public health disaster to rivers choked by pollution and includes a seemingly unstoppable rotting away of transportation infrastructure, educational system, and other basic public services. The Kremlin's weak tools include the disorganization and incompetence of federal bureaucracies—the result of a decade of hemorrhaging talent, low pay, collapsing morale, unclear chains of command, and so forth.

When celebrating or denouncing Putin's consolidation of vertical power, most commentators focus on his strengthening of the executive branch at the expense of the legislature and regional authorities. The most economical way to challenge the assumptions shared by optimists and pessimists, therefore, is to stress another aspect of the problem, namely, the pathological level of fragmentation inside the executive branch itself. Executive agencies and ministries that habitually conceal essential information from one another and work at cross-purposes produce incoherent and self-defeating policies, seize up in periodic deadlocks, and react dangerously slowly to unexpected crises. That Putin's ministries do not always sing from the same songbook is clear from continuing tensions between the Central Bank and the Ministry of Finance, ceaseless rivalries among the Ministry of Justice, the Procuracy, and the Judiciary, and ongoing turf wars among the Ministry of Defense, the Foreign Ministry, and the General Staff. When failures of coordination inside the executive reach such proportions, they signal state weakness. These failures suggest not a consolidation but a progressive degeneration of vertical power.

If Putin can streamline, rationalize, and coordinate relations inside the executive branch, among his central ministries and executive agencies, then he will have made serious progress toward consolidating vertical power. He is obviously trying, but evidence of success in his power-coordinating venture is mixed. So Russia watchers should beware of smoke and mirrors. It is easier to display the outward symbols of consolidated power than to create the real thing, especially when Russian journalists and other sources of information are ominously "encouraged" to accept uncritically the Kremlin's varnish on events.

Thus power in Russia is an elusive subject of research, not to mention nearly impossible to measure. In Russia a vital component of power is the ability to glide under the radar. The capacity to conceal one's power is itself a source or perhaps a form of power. Moreover, the opposite is also true. A facility for bluffing, skill at convincingly exaggerating one's power, is an equally important source or form of power. As a consequence, students of power in Russia, of its successful or abortive consolidation, must become familiar with subterfuge and dissimulation and must learn to cultivate disbelief when besieged by storytellers, impostors, and camouflage artists.

A specifically Russian aspect of the artfully concocted "reputation for power" and its real-world effects is also worth mentioning in this context. Western observers of the last parliamentary election were puzzled by the way Sergei Dorenko, a journalist friendly to the Kremlin, publicly accused Moscow Mayor Yury Luzhkov of all manner of crimes, including murder. How could anyone have believed this inexpressibly vulgar parody of *kompromat*?[1] The answer is revealing. Dorenko had no intention of broadcasting charges that were believable. Indeed, the whole point of vilifying Luzhkov was to illustrate the impunity with which the Kremlin could publicize outlandish charges against its would-be electoral challengers. If the Kremlin permitted itself to treat the Moscow mayor so unjustly, this was visible proof that the Kremlin was strong and Luzhkov weak. Such was the subliminal message that many foreigners missed. To the average Russian listener, the truth of the charges were close to irrelevant; what mattered was the relative strength of the two parties disclosed by the audacity and insouciance with which the charges were leveled. Bandwagoning followed. If given a choice, which team does one join—the winners or the losers? In Russia, vulnerable citizens living from hand to mouth massively prefer to align with probable winners. This bandwagon strategy is popular because it serves as an insurance policy.

Putin and his team continue to emit a stream of "I am in charge" messages to the listening world. But this eulogistic self-presentation is undermined by the Kremlin's palpable anxiety over bad publicity. Putin seems especially upset when the broadcast media reveal the flagrant incompetence of government officials. He was bitter, allegedly, about the way independent television allowed the country to observe the panicky reaction of officials to the tragedy of the *Kursk*. This skittish reaction makes you wonder. Putin's anxiety about being criticized unfairly can be a symptom, suggesting subjectively perceived weakness.

The first response of Putin's Kremlin to the incompetence of state officials is not to fix the problem and improve the quality of public services. On the contrary, Putin's first response is to make the state even less transparent than before. Indeed, it sometimes seems that his main strategy for state building—that is, his principal technique for consolidating vertical power—is a press blackout. Perhaps his extraordinary need for secrecy is not merely a residue of his KGB training but is also a clue. It suggests that Putin recognizes how weak his government remains. It may also suggest that he is aiming to conjure up real power in the future by fabricating the illusion of power now. To admit that this tactic may conceivably work is not to agree that it already has.

Estimating the power of any government so passionately devoted to secrecy and dissimulation is a challenge for observers, both domestic and foreign. One way to approach the issue is to survey the major centers of power outside the Kremlin, including the gubernatorial bureaucracies (such as Moscow city government), the oligarchs, the regional industrialists, the natural monopolies, and the militarized central ministries (which are responsive to the Kremlin but not completely under its thumb). There may be others that are not listed here, but one power center more or less would not change the basic questions to be asked: How much weaker are these rivals to the Kremlin today than they were under Yeltsin? How much of their previous power have they ceded to the Kremlin? Which locally supported authorities have really been unhorsed by pressure from the top? To investigate concrete shifts in relative power is difficult, admittedly, and requires us to ask: power to do what? and power over whom? It also requires us to ask if an ostensibly curbed power wielder really wants to do what he has now been "prevented" from doing. Did the governors, for instance, really want to serve in the Federation Council? What did they concretely gain from such a perch? Has Putin's success in ousting them from that body actually decreased their capacity to pursue local or personal interests, especially when these conflict with national interests as defined by the Kremlin?

Another complication concerns Putin's relation to the security services. Is the *spetzsluzhba,* or special service, his tool, or is he theirs? Do FSB (Federal Security Service)—that is, former KGB—higher-ups snap to attention when he calls, or are they holding him hostage? And if the answer is neither, as is probable, then the cloudy status of the FSB itself reveals volumes about the extent to which Putin has, or has not, consolidated vertical power.

A parallel question can be raised about the oligarchs. Has Putin truly destroyed their power, or has he simply made them less noisy? Has he forced them to keep their heads down, made them feel slightly less secure, while nevertheless leaving them to savor most of their ill-gotten wealth? And what residual powers of sabotage or indirect resistance do they and other powers outside the Kremlin retain? The power to sabotage is intrinsically difficult to quantify or measure accurately because both the saboteur and the sabotaged have an incentive to hide their relationships from public scrutiny.

To gauge the genuine or illusory quality of Putin's consolidation of vertical power is to answer the following question: Does Russia's current president most resemble a boss or a broker? To call the shots in Primorsky Krai or Sverdlovsk regions, or at Gazprom, Minatom, or the Central Bank, in the General Staff and the Procuracy or any other state or quasistate institutions, the Kremlin must be able to replace the holdover cadres who still run things today with new cadres unswervingly loyal to Putin. To consolidate vertical power, the Kremlin needs a reliable staff as well as extensive oversight capacities to keep operational officers steadily in line. Does the Kremlin have such an extended staff and such oversight capacities? Can it replenish the federal bureaucracy with talented and loyal personnel? If not, it will have to back off its pretenses of iron-fisted control. That is to say, without an enormous cadre of reliable Putin loyalists, Putin will be forced to give up his role as either the benevolent or malevolent boss and will necessarily lapse back into acting as a broker, not unlike Yeltsin. He will stop giving orders and start hammering out compromises and bargains.

An important test for Putin's capacity to consolidate or centralize political power is the campaign currently under way to strengthen the court system and foster the rule of law. Jury trials will be extended to all subjects of the federation, and arrests will require procurators to obtain a court warrant. The Kozak plan is designed to create a legal environment that is welcoming to investment—not only foreign but also domestic investment—and of course to quash capital flight, tax evasion, bribery, and other extralegal financial practices.[2]

There is a grave problem, however, with the legal reform ostensibly under way. To put through a reform of this magnitude, the Kremlin needs voluntary cooperation from the main actors in the legal system, including the Procuracy, who have to accept the basic principles of the reform if it is to be successful. One of the most important actors on the current scene, of course, is the FSB. However, the FSB's main strategy for ruling is to inject uncertainty into people's lives; one way it maintains its domination is through fomenting such uncertainty and keeping people off balance. Recent events strongly suggest that this is a highly self-conscious approach. The FSB realizes that people who feel secure are harder to control than those who feel insecure. Indeed, if a property holder feels secure in his or her property, he or she will employ that property as a platform from which to attack the government. Private property can be a staging ground from which to expose the Kremlin's stupidities and crimes. For example, someone could create an independent media outlet (such as the formerly independent NTV television station). Therefore, however eloquently the Kremlin speaks about the need to stabilize property rights, its ability to follow through and render property holders secure remains dubious. Can the Kremlin reliably stabilize property rights while repeatedly destabilizing its critics and potential critics? Its capacity to target insecurity so accurately, to deliver uncertainty so selectively, is questionable. Therefore the Kremlin's real, rather than rhetorical, commitment to the rule of law remains unknown, whatever its spokesmen publicly proclaim.

The motives of, or incentives facing, entrenched government bureaucracies are also relevant to the likely success of Putin's legal reform. These inherited bureaucracies can be usefully described as orphans forsaken by the now defunct Communist Party of the USSR. As fragments broken off from the old system, the FSB and the Procuracy have, yes, been loosed from Communist Party superintendence. Though free of Communist Party domination, they are institutions populated by individuals who have developed strong corporate interests of their own, interests that do not necessarily overlap with those of the Kremlin and that are not always compatible with the rule of law.

Where will Putin find a well-organized constituency inside the country to support the rule of law? What government agency has a strong incentive to make its own behavior predictable? To this question about the government, we need to add a parallel question about the private sector: What profit seeker has a strong motive to stop asking for ad hoc exemptions and special help and to start asking for rules that will be reliably enforced by independent courts? Do such legally minded profit seekers exist in Russia?

Will Russia's rich begin to view Russia's court system in the same amiable way as other privileged groups around the world view their national courts, that is, as more or less effective debt collection agencies, designed to help the wealthy keep their money? There is scant sign of such a revolutionary change in elite attitudes toward binding legality and judicial authority. Russia's chastened but still rapacious oligarchs claim to have been converted to the rule of law. But they have an interest in deception. Remember that most if not all of the truly wealthy Russians have accumulated their wealth under murky and shifting rules that have been fairly easy to evade. They have good reasons to believe that their own rude skills of acquisition would lose value in a system where clear rules were reliably enforced by independent agencies. And they would not be wrong to fear that under such a system, the skills of foreigners, raised in rule-of-law environments, would gain in relative value. So why would most Russian businessmen support the introduction of the rule of law, rather than merely paying lip service to the idea?

For the rule of law to emerge, two conditions must coincide: Power wielders must have an incentive to make their own power predictable, and profit seekers must have an incentive to ask for general rules rather than special deals. If this generalization has any merit, then what is the chance that the rule of law will emerge in Putin's Russia? If the FSB cannot renounce unpredictability and the oligarchs cannot renounce special deals, how then will Putin cobble together a political coalition favoring the rule of law? Where will he find support for this aspect of his consolidation of vertical power? No well-organized constituency for a rule-of-law system exists in Russia today. Putin may sincerely want to introduce the rule of law. He may repeatedly announce that he is going to create it. He may give speech after speech and issue a river of decrees. These subjective intentions are irrelevant, however. The rule of law is going to emerge only if there are strong constituencies supporting it. Students of Putinism need to ask: Where, inside Russia, is he going to locate such political support?

If Putin is having a difficult time cobbling together a political coalition of well-organized social forces to support his attractive-sounding reforms, this is because no powerful groups with a palpable interest in the desired outcome currently exist. Can Putin at least foster a stable investment climate in the country? Doubters suggest that Putin's sway will diminish outright defiance of vertical power while manufacturing a simulacrum of societal order. Putin will not be able to effect the rule of law, despite its foreseeable benefits, because the Kremlin will inexorably continue in making special deals with powerful financial interests. After a few false dawns, Putin will fail to improve the investment climate to any significant degree because his reliance on the FSB will compel him to accept citizen uncertainty as the price for establishing and maintaining order. Pervasive insecurity will make long-term investment unattractive, effectively undermining efforts at stabilization.

Finally, the elusive power of public opinion in today's Russia continues to vex political commentators, both domestic and foreign. Putin apparently believes that his popularity is an important instrument of rule—a significant source of power. At least that is one explanation for his decision to channel recent oil windfalls to pay pensions, despite the fact that the elderly have a negligible capacity to trouble the state. When Yevgeny Primakov became an extremely popular politician in 1999, the Kremlin decided that he had to be destroyed politically. The Kremlin consistently behaves as if popularity— public opinion—is a significant political force. This is true even though "the street" is obviously not an important route to power in Russia. Elites do not fear the mob. Demagogues are not worth jailing or beating up. The people as a whole are disillusioned and alienated from politics, which they accurately view as an insider's game. Russia's citizens are not players in the political system; they are not even especially attentive spectators.

So what can we say about the power of popularity and public opinion in Putin's Russia? And how will it affect the success or failure of the Kremlin's attempt to consolidate vertical power? Perhaps the strongest case for continuity, rather than rupture, between Yeltsinism and Putinism can be made by stressing the still-tenuous connection between the country's elite and its general public. Under Yeltsin, power was in the hands of Russia's "hovercraft elite," its democratically unaccountable ruling and profiteering groups. Under Putin, the same pattern prevails. The rich and powerful remain essentially detached from the population and are focused on their own well-being. The Russian elite can stage democratic rituals, but it has no interest in consulting regularly with civil society. Admittedly, the identity of influential groups may change. Repressive elites may assume a higher profile, while extractive elites may periodically scamper under the table.

These relations will no doubt shift again in unpredictable ways. But experience suggests that, however the identity of power wielders changes from year to year, we are not going to witness any time soon the emergence of a form of power in any way accountable to ordinary citizens. The state will remain detached and nonresponsive to society. It will remain a "corporation" that, however wracked by internal struggles, preserves itself at the expense of governing accountably. This lack of accountability of the Russian state to Russian society is one constant in an ever-churning world. If Putin succeeds, against the odds, he will consolidate unaccountable power. If he fails, unaccountable power will remain fragmented and dispersed.

Notes

1. *Kompromat* is a commonly used term in Russian political dialogue that refers to compromising evidence or material that could be used for blackmail.

2. Dmitrii Kozak is deputy chief of the Putin presidential administration and head of the Commission for Legal Reform. He is one of the main authors of Kremlin-initiated legal and judicial reform packages of 2001.

Part Two

Economic Development

5

Russia's Transition to a Market Economy: A Permanent Redistribution?

Joel Hellman

Reviews are coming in on the first ten years of transition to a market economy in Russia.[1] The occasion has reopened debates about the pace of liberalization and the wisdom of mass privatization. Despite differences, the reviewers tend to share a surprisingly similar diagnosis of Russia's current problems. Russia, they say, lacks "institutions"—a catch-all phrase to connote all the supporting organizations, structures, and practices that make a market function well.[2] Courts, tax inspectors, regulatory agencies, financial intermediaries, among others—these are the institutions that are claimed to have been neglected in the obsession with prices and property that dominated the thinking of the reformers and their advisers in the early stages of the transition. This resulted in a market without the institutional prerequisites for the rule of law—the Achilles heel of the Russian transition. However, it is important to reexamine the initial thinking and underlying assumptions about the development of market-supporting institutions to better understand the current obstacles to reform.

Did the "radical" reformers in Russia ignore the importance of institutions in their rush to liberalize and privatize? The extensive written record of their thinking at the time suggests otherwise. Indeed, rapid liberalization and mass privatization were both strategies designed to create a critical mass of market actors who would not only defend the reforms once introduced but also demand further reforms to create and improve the institutions necessary to support the market economy. Property owners would seek protection for their property and contract rights. Businesses would demand banks to provide a range of financial instruments and services. Taxpayers would want to ensure that unfair exemptions and advantages are not provided to favored firms or individuals. The radical reformers had no plans to impose these institutions from above on the basis of Western models. They believed that liberalization and privatization would generate the demand for effective institutions. They believed that once property rights were established, markets would evolve toward the establishment of more efficient institutions.

This view was particularly prominent in the early thinking about privatization. The overriding imperative of privatization was to "depoliticize" property or, more simply, to get property out of the control of politicians and state bureaucrats.[3] Although the initial privatization plans envisioned transferring ownership to a broad range of the public to create a large constituency with a personal stake in the reform process, it quickly became clear such plans were not politically feasible.[4] Enterprise insiders got the upper hand in the privatization process and forced the reformers to accept privatization options that effectively concentrated property rights and control to existing managers in collusion with workers. Such a compromise, though not ideal from the reformers' point of view, was justified largely because of their beliefs that private ownership generates the incentives for efficiency-enhancing institutions over time. Once a critical mass of private owners had been created, they would, regardless of their past, demand the necessary institutions to protect their newly acquired rights and to create a favorable environment for investment and growth. Even if these new owners did not initially respond to such incentives, they would soon be replaced by those who would, through a liquid secondary market for enterprise shares and an active market for managers.[5]

Paradoxically, the radical reformers behind mass privatization in Russia held an evolutionary approach toward the development of efficient market-supporting institutions.[6] Indeed their belief in this evolutionary approach was so strong that it shaped their assumptions about the initial distribution of property rights. Far from ignoring the importance of market-supporting institutions, the reformers' decisions about privatization were, in part, driven by their desire to create a structure of incentives that would create a constituency for further institutional reforms. While mass privatization—and, in particular, the decision to skew the process toward enterprise insiders—

has become a lightning rod for criticism over the past ten years, the critiques have largely bypassed the assumptions about institutions that shaped the early thinking of the reformers. In reviewing the past decade, we need to go beyond the recognition that Russia lacks adequate market-supporting institutions and ask why the initial assumptions about the evolution toward efficiency-enhancing institutions have not proven valid to date.

In hindsight, several problems with the notion of an evolution toward efficient institutions can be raised. First, reformers assumed that the new stakeholders in the reform process would demand institutions to provide the classic market-supporting public goods—stability, the rule of law, infrastructure, and so on—that bring benefits to the entire society. But was that the only option? Why would the initial beneficiaries of privatization and liberalization not seek to create redistributive institutions to enhance and protect their own interests in the emerging market economy at the expense of other groups in society?[7] Institutions that build barriers to entry into the market, secure individualized protection of property rights, preserve advantageous price distortions, and limit the capacity of the state to collect taxes could be far more advantageous to the initial beneficiaries of reform than those providing classic public goods. Although it is true that the early winners of liberalization and privatization did demand institutions to protect and secure their gains, the notion that such institutions would by definition also be ones that further supported the development of a competitive market economy is certainly questionable.

Second, if enterprise insiders and budding oligarchs were powerful enough to skew the initial distribution of property rights to their own advantage, they would also be powerful enough to skew the further development of market-supporting institutions in a similar direction. Indeed, privatization only strengthened the position of enterprise insiders and the new oligarchs, by turning their initial political influence into economic power. Once property—and the attendant wealth and income—became concentrated in their hands, they had no incentive to support institutions such as liquid secondary markets or minority shareholder protection that threatened to weaken their power and control in the future. By turning their newly acquired wealth into even greater political influence, especially in the absence of any other well-organized collective interests, enterprise insiders and oligarchs had the capacity to tailor the design of new institutions to their own advantage.

Third, it had been assumed that once property rights were redistributed, the new owners would have strong incentives to seek a stable environment and the supporting institutions necessary to protect their newly acquired rights. But what if the opportunities to redistribute state property do not have a clear end point? Reformers were among the first to recognize that the types of political institutions and tactics necessary to redistribute property in transition economies are different from those necessary to protect property rights. Reforms such as mass privatization required a state with considerable discretionary powers that would not necessarily be appropriate once property rights had been fully distributed. Reformers often discussed the need for periods of "extraordinary politics" in which the standard constraints of democratic competition would be temporarily suspended to push through contentious policy choices that face strong opposition from an entrenched status quo.[8] As long as there is valuable property to redistribute, powerful groups will have an interest in preserving the conditions that provide them advantages in the redistributive process, even at the expense of creating the conditions necessary to maximize the value of their previously acquired property rights. This paradox is critical to understanding Russia's transition.

Alternative Approach

In contrast to a theory of transition that relies on the gradual evolution over time of increasingly efficient market-supporting institutions,[9] the Russian transition suggests an alternative approach, which could be called a theory of "permanent redistribution"—with apologies to Trotsky's famous theory of "permanent revolution."[10] This alternative approach explains why the initial successes of liberalization and mass privatization in Russia *did not* generate the expected demand for more efficient institutions, but instead resulted in the transition being stalled by the very groups that benefited most from liberalization and privatization. There are five main features of a transition of permanent redistribution.

First, the basic distribution of property rights is incomplete and subject to constant renegotiation. In contrast to the view that mass privatization is a one-off redistribution of state-owned property following which private owners seek to protect their newly acquired rights, this approach suggests that there is no clear, finite end to the redistribution of formerly state-owned property. Even after mass privatization and the infamous "loans-for-shares" deals in Russia, the state continued to maintain substantial holdings of industrial assets that would eventually be subject to some form of privatization.[11] These stakes encompassed both minority and majority blocs of some of the most valuable assets in the country, including energy and natural resources, banking, and real estate.[12] Though continued state ownership of key assets is a standard feature of most market economies, the key difference is that in Russia it is widely assumed by market actors that many of these valuable state-owned assets will eventually be privatized in some form. As a result, potentially substantial payoffs are still possible by taking advantage of opportunities in the privatization of remaining state assets.

More important, a theory of permanent redistribution suggests that even assets that have been privatized are subject to renegotiation. This does not mean that there is a lively resale market for privatized assets, which would be a natural and welcome feature of any transition economy. Instead, permanent redistribution presumes that the initial privatization of assets is open to constant contestation through such methods as legal challenges to the legitimacy of the initial privatization deal, expropriation of rival stakeholders, tunneling of assets, or political interference in the disposition of privatized property. In Russia, such contestation over previously privatized assets is a permanent feature of the transition landscape. Courts in far-flung regions overturn earlier privatizations by the Federal State Property Committee. Minority shareholders turn up at annual meetings only to find the location suddenly changed to a remote city and their voting rights diluted by new share issues. Assets from companies with continued large state holdings are systematically shifted to offshore companies controlled by management through transfer pricing schemes, asset stripping, and other nontransparent procedures. And most prominently, the threat constantly hovers over the loans-for-shares deals that the state will reopen these cases and, in so doing, start a new scramble for some of Russia's most prized assets.

Second, new market actors are primarily focused on the accumulation and redistribution of property rather than other maximizing strategies. This suggests that in the environment of permanent redistribution, the returns to acquisition of new property rights over additional assets exceed those of investment in existing privatized assets. This is particularly true if the new property can be acquired not in a liquid and competitive secondary market for assets, but through nonmarket means such as political intervention, manipulation of the court system, or nontransparent forms of tunneling through which property can be acquired at below-market prices. Especially after the 1998 financial crisis in Russia, when foreign investors largely abandoned the market and numerous potential domestic competitors were eliminated, the opportunities to acquire assets in a noncompetitive environment were enormous. The financial-industrial groups that survived the crash have tended to gobble up assets indiscriminately through both market and nonmarket means. Indeed, it has been the most dynamic entrepreneurs in Russia who have invested their talents in acquisition of new assets over investment in existing assets, thus setting the standard for innovation in the Russian market.

Third, the permanent redistribution of property relies heavily on the capacity of economic actors to influence the state. As discussed above, permanent redistribution in Russia has not been largely market-driven. Instead, economic actors seeking to acquire existing state-owned assets or previously privatized assets are often reliant on state intervention. Firms "convince" local or regional governments to challenge prior privatizations. Regional courts uphold various schemes to expropriate minority shareholders. Privatizations of remaining state holdings in attractive enterprises have been structured to the advantage of particular firms. What distinguishes an environment of permanent redistribution from a normal secondary market for assets is the extent to which the redistributions are a function of nonmarket interventions. The insecurity of property rights underlying permanent redistribution is a function of the state's willingness to intervene in the disposition of privatized assets.

Fourth, economic actors who can capture state institutions have substantial advantages in the constant renegotiation over property rights. In the game of permanent redistribution, the main currency is influence over the state. Though influence is largely dependent on economic resources, as in any political system, it also relies on personal ties and networks—some inherited from the past, others newly sprung from the transition. Economic actors that can utilize wealth and influence to "capture" politicians and even entire state institutions will be able to use the state to shape the process of permanent redistribution to their own advantage.[13] Moreover, in Russia, as in many post-Soviet systems, there are few collective actors who can serve as countervailing interests to powerful oligarchs and firms with the capacity to capture the state. Political parties, trade unions, consumer groups, and nongovernmental organizations are extremely weak. In such an environment, politicians are dependent on large firms and wealthy businessmen to fund their campaigns, to provide an organizational network of support, and, in many cases, to provide a range of private benefits as well. What these businesses get in return is an opportunity to use the state to enhance their capacity to acquire additional assets.

And, finally, permanent redistribution is not contained within Russia's borders. In his theory of permanent revolution, Trotsky recognized that the success of Russia's essentially peasant revolution depended on the spark it would generate for revolutions around the world. Similarly, the imperative for permanent redistribution appears to be driven from outside Russia. As the stock of available assets to acquire or redistribute goes down, the interest in acquiring assets through similar means in other transition countries increases. As a result, Russian firms seek to export their redistributive strategies abroad in countries where the state is highly susceptible to capture, and property rights can be easily manipulated by political intervention.

In recent years, Russian firms have been particularly active in acquiring assets in neighboring transition countries. In many cases, these acquisitions are the result not of competitive international tenders but of negotiations between governments in the form of debt-for-equity swaps or other barter-equity deals. Again, these deals rely on state intervention and are often structured to benefit private firms as opposed to state entities.

The proponents of mass privatization believed that the distribution of formerly state-owned property would have a number of "lock-in" effects. It would shift control over assets away from state bureaucrats to private owners who would not easily cede these control rights back to the state, thus locking in a constituency with an interest in making economic reforms irreversible. It would create a new set of stakeholders with an interest in defending their assets from encroachments, thus locking in a constituency for the rule of law. At the same time, by spreading property rights to the public through vouchers, the reformers believed that they were building the foundation of a liquid and competitive secondary market for assets that would prevent the initial recipients from locking in any permanent advantages in the new market economy. This was especially important, as political considerations had compelled them to give preferences to enterprise insiders who were not the best suited to making the most productive use of those assets, given their previous track record in the command economy. Once the rounds of mass privatization had been completed, the reformers immediately turned their attention to the development of the securities market to ensure that assets would eventually flow to the most efficient users.

But what the reformers did not anticipate was that mass privatization by itself would not be sufficient to prevent the state from intervening in the disposition of assets, that is, to achieve the depoliticization of property in the reformers' own terms. The same constituencies that compelled the reformers to skew the initial distribution of state property to their advantage also influenced the state to continue intervening in the dispensation of property rights. Instead of a liquid secondary market, mass privatization launched a process of constant renegotiation of property rights in which the state continued to play a critical role. As key assets in the economy remained up for grabs, new market actors had strong incentives to focus on further acquisitions to lock in advantaged positions in the emerging market economy. These acquisitions largely depended on one's capacity to capture politicians and bureaucrats. The most dynamic entrepreneurs who thrived in this environment were driven to invest their resources and talents in capturing the state to use the state's power to acquire more and more resources.

Demand for Institutions

The reformers correctly assumed that mass privatization would generate a demand for institutions. But what type of institutions? What are the consequences of permanent redistribution on the demand for market-supporting institutions and for further reforms in Russia? In an environment of permanent redistribution, demand for the rule of law is weak. The most powerful actors in the new market economy have a strong interest in minimizing any legal constraints on their capacity to acquire additional assets through methods such as tunneling, expropriation of minority stakeholders, and other forms of asset stripping. If property rights were properly protected, then the opportunities for redistributing already privatized assets would be limited to legitimate market mechanisms. Because permanent redistribution depends on complicit intervention by the state or, at the very least, tacit agreement by relevant legal and regulatory authorities, an environment that adequately curbed corruption and other forms of illicit influence on public officials would seriously undermine the capacity to redistribute property. In contrast to the initial hopes of the reformers, privatization created a powerful constituency that gains from the absence of a rule of law. Such a constituency prefers state institutions that maintain a high degree of discretionary power, that are susceptible to influence through corruption, and that are incapable of enforcing secure property rights for all.

The World Bank and the European Bank for Reconstruction and Development (EBRD) recently conducted a survey of firms in twenty-two transition countries called the Business Environment and Enterprise Performance Survey, or BEEPS. The survey provides evidence of the concentrated advantages that selected firms can gain from engaging in various forms of grand corruption at the highest levels of the political system.[14] The survey is able to identify those firms that engage in "state capture," defined as paying bribes to public officials to influence the content of laws, regulations, or decrees. Then the performance of these "captor" firms can be compared with the performance of ordinary firms without such influence. Figure 5.1 compares the average reported growth in revenues over a three-year period (from 1997 to 1999) for captor firms and ordinary firms in Poland and Russia. In Poland, where privatization progressed gradually and the perils of permanent redistribution were largely avoided, firms that engage in this form of grand corruption show little systematic benefit from this activity in comparison with other firms. In Russia, the captor firms grow at more than twice the rate of ordinary firms.[15] This suggests a substantial payoff in terms of growth to the firms that can manipulate the instruments of the state through grand corruption. Such firms will seek to preserve these advantages for as long as possible.[16]

Of course, those who gain from the process of permanent redistribution have an interest in protecting their own property rights even as they seek ways to expropriate the property of others. The reformers, however, were mistaken in believing that such an interest would lead to the demand for institutions that protect property rights *as a public good.* Instead, those who benefit from the permanent redistribution seek to purchase protection of their own property rights à la carte from the state.[17] In other words, they seek individualized protection for their own property rights usually through the provision of some form of private payment to individual state officials. But this de facto privatization of the provision of a key public good weakens the security of property rights for everyone else. If public officials can extract private payments from the firms for selected guarantees of security, why should they provide this good to everyone else?[18]

The BEEPS provides direct evidence of the selective provision of security of property rights for powerful firms in transition economies.

Figure 5.1 Gains to State Capture

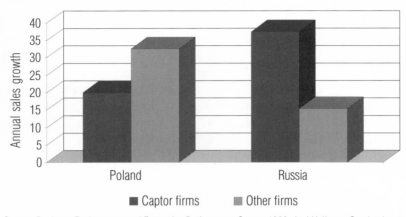

Source: Business Environment and Enterprise Performance Survey 1999; Joel Hellman, Geraint Jones, and Daniel Kaufmann, "Seize the State, Seize the Day: State Capture, Corruption, and Influence in Transition," Policy Research Working Paper no. 2444 (Washington, D.C.: World Bank, 2000).

Figure 5.2 compares the responses of firms across countries on the extent to which they are confident in the security of their property and contract rights. In Russia, more than 70 percent of the firms interviewed reported doubts about the security of their property rights. Yet if we examine how the security of property rights has changed over time, an interesting pattern emerges. In all countries, firms that engage in state capture and other forms of grand corruption are much more likely to have reported gains in the security of property rights than are other firms. As the level of grand corruption increases in the country, the difference becomes more stark. In countries such as Russia, where the state is highly susceptible to capture, the captor firms were more than five times more likely than other firms to have reported improvements in the security of their property rights over time. In these countries, powerful firms have been able to buy individualized security from the state, while at the same time weakening the security of property rights for everyone else.

For those who benefit from permanent redistribution, the ideal state is weak at home but strong abroad. In a weak state, individual public officials generally have considerable discretionary authority, while the state itself cannot effectively enforce laws. This makes the state particularly susceptible to capture and other forms of illicit influence by powerful firms. A strong state at home might be less willing to undertake policies that give advantages

Figure 5.2 Security of Property Rights

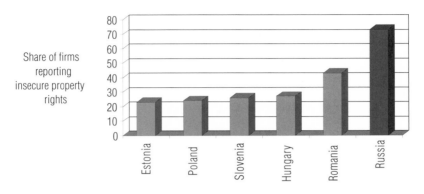

Share of firms reporting insecure property rights

Source: Business Environment and Enterprise Performance Survey 1999; Joel Hellman, Geraint Jones, and Daniel Kaufmann, "Measuring Governance and State Capture: The Role of Bureaucrats and Firms in Shaping the Business Environment," Policy Research Working Paper no. 2312 (Washington, D.C.: World Bank, 2000).

to particular firms while imposing substantial social costs. Moreover, a strong state might be tempted to reclaim property rights for itself, thus threatening existing private owners. Weak states are generally unable to exercise effective control over their own holdings, thus opening up lucrative opportunities for acquiring nominally state-owned assets through a variety of illicit or informal methods.

However, if the process of permanent redistribution can be extended beyond Russia's borders, then it generates a preference for a strong state abroad. Most efforts by Russian firms to acquire assets in other transition countries depend not on competitive market tenders but on bilateral deals between Russia and the respective governments. Assets are acquired through debt-for-equity swaps, in barter deals for state-provided services (such as border control), and by other political agreements between states that are then channeled to selected firms. Such deals depend on the strength of the Russian state to enter into and enforce agreements in its relationships with other transition countries. In particular, Russia's increasing assertion of authority in the so-called near abroad (a term sometimes used by Russian officials to refer to the new independent states that occupy former Soviet territory) has netted a wide range of asset acquisitions for important Russian firms.

Figure 5.3 Exporting State Capture Abroad

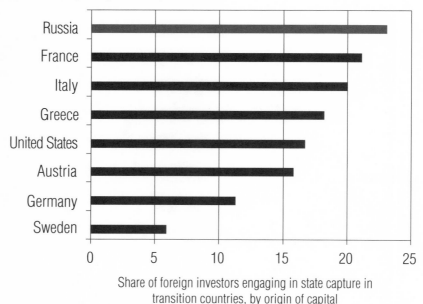

Share of foreign investors engaging in state capture in transition countries, by origin of capital

Source: Business Environment and Enterprise Performance Survey 1999; Joel Hellman, Geraint Jones, and Daniel Kaufmann, "Far from Home: Do Foreign Investors Import Better Standards of Governance in Transition Economies?" available at http://www.worldbank.org/wbi/governance.

The BEEPS adds to the growing anecdotal evidence of efforts by Russian firms to expand the process of permanent redistribution to other transition countries. The survey included nearly five hundred foreign direct investors in the transition countries.[19] When investing in other transition countries outside of Russia, Russian-owned firms are more likely than any other foreign direct investors to use illicit methods of influence at the highest levels of the political system to promote their activities. Figure 5.3 shows the share of all foreign investors that engage in state capture sorted by origin of the firms' capital. Nearly a quarter of all Russian firms investing in other transition countries resort to capturing the state in building their investment portfolios. As the Russian state under President Putin has begun to play a much stronger role in the near abroad, Russian firms have been more aggressive in expanding their holdings in other transition countries. This has created vast new opportunities for acquisition of assets, thus further prolonging the dynamics of permanent redistribution in Russia and across the region.

The first ten years of Russia's transition have shown that the belief of reformers that liberalization and mass privatization would create demand for institutions to provide key public goods necessary for a well-functioning market economy rested on a number of assumptions about the incentives of the new market actors that ultimately proved inaccurate or incomplete. Although it is clear that society as a whole would have gained from the development of market-supporting institutions, what few reformers recognized at the time was that some would also lose as a result of such institutions. Periods of uncertainty, instability, and discretion can be very conducive for some groups to rapidly accumulate resources and power. An environment of insecure property rights creates opportunities for some to expropriate the assets of others. A weak state unable to enforce the rule of law generates opportunities for grand corruption that can aid in the building of future economic empires. Such distortions in the emerging market economy impose high costs on society, but they also can bring extraordinary gains to those in a position to take advantage of them through close ties with politicians and state bureaucrats. Institutions that reduce these distortions eliminate opportunities for those who can make the most out of periods of uncertainty. As long as there are valuable assets that can be acquired through nonmarket means (and hence at below-market prices), there will be powerful groups that oppose any institutions that reduce these distortions. These are the groups that gain from prolonging the process of permanent redistribution.

In an environment of permanent redistribution, the most dynamic and successful entrepreneurs invest their talent and resources in capturing politicians and bureaucrats to use their discretionary authority and the absence of countervailing restraints to acquire more assets. For such entrepreneurs, this environment constitutes a real window of opportunity that they seek to prop open for as long as possible. Although the weaknesses in the functioning of the market economy also impose costs on the entrepreneurs themselves, the costs are far outweighed by the potential gains generated by the additional accumulation of assets. Eventually the balance of costs and benefits will shift, but in large, natural resource–rich economies such as Russia's with plenty of "jewels in the crown" to redistribute, this could be a long time coming.

Some Thoughts for the Next Ten Years

The social costs of this permanent redistribution over the past ten years are well known. Although Russia has finally returned to growth, much of the economic contraction of the last decade can be attributed to asset stripping and theft, capital flight, declining investment rates, barriers to new market entry, deteriorating physical and human capital, and other problems generated by the process of permanent redistribution.[20] This has pulled many people into poverty. The pattern of redistribution has concentrated gains to a narrow constituency while imposing high costs on the rest of society, bringing the inequality rate in Russia close to that of the most unequal countries in the world. Comparisons between the present and the pretransition past are futile in Russia, given the vastly different political, social, and economic context of the former communist system; however, it is clear that permanent redistribution has substantially constrained the potential inherent in the reform process.

The return to growth, the increasing investment rate, and the newfound political and economic stability that have followed the Russian financial crisis in 1998 are signs that the worst excesses of permanent redistribution may be abating, although constant renegotiation over property rights continues. Those financial-industrial groups that survived the crisis have been on hyperactive acquisition mode. While some of this acquisition has come through legitimate market mechanisms, there remain daily stories of political and legal challenges to past privatizations, expropriations of existing stakeholders, systematic tunneling and asset stripping, and other unchecked violations of property rights. New voices within the business community have been raised to demand that institutions provide the key public goods still lacking in Russia's emerging market economy. Recently proposed reforms to strengthen the judiciary, to reduce regulatory obstacles, and to improve the quality of public administration are encouraging signs. But these developments are still in their infancy, and implementation has always been one of the key weak spots in Russia's transition.

When looking toward the next ten years of transition, few have considered what might be the most important legacy of this process of permanent redistribution—the potential illegitimacy of the initial distribution of property rights in Russia. If the dominant financial-industrial groups in Russia were forged in questionable privatization deals, in acquisitions tainted by political interference and corruption, and in an environment marked by lawlessness, how will they stand up to challenge in the future? Will every future anticorruption campaign threaten forcibly to redistribute previously acquired assets? As the state gains strength, will it seek to reclaim its stake-holdings in key assets frittered away by previous governments? If populism ever takes hold in Russia, will the earlier distributions of property rights have enough legitimacy to withstand any potential backlash? No one has considered, in the context of the transition, the implications of a market economy built on an initial distribution (and redistribution) of property rights whose legitimacy is open to challenge. Of course, similar questions could be raised about the origins of most modern market economies, but the compressed time frame of the transition—in which developments over generations have been squeezed into a decade—makes these risks seem far more relevant.

As long as such questions remain, the security of property rights in Russia will be compromised, with negative consequences for investment and growth. Recognizing this problem, some voices within Russia are already calling for blanket amnesties or other methods to secure ex post facto legitimization for the frenzied redistribution of property rights in the first decade of transition. But perhaps more important are the potential political consequences. In the quest to make reforms irreversible, the reformers may have unintentionally planted the seeds for future political challenges in the very structure of property rights in the new market economy.

Notes

1. The views presented here are those of the author and do not necessarily reflect the views of the World Bank.

2. For a representative argument that goes well beyond Russia but nevertheless makes frequent references to the Russian case, see the World Bank's *World Development Report 2002: Building Institutions for Markets* (New York: Oxford University Press, 2001). Similarly, see the European Bank for Reconstruction and Development's (EBRD) ten-year review of transition, *Transition Report 1999* (London: EBRD, 1999).

3. The clearest statement of this view comes from Maxim Boycko, Andrei Shleifer, and Robert Vishny, *Privatizing Russia* (Cambridge, Mass.: MIT Press, 1995). See also Anders Åslund, *How Russia Became a Market Economy* (Washington, D.C.: Brookings Institution Press, 1995).

4. For an interesting ex post explanation of the political tactics of economic reform in Russia, see Daniel Treisman and Andrei Shleifer, *Without a Map: Political Tactics and Economic Reform in Russia* (Cambridge, Mass.: MIT Press, 1999).

5. This is a rather broad generalization of what was a wide divergence of views at the time. For an approach to privatization that started with recognition of the potential pitfalls inherent in this approach, see the work of Roman Frydman and Andrzej Rapaczynski. For an example, see Roman Frydman, Andrzej Rapaczysnki, and John Earle, *Privatization in the Transition to a Market Economy* (Budapest: Central European University Press, 1993).

6. At the time, however, the evolutionary approach was used primarily to argue against rapid privatization. See in particular the work of Peter Murrell, including, "Conservative Political Philosophy and the Strategy of Economic Transition," *East European Politics and Societies*, vol. 6, no. 1 (1992), pp. 3–16.

7. For an earlier statement of this argument, see Joel Hellman, "Winners Take All: The Politics of Partial Reform in Post-Communist Economies," *World Politics*, vol. 50, no. 2 (1998), pp. 203–34.

8. This was the underlying political theory that motivated the shock therapy approach. One of the clearest statements of this approach is Leszek Balcerowicsz, "Understanding Postcommunist Transitions," *Journal of Democracy*, vol. 5, no. 4 (October 1994), pp. 75–89. Such views also come out in many of Jeffrey Sachs' statements of the period. For an example, see "Life in the Economic Emergency Room," in *The Political Economy of Policy Reform*, ed. John Williamson (Washington, D.C.: Institute for International Economics, 1994).

9. Although he did not write about Russia and the transition, such a theory of institutional development is most prominently associated with the work of Douglass North. In particular, see his *Institutions, Institutional Change and Economic Performance* (Cambridge, U.K.: Cambridge University Press, 1990).

10. Trotsky's theory of permanent revolution, though initially welcomed as a major contribution to Marxist thinking, ultimately became the heresy upon which his fall was based. The theory simply stressed that Russia, at the time of revolution still largely a peasant country, needed to go through a bourgeois phase before reaching the socialist phase of development. As a result, Trotsky argued that the survival of the Russian revolution depended upon its success in sparking proletarian revolution in the more advanced capitalist countries around the world. See the classic work of Isaac Deutscher, *The Prophet Unarmed, Trotsky: 1921–1929* (Oxford, U.K.: Oxford University Press, 1959). One could argue that Trotsky's warning that Russia cannot simply skip key phases of development remains relevant to the development of a market economy as well.

11. This was an arrangement by which many of Russia's oligarchs made loans to the government with shares in government-owned enterprises as collateral. When the federal government was unable to repay the businessmen, they gained control of key state enterprises as a result of the government's default.

12. One need only refer to existing valuable state stakes in Gazprom, United Energy Systems of Russia (UES), Lukoil, Sberbank, Vneshtorgbank, and extensive real estate holdings, particularly at the regional and municipal levels.

13. For an application of the conventional concept of capture to the political economy of transition, see Joel Hellman, Geraint Jones, and Daniel Kaufmann, "Seize the State, Seize the Day: State Capture, Corruption and Influence in Transition," Policy Research Working Paper no. 2444 (Washington, D.C.: World Bank, 2000).

14. For a review of the BEEPS and its main results, see Joel Hellman, Geraint Jones, Daniel Kaufmann, and Mark Schankerman, "Measuring Governance and State Capture: The Role of

Bureaucrats and Firms in Shaping the Business Environment," Policy Research Working Paper no. 2312 (Washington, D.C.: World Bank, 2000).

The results are also reported in the World Bank study, *Anticorruption in Transition: A Contribution to the Policy Debate* (Washington, D.C.: World Bank, 2000).

15. For a much more detailed statistical test of this relationship controlling for all the other variables that might affect firm performance, see Hellman, Jones, and Kaufmann, "Seize the State."

16. It is important to recognize that the performance indicator is sales growth and not profits (which are notoriously underreported in transition economies and therefore unreliable). As sales growth is a rough measure of the size of the firm, and as additional evidence in the survey shows no greater productivity gains for captor firms in comparison with ordinary firms, it may be assumed that one possible explanation of this growth is increasing accumulation of assets through gains associated with the process of permanent redistribution.

17. For a more extensive discussion of this concept, see Hellman, Jones, and Kaufmann, "Seize the State."

18. A standard answer to this question would be to maximize the collection of tax revenue. But while this would be collectively rational for the state as whole, it is unlikely to be rational for the individual bureaucrat in an environment of considerable uncertainty about the future.

19. For an analysis of the state capture among foreign investors, see Joel Hellman, Geraint Jones, and Daniel Kaufmann, "Far From Home: Do Foreign Investors Import Better Standards of Governance in Transition Economies?" available at www.worldbank.org/wbi/governance.

20. For an exploration of the link between poverty and these issues, see World Bank, *Making Transition Work for Everyone: Poverty and Inequality in Europe and Central Asia* (Washington, D.C.: World Bank, 2000).

6

Ten Myths about the Russian Economy

Anders Åslund

Few topics are as politicized as Russia and its transition from communism. This politicization arouses emotions, often rendering reality the victim. Russia's legacy as a closed society aggravates popular mythology because in the Soviet times, anything could be alleged without being exposed as wrong. Fortunately, after ten years of transition, Russia is much more transparent, and it is possible to vanquish many myths that have arisen. Let us examine ten statements of conventional wisdom about Russia.

Myth 1: The Russian Economy Has Collapsed

According to official Russian statistics, gross domestic product (GDP) plummeted 44 percent from 1989 to 1998.[1] However, this figure is grossly exaggerated because of the peculiar quirks of communist and post-communist statistics. Under communism, everybody padded output to reach plan targets, while nobody cared about the quality (or even the usefulness) of the items produced. Inputs were wasted on a massive scale. For instance, even though the Soviet Union manufactured more than six times as many tractors as the United States, its agricultural output lagged far behind because production was so substandard and wasteful.[2] Much of Soviet manufacturing was unfit for consumption, and Russians flocked to alternative, imported goods that flooded the market following the liberalization of foreign trade. The subsequent decline in the production of useless final goods and unneeded inputs was not a tragedy but a desirable change.

East Germany offers an enlightening comparison. The German Institute of Economic Research in West Berlin assessed East German GDP per capita steadily at about 60 percent of the West German level.[3] When the wall fell in 1989, the GDP level, as well as consumption and public investment, was boosted by large West German subsidies, while production collapsed because of excessive wage increases imposed by West German trade unions. Therefore, the most relevant indicator of East German production appears to be productivity, which was barely 30 percent of the West German level.[4] Thus, the West thought East German production was twice as large as it really was. A similar overestimation for Russia appears likely. At least one-fifth of Soviet Russian output and probably half of the estimated GDP of the Soviet era should be eliminated if we want to achieve a true picture of Soviet-era GDP at market prices.[5]

After communism, the statistical measurement of output shrank far more than its actual level. According to the best estimates, the increase of the underground economy accounts for at least one-quarter of GDP.[6] Thus, the Russian economy has not collapsed. Rather, it is more accurate to say that until 1998 the economy stagnated because of sluggish and incomplete reforms. Russia's level of economic development remains where it was during the Soviet era, roughly on a par with that of Brazil.[7]

Nor has Russia developed a new "virtual economy" based on barter rather than money. The share of barter transactions in Russian industry peaked at 54 percent in August 1998, but the financial crash curtailed this system of hidden subsidies that had been the norm for Russian enterprises. Non-monetary transactions fell like a stone, as Russian industry realized it could no longer depend on the state and would have to earn real money in the marketplace. Today, the virtual economy is marginal.[8]

According to the latest official data, Russia achieved a GDP growth of 5.4 percent in 1999, 9.0 percent in 2000, and 5.2 percent in 2001, and growth continues abreast. Although many systemic problems remain, Russia appears to have attained a critical mass of market reforms and privatization. (The same is true of several other countries in the region, such as Ukraine and Kazakhstan, which are also booming.) Considering the enormous distortions left behind by communism, that is a splendid achievement.

Myth 2: Shock Therapy Was a Failure

The new conventional wisdom is that Russia's economic and social troubles are the result of radical economic reforms (such as price liberalization and privatization) that were launched too fast and too soon, but this is simply wrong. Many argue that Russia, like China, should have opted for a gradual reform. There are several flaws in this argument.

First, Soviet Russia did follow the Chinese example by trying gradual reforms from 1985 through the end of the Gorbachev era, but they did not work because the preconditions were completely different. Notably, the Soviet Union was ruled by a large antireformist bureaucracy that only selectively obeyed central orders, and the economy was dominated by large-scale industry that could not be left aside as in China. Moreover, the Soviet Union had experimented with economic reforms in the 1920s, the 1950s, and the 1960s. The obvious conclusion was that piecemeal reforms did not work. Even so, Soviet President Mikhail Gorbachev tried again, and the results were truly disastrous, leading to output collapse and near hyperinflation. But a severe economic crisis contributed to the collapse of the Soviet Union—the legacy of years of gradual, inadequate reforms—leaving former Russian president Boris Yeltsin with little choice.

Second, Russia did not undertake very radical reforms, as is illustrated in table 6.1. More than twenty other former communist countries carried out market economic reform in parallel with Russia, and Russia comes out in the middle. Nearly all East Central European countries initially undertook more radical reform than Russia, and later on Russia was lagging even among former Soviet republics. Virtually all the problems in Russia today—excessive state intervention, corruption, lingering inflation, and limited rule of law—are indications of insufficient reform efforts.

Third, the correlation between systemic reforms and growth is strong and positive. The most successful countries with high growth and contained corruption (notably Poland and Estonia) undertook some of the most radical reforms.

Fourth, for three years Russia has experienced substantial economic growth and considerable structural improvements in the wake of the horrendous financial crash that shook the world in August 1998. That financial crisis reduced the financial wealth and political power of two of the most corrupt groups in Russia: the oligarchic tycoons and the regional governors. More surprisingly, it convinced both the communists and the popu-

Table 6.1 World Bank/EBRD Structural Reform Index, 1990–2000

	1990	1991	1992	1993	1994	1995	1996	1997	1998	1999	2000
Central Europe											
Poland	0.68	0.72	0.82	0.82	0.83	0.79	0.79	0.81	0.86	0.86	0.86
Czech Republic	0.16	0.79	0.86	0.90	0.88	0.82	0.82	0.82	0.90	0.90	0.93
Slovakia	0.16	0.79	0.86	0.83	0.83	0.79	0.79	0.77	0.90	0.90	0.89
Hungary	0.57	0.74	0.78	0.82	0.83	0.82	0.82	0.87	0.93	0.93	0.93
Southeast Europe											
Romania	0.22	0.36	0.45	0.58	0.67	0.65	0.64	0.66	0.76	0.82	0.82
Bulgaria	0.19	0.62	0.86	0.66	0.63	0.61	0.57	0.67	0.79	0.79	0.85
Baltics											
Estonia	0.20	0.32	0.64	0.81	0.83	0.77	0.78	0.82	0.90	0.93	0.93
Latvia	0.13	0.29	0.51	0.67	0.71	0.67	0.74	0.74	0.86	0.86	0.82
Lithuania	0.13	0.33	0.55	0.78	0.79	0.71	0.74	0.74	0.82	0.82	0.86
Commonwealth of Independent States											
Russia	0.04	0.10	0.49	0.59	0.67	0.64	0.71	0.72	0.64	0.64	0.64
Belarus	0.04	0.10	0.20	0.33	0.42	0.50	0.44	0.37	0.37	0.37	0.43
Ukraine	0.04	0.10	0.23	0.13	0.33	0.54	0.57	0.59	0.65	0.65	0.68
Moldova	0.04	0.10	0.38	0.51	0.54	0.64	0.64	0.64	0.76	0.76	0.75
Armenia	0.04	0.13	0.39	0.42	0.46	0.54	0.61	0.61	0.76	0.76	0.72
Azerbaijan	0.04	0.04	0.25	0.31	0.33	0.40	0.44	0.51	0.61	0.61	0.65
Georgia	0.04	0.22	0.32	0.35	0.33	0.50	0.61	0.66	0.79	0.79	0.79
Kazakhstan	0.04	0.14	0.35	0.35	0.42	0.50	0.64	0.66	0.79	0.72	0.71
Kyrgyzstan	0.04	0.04	0.33	0.60	0.71	0.71	0.67	0.70	0.82	0.79	0.79
Tajikistan	0.04	0.11	0.20	0.26	0.42	0.40	0.40	0.39	0.55	0.58	0.61
Turkmenistan	0.04	0.04	0.13	0.16	0.29	0.27	0.27	0.36	0.36	0.36	0.35
Uzbekistan	0.04	0.04	0.26	0.30	0.50	0.57	0.57	0.54	0.57	0.50	0.49

Sources: Martha De Melo, Cevdet Denizer, and Alan Gelb, "From Plan to Market: Patterns in Transition," in *Macroeconomic Stabilization in Transition Economies*, ed. Mario Blejer and Marko Skreb (New York: Cambridge University Press, 1997); Oleh Havrylyshyn and Thomas Wolf, "Growth in Transition Countries: 1991–1998: The Main Lessons," paper presented at the conference on "A Decade of Transition," International Monetary Fund, Washington, D.C., February 1–3, 1999, p. 34; and author's own calculations from European Bank for Reconstruction and Development (EBRD), *Transition Report 1998* (London: EBRD, 1998), p. 26; EBRD, *Transition Report 1999* (London: EBRD, 1999), p. 24; and EBRD, *Transition Report 2000* (London: EBRD, 2000), p. 14.
Note: See note 9, p. 124.

lation at large that there was no alternative to a real market economy. Thus, Russia's reforms started working only after a new shock. Russia's real problem was too little shock and too much corrupt state therapy in the form of subsidies to the country's elite.

Myth 3: Privatization Has Only Generated Corruption

Rather than generating corruption, privatization has generated national wealth. Since 1997, Russia's private sector has created no less than 70 percent of the country's GDP. Corruption is usually defined as "the misuse of public power for private gain," but privatization permanently deprives public servants of public property, so they can no longer charge money for the privilege of using it. Logically, privatization should swiftly diminish corruption, although the process inevitably involves some corrupt practices. Today, the bribery that plagues Russia is not related to privatization but is overwhelmingly connected with law enforcement, tax collection, and state intervention.

In general, the higher the level of privatization that an ex-communist country has attained, the higher the economic growth it has achieved. Russia is atypical in having been more successful in privatization than in other market reforms such as price liberalization (see table 6.2). Therefore, people tend to blame Russia's privatization for the country's shortfalls, while it would be more logical to complain about the dearth of other reforms. The scourge of Russian enterprises is scores of state inspectorates that regularly extort money from businesspeople.

Strangely, the standard comparison is between privatization in Russia and that in Poland, with the allegation that Poland privatized more slowly. In fact, Poland started off with a large private sector that was much bigger than Russia's, and it undertook more reforms in nearly all spheres than did Russia. This suggests that if Russia had not privatized so fast it would probably have suffered far worse economically. In contrast, Ukraine has implemented most reforms, including privatization, more slowly than Russia. As a consequence, Ukraine's privatization has been of worse quality than Russia's, with more ownership going to managers and employees and less being sold on open markets. Not surprisingly, Ukraine has been slower to return to economic growth. Ukrainian corporate governance remains far worse than in Russia, where nearly 800 enterprises actually paid dividends to their shareholders in 2000.

Table 6.2 Private Sector as Share of GDP, 1991–2000 (EBRD estimates, mid-year, percentage of GDP)

	1991	1992	1993	1994	1995	1996	1997	1998	1999	2000[a]
Central Europe										
Poland	40	45	50	55	60	65	65	65	65	70
Czech Republic	15	30	45	65	70	75	75	75	80	80
Slovakia	15	30	45	55	60	70	75	75	75	75
Hungary	30	40	50	55	60	70	75	85	80	80
Southeast Europe										
Romania	25	25	35	40	45	55	60	60	60	60
Bulgaria	20	25	35	40	50	55	60	65	70	70
Baltics										
Estonia	10	25	40	55	65	70	70	70	75	75
Latvia	10	25	30	40	55	60	60	65	65	65
Lithuania	10	20	35	60	65	70	70	70	70	70
Commonwealth of Independent States										
Russia	5	25	40	50	55	60	70	70	70	70
Belarus	5	10	10	15	15	15	20	20	20	20
Ukraine	10	10	15	40	45	50	55	55	55	60
Moldova	10	10	15	20	30	40	45	50	45	50
Armenia	30	35	40	40	45	50	55	60	60	60
Azerbaijan	10	10	10	20	25	25	40	45	45	45
Georgia	15	15	20	20	30	50	55	60	60	60
Kazakhstan	5	10	10	20	25	40	55	55	60	60
Kyrgyzstan	15	20	25	30	40	50	60	60	60	60
Tajikistan	10	10	10	15	15	20	20	30	30	40
Turkmenistan	10	10	10	15	15	20	25	25	25	25
Uzbekistan	10	10	15	20	30	40	45	45	45	45

a. Preliminary figures.

Source: European Bank for Reconstruction and Development (EBRD), *Transition Report 2000* (London: EBRD, 2000).

Belarus, which privatized little and undertook few reforms, is now the only full-fledged dictatorship in Europe. That was the real threat that Russia's swift privatization jeopardized. Today Russia's corporate sector is undergoing a swift restructuring with many mergers and acquisitions that would have been impossible without large-scale privatization. In the end, the effects of privatization appear to be as enormous as expected, although they have taken a few years to materialize.

Myth 4: Russia Cannot Collect Taxes

Russia collects steadily one-third of its official GDP in general government revenues, slightly more than the United States, whose citizens complain that taxes are too high. Not only has Russian tax collection been high, it has also been stable (see figure 6.1). The misperception over Russian taxation is the result of superficial observations. Most outsiders, including the International Monetary Fund (IMF), tend to focus on federal revenues—but those represent only a part of total state revenues, which also include regional and local tax revenues, as well as several extrabudgetary funds, notably the pension fund. Another source of confusion is that many observers, including some Russians, take for granted that Russia should have state revenues as high as Western Europe or the former Soviet Union, ignoring that such taxation harmed growth in both places. For Russia, a more plausible tax burden, in line with its level of economic development, would be 15 to 25 percent of its GDP. The real problem is not that Russia cannot collect taxes, but that the government collects too much. These revenues are improperly spent and aggravate corruption. According to the World Bank, enterprise subsidies comprised no less than 16 percent of Russia's GDP in 1998. Small wonder that state finances crashed. Russian tax rates had long been very high by most comparisons, and tax collection was ruthless. For those who actually paid the taxes, the situation was close to unbearable. A large survey of start-ups in Poland, Slovakia, Romania, Russia, and Ukraine in 1997 showed that such enterprises paid 16 percent of their turnover in taxes in Central Europe but 24 percent in Russia and Ukraine.[10] As a natural consequence, entrepreneurs in Russia and Ukraine were also extorted to pay 50 percent more bribes than their Central European counterparts; the lawlessness of the tax inspectors has emerged as one of the most serious concerns of the post-Soviet era.

Figure 6.1 General Government Revenue and Grants for Russia, 1992–1999
(percentage of GDP)

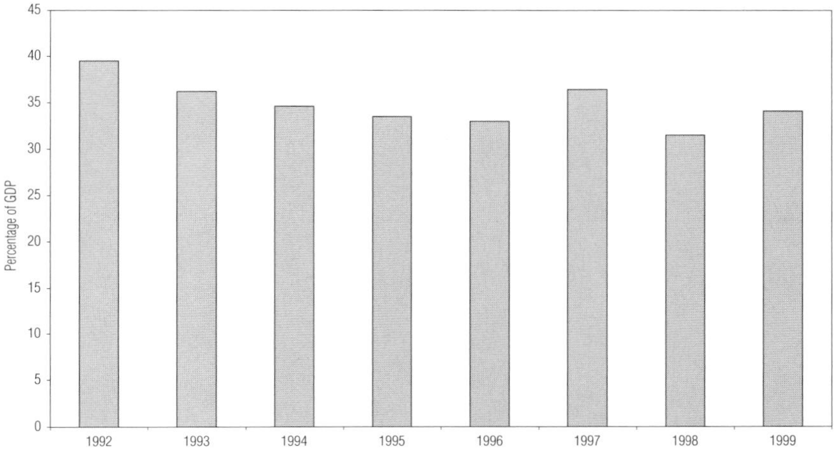

Sources: Vito Tanzi, "Transition and the Changing Role of Government," mimeo, paper presented at the conference on "A Decade of Transition," International Monetary Fund, Washington, D.C., February 1–3, 1999; United Nations Economic Commission for Europe, *Economic Survey of Europe* (New York: United Nations, 2000); European Bank for Reconstruction and Development (EBRD), *Transition Report 2000* (London: EBRD, 2000).

The solution has been radical tax cuts. As of 2001, Russia introduced a flat income tax of only 13 percent (a rate that the United States and Western Europe can only dream about). Instantly, income tax revenues rose sharply as people abandoned expensive tax-avoidance schemes. The corporate profit tax was reduced to 24 percent in 2002, and deductions of costs from profit have been boosted.

Myth 5: Russia's Infrastructure Is Falling Apart

Dramatic news stories, such as the tragic sinking of the submarine *Kursk* and the fire that engulfed the Ostankino television tower in Moscow, have created the impression that Russia is coming apart at the seams. In fact, Russia has seen an extraordinary improvement in its infrastructure. Investment in fixed assets (that is, buildings, equipment) increased by 18 percent in 2000—a healthy investment ratio of nearly 20 percent of GDP (higher than the standard U.S. ratio of 16 percent). Admittedly, the USSR had an investment ratio of about 30 percent of GDP, but that was an indication of waste. Even given that expenditure, the Soviet Union was notorious in its neglect of infrastructure and its maintenance.

Today, privatization and market pricing have revived much of the country's infrastructure. Free market competition has fostered an incredible expansion in the telecommunications industry. The oil industry has been broken up into a dozen viciously competitive and predominantly private oil companies, which boosted oil production by 11 percent in 2001. Airports and airlines have likewise improved. Road construction is up. The number of cars has doubled from 1990 to 1997. New ports have been built around St. Petersburg. Whereas ruins once blighted the landscape of even the Soviet capital, modern-day Russia has initiated a widespread building boom. Problems of maintenance persist where state or semi-state monopolies linger, notably in the natural-gas monopoly Gazprom, in the state-owned oil pipeline monopoly, and partly in the public utilities. As is often the case, a profound problem of the Soviet system is perceived as a novel problem of Russian capitalism.

Myth 6: Russia Desperately Needs Foreign Investment

Throughout the world, from East Asia to post-communist Eastern Europe, exports, not foreign direct investment (FDI), have led all economic takeoffs. Even Poland, the most successful transition economy, did not see annual FDI rise over $100 per person until 1998. In contrast, Hungary and the Czech Republic succeeded in attracting large foreign investments early on, but those investments did not prove to be too beneficial for economic development. Most investment is nearly always domestic.

Russia does not need foreign capital to boost its investment rate. Although the country has a persistent large capital flight of more than $20 billion a year, it has a higher investment ratio than the United States. This capital flight reflects the country's high level of savings being invested abroad—a resource for the future. Enterprises, as well as wealthy individuals, prefer to keep their money in safe banks outside of Russia where the legal systems are stronger. Yet the Russian investment climate remains poor because of excessive bureaucracy and corrupt law enforcement. Russia has to solve this problem to make its fledgling economic growth sustainable. The capital flight is a good indicator of the investment climate.

Myth 7: Russia Suffers from a Terminal Health Crisis

Granted, the statistics from Russia today are shocking: Male life expectancy plummeted from sixty-four to fifty-seven years from 1989 to 1994, and the country's population is declining by over half a million each year. These statistics alone, however, do not tell the whole story. The population decline has two causes. The first is low birthrates, which are typical of Europe as a whole. The communist economic incentives for young people to have children early have disappeared. Today, as in most Western countries, Russian women postpone childbearing, and it is too early to say what the post-communist reproduction rate will be. The other cause is high death rates. The population pyramid is badly skewed since there were so few births from 1930 to 1945 on account of government terror and war; the large age group born before 1930 is now dying.

According to the most recent U.N. projections, Russia's population decline (28 percent through 2050) is not drastically worse than that in parts of Western Europe. Thus, population decline is not a particular Russian problem, but an issue across Europe. The situation is far worse for Estonia and Bulgaria where the United Nations projects a natural population decline of more than 40 percent through 2050. The drop in male life expectancy, even as women thrive, is common not only in Russia but in East Slavic and Baltic countries as well. (Strangely, the war-ridden and truly impoverished countries of Georgia and Armenia have not recorded any such decline.) The direct causes are cardiovascular disease and accidents, fueled in part by alcoholism.

The appearance of a dramatic decline in life expectancy can be explained by the temporary effects of former Soviet president Mikhail Gorbachev's anti-alcohol campaign—which limited access to alcohol and thus boosted life expectancy by a couple of years—followed by a sudden increase in alcohol consumption when the exorbitant Soviet-era sales taxes on vodka disappeared. Nothing suggests that average health care standards in Russia have fallen. The quality of health care is closely linked to infant mortality, which plunged by 17 percent from 1993 to 1998. Both public and private expenditures on health have risen sharply as a share of GDP. Capitalism has made medicines widely available that were unknown during the Soviet era, and the equipment at hospitals has greatly improved.

Nevertheless, some problems are cause for genuine concern. One is the proliferation of drugs and AIDS, both of which are the inevitable consequences of becoming an open society. The other worry is the tuberculosis epidemic (a new drug-resistant strain of the disease is particularly troubling). Moreover, because the health care system remains predominantly public, it suffers from all the problems of low salaries, low efficiency, and bribery that were typical of the public sector under communism.

Myth 8: Russia Has Been a Black Hole for Western Aid

A profound misperception prevails that Western aid to Russia has been enormous when truly it has been trivial. From 1992 to 2000, total U.S. Agency for International Development (USAID) commitments to Russia amounted to $2.6 billion. But actual disbursements are always less: Russia has received only about $200 million a year in grant aid from the United States, while the European Union gave barely $150 million a year.

In addition, the United States has given food aid, partly in grants, partly in credits—but that has been at the behest of the U.S. agricultural lobby and qualifies more as financial aid for U.S. farmers. (In fact, it has hampered agricultural reform in Russia.) The United States has also financed denuclearization in the former Soviet Union, but that is driven predominantly by U.S. security interests. Russia has drawn nearly $20 billion in stabilization credits from the IMF, all of which must be paid back with interest, and Russia has already returned two-thirds of that amount. The World Bank has committed a total of $12 billion, but that is also in the form of credits and must be repaid with interest.

Thus, since the Cold War ended, the Western public grants of real assistance to Russia come to a grand total of about $5 billion (equivalent to the total U.S. foreign aid to Israel and Egypt in a single year), most of which has been spent on Western consultants.

For its part, the United States has benefited enormously from the peace dividend that came with the disappearance of the Soviet military threat. In the 1980s, the United States spent 6 percent of its GDP on defense, compared with 3 percent ($300 billion a year) in 2000. Americans should thank Presidents Gorbachev and Yeltsin, not former President Bill Clinton or the U.S. Congress, for wiping out the U.S. budget deficit. Russia's gift to the United States of $300 billion a year by 2000 should be compared with the much discussed U.S. compensation of a measly $200 million a year.

Even so, Western aid has accomplished a lot in Russia. The IMF has assisted in the Russian financial stabilization at no cost to U.S. taxpayers, and so the fund can now declare victory and go home. At minimal cost, USAID and the World Bank have contributed to the largest privatization effort the world has ever seen, which may yet emerge as a great success. Consultants have helped foster such a profound change in Russian economic thinking that the prevailing mind-set is now even more market-oriented than Western Europe's.

In short, Western assistance to Russia has been an astounding success considering the paltry amounts. Rarely has so little money made such a difference. Yet, if more had been given early on, much more could have been attained.

Myth 9: Russia Needs a General Pinochet

Many Russians and foreigners alike think Russia's problem is a lack of a strong leader, and quite a few consider democracy an impediment to arduous economic reforms (the arguments of the modernization school). Similarly, proponents of a Chinese model for Russia favor dictatorship over democracy. Worse, these ideas are popular among the Russian elite. Throughout the world, democracy and market reform are positively correlated, and in the former communist world this correlation is extremely close (see figure 6.2). The reason is obvious: The main threat to successful transformation comes from the old, powerful elite, which usurped the state for private gain. Democracy and vibrant media are the best checks on that elite. Strong presidential power is not beneficial to reforms. The transitional countries with the least amount of reform are all under presidential rule, while the most liberal countries have parliamentary systems, which can check the power of centralized government. Without exception, the countries with presidential systems are less democratic than those with parliamentary rule. Much of the antidemocratic sentiment stems from the perception that political stability is good for reforms. But in practice, the opposite is true. The long tenure of the infirm President Yeltsin and the passive Prime Minister Viktor Chernomyrdin provided Russia with a "stability" that favored the corrupt elite. Poland, the three Baltic countries, and Bulgaria have changed governments on average every year for the last decade, and they are among the most successful reformers. Contrary to common opinion, communists

Figure 6.2 Democracy and Market Reform, 2000

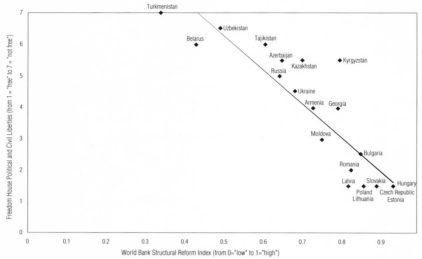

Sources: European Bank for Reconstruction and Development (EBRD), *Transition Report 2000* (London: EBRD, 2000); Freedom House, *Freedom in the World: Annual Survey of Political Rights and Civil Liberties* (New York: Freedom House, 2001), also available at http://www.freedomhouse.org/survey/.

do not threaten truly radical reforms, such as in Poland and Estonia. The Russian and Ukrainian communists have remained relatively strong because of the slowness of Russia's reforms. Yet these reforms have progressed far enough to keep the communists at bay. The idea that democracy is bad for reform presumes that the elite is good and wise, while the common people are stupid and shortsighted. All evidence, however, suggests that the unlawful enrichment of the elite is the problem. The population needs to be mobilized and organized to check the elite's excesses, and the most effective means of popular control we know is democracy and the freedom of the press. The widespread disregard for democracy and the repression of media are the greatest dangers in Russia today.

Myth 10: President Clinton Lost Russia

Russia is by no means lost—except in some people's imagination. While many processes have taken some time, a great deal has been accomplished in the last decade. If not a very liberal country, Russia is at least an electoral democracy with substantial participation and clear electoral patterns. Even if under threat, Russian media remain of good quality and highly pluralist. Prices are free and reasonably stable, as is the exchange rate. The economy is largely privatized, and radical tax reform is likely to improve governance. Barter and nonpayments have dwindled to an ordinary level. While the legal system is highly corrupt, substantial judicial reform was legislated at the end of 2001. By and large, obvious popular demands are being satisfied, and public opinion is swiftly becoming more informed. It would be strange if something as terrible as Soviet communism could be obliterated without a trace within a few years, and it is amazing how much has already been corrected.

Furthermore, it is both pretentious and incorrect to think that the United States could have dictated what happened in Russia. Although Russia no longer is a superpower, it remains a huge sovereign country with great influence on world affairs. The very idea that the United States "lost Russia" suggests disrespect for other countries' sovereignty. Considering that the United States spent only a pittance on Russia, it is amazing that any Americans can believe that the United States could determine events in Russia. The United States had one extraordinary, though brief, opportunity to influence Russia's future. That was in early 1992, when Russia had a government under Prime Minister Yegor Gaidar that was serious about attempting radical economic reform. The United States, however, did nothing to support these efforts when a little assistance could have changed the course of history. Instead of promoting reform, the United States discussed the perfection of humanitarian assistance. Yet the U.S. president at the time was not Bill Clinton but George Bush Sr. No such historical chance returned, and George Bush Sr.'s epitaph should be "the man who slept when the Cold War ended."

Russians increasingly believe that President Yeltsin was wrong in trying to establish too friendly relations with the United States, complying with its many demands, while China's hard-line foreign policy toward Washington was more successful. The United States expanded the North Atlantic Treaty Organization (NATO) against Russia without offering anything in return. The U.S. media and Congress persistently criticize Russia more often than China. Many Russians even argue that China has been wise to maintain a hard dictatorship in the face of U.S. hegemony. These examples could be multiplied, but they illustrate how poorly informed much of the Western discussion about Russia actually is. Emotions substitute for reality.

Notes

1. UN Economic Commission for Europe, *Economic Survey of Europe,* no. 2/3 (New York: United Nations, 2000).

2. *Narodnoe Khoziaistvo SSSR v 1989 g.* (The National Economy of the USSR in 1989) (Moscow: Goskomstat, 1990).

3. Deutsches Institut für Wirtschaftsforschung, *Handbuch DDR-Wirschaft* (Manual of the GDR Economy) (Reinbek at Hamburg: Rowohlt, 1977).

4. Horst Siebert, *Das Wagnis der Einheit* (The Daring of Unity) (Stuttgart: Deutsche Verlags-Anstalt, 1992), p. 39.

5. Anders Åslund, "How Small Is the Soviet National Income?" in *The Impoverished Superpower: Perestroika and the Soviet Military Burden*, ed. Henry S. Rowen and Charles Wolf Jr. (San Francisco: Institute for Contemporary Studies, 1990), pp. 13–61, 288–305.

6. Simon Johnson, Daniel Kaufmann, and Andrei Shleifer, "The Unofficial Economy in Transition," Brookings Papers on Economic Activity no. 27 (Washington, D.C.: Brookings Institution Press, 1997), pp. 159–239.

7. Åslund, "How Small Is the Soviet National Income?" pp. 13–61, 288–305.

8. *Russian Economic Barometer* (III Quarter), 2000.

9. This index was originally set up by Martha de Melo, Cevdet Denizer, and Alan Gelb (1997), with World Bank assessments for 1990–1994. They also indicated how their assessments were related to EBRD indices. Havrylyshyn and Wolf (1999) updated their series for 1995–1997, while the author has updated correspondingly for 1998 and 1999. The formula is rather simple. The first element is 0.3 times EBRD's index for price liberalization and competition policy. The second element is 0.3 times EBRD's index for trade and foreign exchange liberalization. The third element is 0.4 times EBRD's index for large-scale privatization, small-scale privatization, and banking reform. Each index is normalized to reach a maximum of 1. Thus, this index represents liberalization to 73 percent, while the rest is privatization. The weights have been arbitrarily selected, but actually it does not matter much what weights are chosen for the countries' relative standing to one another, as the covariance is great.

10. Simon Johnson, John McMillan, and Christopher Woodruff, "Entrepreneurs and the Ordering of Institutional Reform: Poland, Slovakia, Romania, Russia, and Ukraine Compared," *Economics of Transition 2000*, vol. 8, no. 1 (2000), pp. 1–36.

7

Has Russia Entered a Period of Sustainable Economic Growth?

Clifford G. Gaddy

Russia's financial crash of August 17, 1998, was a turning point. What happened in the three years since has changed the economy, pushing it into a distinctly new phase of economic evolution. It has altered some of the institutional features and organization of the economy, as well as the behaviors and expectations of agents. But in the most fundamental aspects, there has been much less change in the underlying structure and location of physical and human capital. Misallocation remains the hallmark of the Russian economy. At best, the changes have made the economy more technically efficient—that is, able to obtain more output from given inputs—but not more competitive.

The enhanced efficiency is likely to provide for a few years of measurable growth in output. The growth will be hard-won. It will be based on careful husbanding of resources and will require tough management. The growth will also be fairly modest in quantity. But most important, its quality will remain questionable because part of the recorded growth will not be truly competitive output. It is therefore difficult to describe it as sustainable, at least if that term is taken to imply "self-perpetuating."

Brief Review

The Russian government's August 1998 default on its domestic debt and the subsequent paralysis of its payments system shocked an already very weak economy. Output plunged to the lowest levels ever in an already disastrous decade. By December 1998 Russian industry was producing barely 50 percent of its output a decade before. But then the rebound began. For one full year, the economy showed not just steady but accelerating growth. As the gross domestic product (GDP) growth rates moved into the range of 10 to12 percent on an annualized basis in late 1999, a sense of near-euphoria affected everyone. Vladimir Putin, whose accession to power happened to coincide with those peak rates, reflected the overall mood. When he declared his vision for Russia in a special Internet message issued in the final days of the millennium, he posited that a reasonable goal for the country would be fifteen years of 8 to 10 percent annual GDP growth.

Since then, the economy's performance has moderated and so have the predictions. Although it is natural that the economic rebound would gradually attenuate, and although the balance is still positive, there are worrisome signs. In 2001 major sectors of industry began to show declines in output, profits, and investment. As expectations come down for a somewhat soft landing, it is a good time to pause and ask what is it that has happened to the Russian economy after 1998? And what can we expect over the longer term?

It may be useful to refresh our memories of the past three and a half years, from the beginning of 1998 through the middle of 2001. Figures 7.1–7.3 are an attempt to give such a snapshot of the economy. They use selected official Russian government statistical series to illustrate production as well as welfare. The figures are based on monthly statistics for year-to-year growth or decline. To smooth temporary fluctuations and better show the trends, they are presented in the form of six-month rolling averages. Thus, each data point is the mean of the values for the preceding six months. (Smoothing the data in this way not only permits us to discern actual trends more clearly. It also helps minimize the measurement and reporting errors that plague Russian statistics.)

Figure 7.1 shows production. The two curves show industrial output and freight transport—both measured in physical units. Although the industrial output measure is more volatile, the two data series show the same general pattern: They were negative in 1998 (even before the August financial col-

Figure 7.1 Industry and Transport, June 1998–June 2001

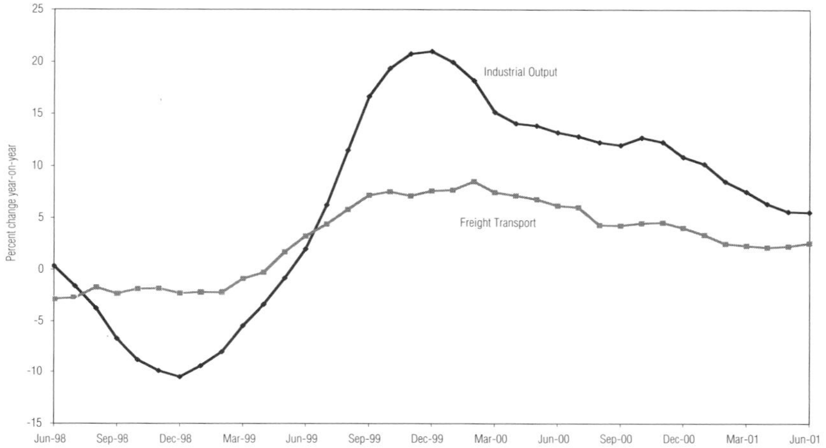

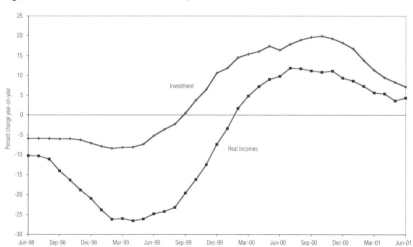

Source: "Osnoynyye sotsial'no-ekonomicheskiye pokazateli po Rossiyskoy Federatsii za 1996–2001 gg. (po materialam Goskomstata Rossii)," *Voprosy statistiki*, no. 12 (2001), pp. 27–38.

Figure 7.2 Investment and Incomes, June 1998–June 2001

Source: "Osnoynyye sotsial'no-ekonomicheskiye pokazateli po Rossiyskoy Federatsii za 1996–2001 gg. (po materialam Goskomstata Rossii)," *Voprosy statistiki*, no. 12 (2001), pp. 27–38.

Figure 7.3 Investment, Industry, Incomes, and Transport, June 1998–June 2001

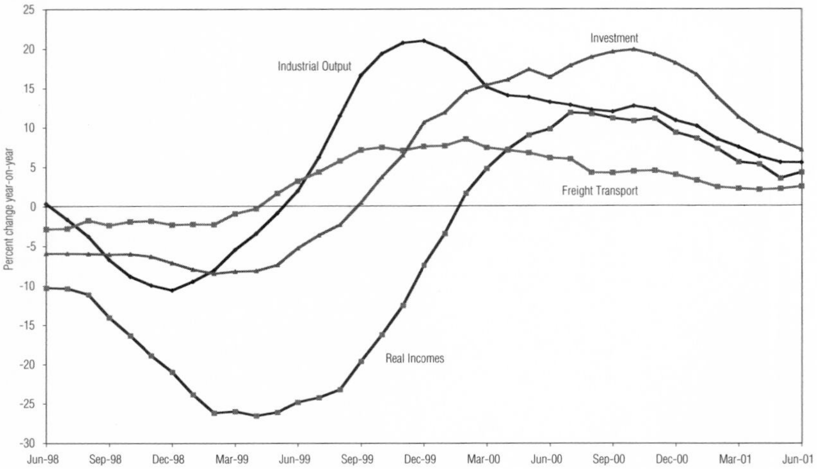

Source: "Osnoynyye sotsial'no-ekonomicheskiye pokazateli po Rossiyskoy Federatsii za 1996–2001 gg. (po materialam Goskomstata Rossii)," *Voprosy statistiki*, no. 12 (2001), pp. 27–38.

lapse); they rebounded strongly in 1999; and finally they tapered off in 2000 and 2001, while so far remaining positive.

Figure 7.2 shows some of the follow-on effects of the trends in the production sphere. It looks at household incomes and capital investment. Note that the pattern is the same as in the production measures: decline, rebound to ever-higher growth rates, and tapering off. As would be expected, there is a difference in timing—a lag of six months to one year—as compared to figure 7.1. This becomes clearer when we superimpose the two figures and look at the four indices together (figure 7.3). Despite the variation in volatility and in the timing over the entire three-year period, there is in the end a convergence. So far, all four indices remain positive. In the next section, we will consider some explanations for the patterns shown by these curves.

Accounting for Growth

Before examining the effect of purely economic factors, we need to remember one simple statistical fact: Russia began its recovery from a very low base. Because output in 1998 was very low relative to levels of only a few years before, merely resuming a modest amount of old production showed up as

Figure 7.4 Production of Grain Harvesting Combines, 1995–2000

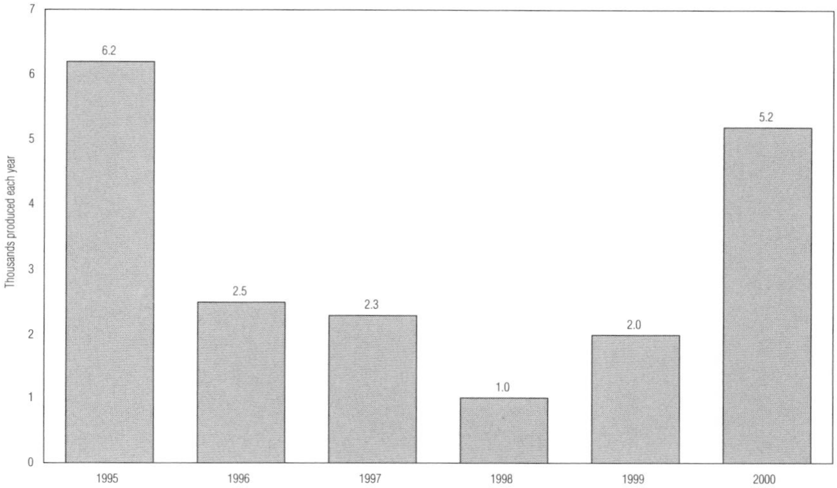

Source: Data from *Interfax Statistical Report,* no. 5 (2001).

large percentage growth. The core sector of heavy manufacturing, for instance—what the Russians call machine building and metalworking—is illustrative. Consider its situation as shown in the output data for one particular product, the large grain-harvesting combines used on the giant collective and state farms of the former USSR. In 1999 and 2000, production of combines in Russia rose by 100 percent and 160 percent, respectively (figure 7.4). This appears impressive until we put the recent years' development in a longer-term perspective. In 2000 the industry produced slightly more than 5,000 combine units. As recently as 1986, Russian factories had been producing well over 100,000 units a year (figure 7.5). While all heavy manufacturing output did not fall as far as this particular product, it still suffered a decade of unprecedented collapse of output without a corresponding shrinkage of either employment or physical production capacity.

Oil Prices

The world price of oil is extremely important for the Russian economy. Russia exports such large quantities of crude oil and various oil products that every dollar increase in the price of a barrel of petroleum translates into

Figure 7.5 Production of Grain Harvesting Combines, 1986–2000

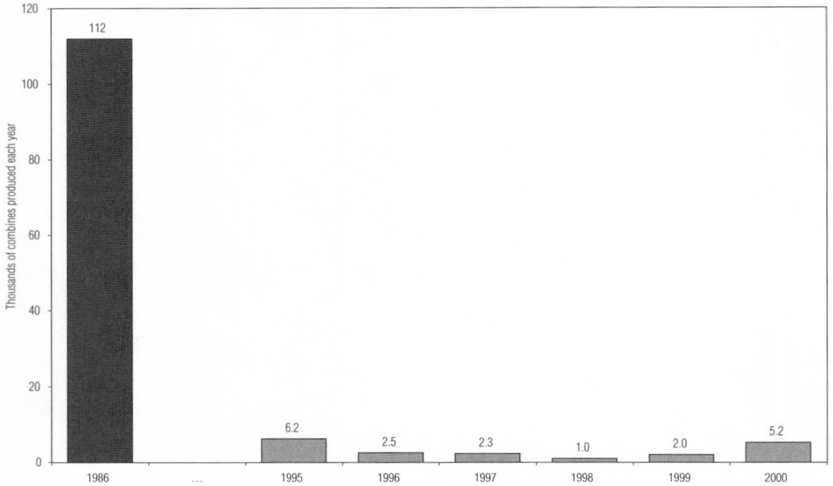

Sources: Data for 1986 from *Narodnoye khozyaystvo RSFSR v 1988* g. (Moscow: Goskomstat RSFSR, 1989), p. 372; data for 1995–2000 from *Interfax Statistical Report,* no. 5 (2001).

roughly \$1.5–\$2.0 billion of additional yearly export revenues. The world oil price rose from barely \$10 a barrel in February 1999 to over \$27 a barrel a year later, and rose again to more than \$30 before gradually declining. This is roughly the same trend as noted in Russia's industrial output. Examining the year-to-year change in world oil prices and Russia's industrial growth, there is little doubt about a strong positive statistical correlation between the two (see figure 7.6).

The traditional "goodness-of-fit" measure for this relationship, the coefficient of determination or R^2, is quite high. It indicates that about 80 percent of the variation in industrial growth is "explained" by oil prices alone. Another test of the explanatory power of the oil price changes is to graph actual industrial growth against what would have been predicted by oil price data alone. That is, imagine that on December 31, 1999, the econometrician knew only the relationship between the two variables for each month of 1998 and 1999. Then suppose that the analyst was given only the monthly oil price data for the year 2000 and asked to predict the year's industrial performance. Figure 7.7 shows the prediction for Russia's industrial growth in the year 2000. Figure 7.8 compares the prediction to what really happened. The fit is striking.

Figure 7.6 Oil Price Change versus Industrial Growth, January 1998–February 2001

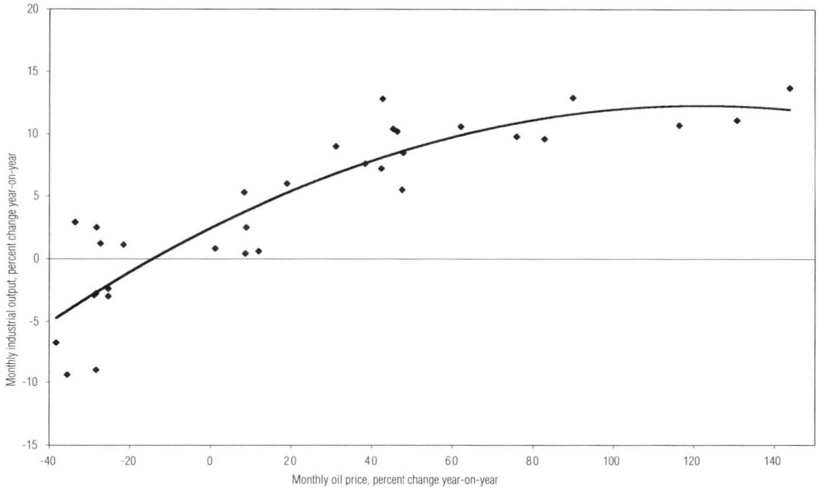

Sources: Industrial output data from "Osnoynyye sotsial'no-ekonomicheskiye pokazateli po Rossiyskoy Federatsii za 1996–2001 gg. (po materialam Goskomstata Rossii)," *Voprosy statistiki*, no. 12 (2001), pp. 27–38; oil price data are monthly averages of NYMEX futures prices for crude iol from the U.S. government's Energy Information Administration, available at http://www.eia.doe.gov.

The statistical relationship between oil prices and industrial output is so close that it is tempting to ascribe virtually all of Russia's post–August 1998 economic performance to oil. All the other factors that are assumed to influence economic performance—exchange rate dynamics, monopolies' pricing policy, taxes, investment rates, competition policy, capital flight, banking reform, monetary policy, and progress on corporate governance and rule of law—would be irrelevant. It would, however, be a mistake to ignore these factors. It is unfortunately not possible to make a rigorous statistical analysis of the effect of those factors, but there is no doubt that policy has made a difference. Without the oil price rise, Russia would not have had its boom. It was sound economic policy that allowed the Russian economy to take advantage of the oil price increases, but sound policy alone could not have substituted for the oil price effect.

Devaluation

The real devaluation of the ruble that occurred in the August 1998 crisis is a second important economic factor in the post-1998 economy. This was the

Figure 7.7 Industrial Growth Forecast, March 2000–February 2001

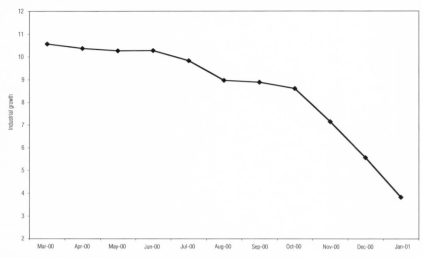

Note: Forecasted industrial growth rates are three-month rolling averages.
Source: Forecasts are author's calculations based on the regression results in Figure 7.6.

Figure 7.8 Industrial Growth Forecast and Actual, March 2000–February 2001

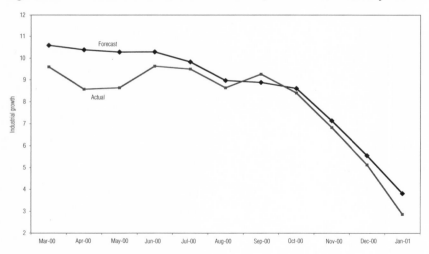

Note: Forecasted and actual industrial growth rates are three-month rolling averages.
Sources: Forecasts are author's calculations based on the regression results in Figure 7.6. Actual industrial growth rates are from "Osnoynyye sotsial'no-ekonomicheskiye pokazateli po Rossiyskoy Federatsii za 1996–2001 gg. (po materialam Goskomstata Rossii)," *Voprosy statistiki,* no. 12 (2001), pp. 27–38.

consequence of a nominal depreciation that exceeded ensuing inflation. By December 1998 the real value of the ruble relative to the U.S. dollar was about 36 percent of its July value. This was the maximum extent of real depreciation. Since the beginning of January 1999, the ruble has gradually, but steadily, increased in value.

This dramatic devaluation benefited many Russian producers. For exporters of commodities whose prices were denominated in dollars on world markets, the effect was immediate. Their costs were primarily ruble based, while each dollar they earned was now worth many more rubles. Even without making any changes in the way they did business, the exporters saw dramatic improvement in their profit and loss statements.

The devaluation effect had provided a boost to Russia's oil exporters even before the world oil price began its sharp rise. But by the spring of 1999 the two effects were working together to give the oil producers an unprecedented windfall. The currency depreciation meant that each dollar they earned was worth more than twice as much inside Russia. The oil price increase meant that by the end of 1999 they were earning three times as many dollars for each barrel of oil.

The devaluation was also important for Russian producers that sold their products on the domestic market in competition with imported goods. Before August 1998, the ruble was quite expensive, trading at a rate of around 6 rubles to the dollar. This made it possible for a significant number of Russians to afford foreign-made goods at relatively low ruble prices. The devaluation pushed those prices out of reach for many. Before August the average Russian worker could have purchased one kilogram of imported American chicken for the equivalent of one hour's wage. Afterwards, that same chicken would cost the equivalent of three hours' worth of wages.

In response to this dramatic rise in prices of imported goods, Russians turned to cheaper domestic products. That in turn led to a boost in output and profits in the domestic consumer goods sector (mainly in the food and in the so-called light industries of textiles and apparel). Nevertheless, the boost was not sustainable. Output in these sectors is now flat or down. In 2000, real profits in light industry were down 20 percent from 1999 levels; in the first half of 2001 they dropped another 34 percent. In the food sector, many imported goods are now beginning to reclaim their lost markets. In the first quarter of 2001 poultry imports from the West were up 430 percent, butter imports were up 220 percent, and meat and fish imports were up 100 percent.

Figure 7.9 Russian Hourly Wage in Dollars, January 1998–July 2001

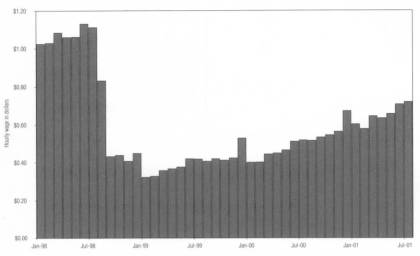

Sources: Author's calculations based on nominal average monthly wages due and official ruble-dollar exchange rate at the end of the month. Wage and exchange rate data taken from "Osnoynyye sotsial'no-ekonomicheskiye pokazateli po Rossiyskoy Federatsii za 1996–2001 gg. (po materialam Goskomstata Rossii)," *Voprosy statistiki*, no. 12 (2001), pp. 27–38.

Overall, the effect of the cheap ruble has been fairly small relative to the extent of the real depreciation. The reason why is clear: The sharp decline in real household incomes that was caused by the currency devaluation put a limit on the import substitution effect. Compared to July 1998, the average wage in September 1999 was still more than 35 percent lower in real terms than it had been before the crisis (see figure 7.9). As a cumulative phenomenon month after month, this "wage gap" added up to an amount equal to 18 percent of GDP between October 1, 1998, and October 1, 1999, alone.

Russians responded to the devaluation in two ways. First, they did indeed substitute some cheaper domestic products for the imported goods they had previously been buying. But second, owing to reduced incomes, they had to cut down on retail spending overall. Most Russians made up the difference in their usual way: They drew upon family and social networks of support and, to the extent possible, they engaged in direct self-production. The old and tested method of growing one's own food in a family garden plot once again was the ultimate safety net. In the face of all the ups and downs of the Russian economy in the 1990s, one robust (but negative)

Figure 7.10 Household Sector's Share of Potato Production, 1971–2001

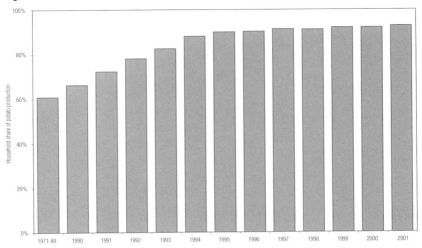

Sources: Data for 1971–1995 taken from Russian statistical yearbooks for various years; data for 1996–1999 from *Interfax Statistical Report,* no. 6 (2000), and *Interfax Statistical Report,* no. 1 (2001). Note: The output of the backyard and dacha plots is about 30 million tons a year. This means that ordinary Russian families produce more potatoes than all the farmers of the United States, Canada, Australia, Italy, and France put together.

index of the extent to which Russian households have seriously integrated themselves into the market economy is the amount of effort they put into working on their family garden plots. By this "garden plot index," the past two years' economic growth has not been sufficient to persuade Russian households to reduce their reliance on nonmarket activities. Figure 7.10 shows the share of the national annual potato crop—Russia's "second bread"—that is grown by individual households on their plots. In 2000, the household share of the production of the potato crop was slightly over 90 percent. Data on other food products such as vegetables, fruits, and even meat would show the same pattern over time. (Russians produce close to 80 percent of all vegetables and fruits and over 50 percent of all meat they consume on their garden plots.)

There is, moreover, no reason to think that household behavior will change this year. Real incomes remain substantially below what they were before the 1998 crisis. And while official statistics claim that incomes are rising, this contention needs qualification. First, there is strong regional differentiation in income trends. For instance, in one out of five of Russia's regions, the officially computed real disposable income per capita was lower in June 2001 than in June 2000. Second, and more serious, the inflation index used to calculate real incomes appears to be biased against the price increases on the basket of goods and services actually purchased by the majority of the population. Consequently, it is entirely possible that incomes nationwide, not just in certain regions, are declining.

Officially, the mean per capita nominal income was up 33.5 percent from June 2000 to June 2001, which translates into a real increase (in disposable monetary income) of 7.4 percent if one uses a deflator based on the consumer price index of 1.243. If, on the other hand, one deflates nominal incomes by the price index of the so-called subsistence consumption basket of goods and services for the same period (1.443), then the value of cash income was *down* in nearly nine out of ten regions from June 2000 to June 2001. By that index, the average cash income of Russians in June 2001 could buy 7.5 percent less basic goods and services than it did one year before.[1]

What Remains?

Both the oil price and the devaluation effects are temporary. Although they provide a windfall while they last, they cannot contribute to making the economic recovery sustainable except to the extent that they change the underlying structure of the economy and the way agents in it behave. What we need to know is whether the windfalls from high oil prices and the cheap ruble were used to make the economy more competitive than it was prior to 1998.

Currency devaluation is a classic example of a policy that can be used to increase competitiveness. When a country depreciates its currency as a conscious instrument of economic policy, the intent is to allow its producers to sell cheaply abroad and at home in competition with the rest of the world. This works because domestic costs—wages in particular—are kept low. The strategy is to sacrifice consumption today for the sake of investment in the future. Companies can gain market share and earn higher profits. They use those profits to modernize so that when the price ratios even out (that is, when domestic price levels rise faster than the devaluation of the currency), the companies will be more competitive compared to the predevaluation situation. The key, then, is that the windfall profits are used for modernization. Additional oil revenues could serve the same purpose but without lowering current consumption.

To what extent have the windfalls been used for modernization in Russia? One obvious indicator is spending on new plant and equipment. However, this is an imperfect measure. It does not distinguish the quality of the investment. It also misses many important dimensions of the necessary reallocation of resources required. But it is a beginning for understanding. As figure 7.2 shows, investment picked up in late 1999 and continued to grow vigorously through 2000. Here, too, we must remember that the economy began from a low base. Investment in the Russian economy fell in the 1990s even more than output. By 1997, spending on new plant and equipment was only one-quarter of what it had been in 1990. This means that even the growth rates of 20 percent per year that were reached in the second half of 2000 were quite modest in absolute terms. The current rate of growth—6 to 7 percent per annum—is all the more inadequate.

Moreover, the rates of fixed capital investment continue to drop. Recent figures show that more than a third of Russia's regions invested less, not more, in the first half of 2001 than they did in the first half of 2000. The regions that showed declines in capital investment included such important economic centers as the cities of Moscow and St. Petersburg and the regions of Krasnodar, Stavropol, Nizhny Novgorod, Saratov, and Sverdlovsk.[2]

Similarly disturbing trends emerge when investment is disaggregated by sector. The food industry, for instance, invested 15 percent less in the first half of 2001 than it did the previous year. Investment by machine-building and metalworking enterprises was down 18 percent. As of fall 2001, oil and gas continued to account for most investment. The oil and gas sector invested 19 percent more in 2001 than in 2000. Overall, the oil and gas sector invests about ten times more than either heavy manufacturing or the food industry. Thus, not even as measured by gross capital spending (the crudest measure) has the opportunity afforded by the devaluation and oil price rise been used to appreciably upgrade production capacity in the economy.

In fact, the situation is even worse than this. As bad as the underinvestment problem is, it is not the main problem. *Under*investment is the legacy of the 1990s. A much weightier negative legacy is the massive *mis*investment that marked the six decades of communist central planning in the USSR. The latter problem greatly magnifies the investment shortfall of the 1990s, since today's Russia must now reallocate what the Soviet economy misallocated. The entire structure of the Soviet economy was flawed. It was configured not just to produce things in the wrong way. It was structured to produce the wrong things. (And it produced them in the "wrong place" as well.) To right these wrongs requires huge new investments in physical and human capital. But above all, it requires the right kind of investment in the right places. Even when today's Russian economy does invest, it is not clear that this is good. For example, taking into account opportunity cost, modernizing a plant or building a school or hospital in a location that should never have been developed in the first place is simply a further waste. Yet the hospital or plant upgrade will appear in statistics as positive.

The importance of overcoming past misallocation suggests how critical it is to try to measure its extent. One attempt is a Brookings Institution project on "The Cost of the Cold." The premise of this work is that one important component of Russia's past misinvestment is spatial misallocation, notably, industrial location and labor migration. A major component of the spatial misallocation problem relates to location in "thermal space," that is, people living and working in very cold places. The concept of "temperature per capita" (TPC) is useful in studying the problem. TPC, which is a population-weighted average temperature for a country or region, permits comparisons across countries and over time. A country's TPC changes as a result of economic location decisions in the economy. When businesses and people move to locations with more moderate climates, production costs are lowered and the TPC rises. The TPC can thus be treated as an "economic rationality index." When applied to Russia, the results are striking. Figure 7.11 shows that when the Communist Party launched its grand plan to restructure the economy of the USSR, Russia was indeed a "cold country" in the precise sense that it had a very low TPC, much lower than far northern European countries such as Sweden. Canada's TPC, however, was much closer to Russia's.

Figure 7.12 shows the net effect of Soviet spatial allocation policies on the Russian TPC: a drop of almost one full degree centigrade. Canada, in contrast, raised its TPC by an even greater amount during the same period (figure 7.13). In fact, the Canadian pattern of a rising TPC is the normal one for all of the Northern Hemisphere industrialized nations studied in the project. While further research will be required to begin to compute the actual "cost of the cold"—what we might term the "marginal temperature cost," or the amount by which a nation's GDP changes as its TPC drops by one degree—it is clear from work already done that (1) Russia's cold is costly; (2) the policies of the past that lowered its TPC increased Russia's cost of production; and (3) as long as Russia does not warm up (that is, raise its TPC), it will bear a continuing cost.

Figure 7.11 January Temperature Per Capita for Selected Countries

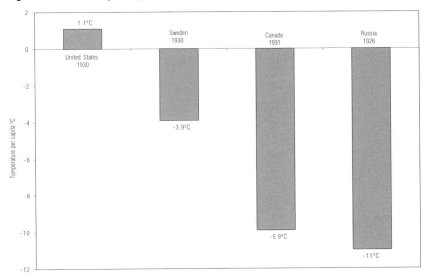

Source: Author's calculations from the Brookings Institution project on "The Cost of the Cold," Brookings Institution, Washington, D.C.

Here, too, very recent trends are not good. There was a small warming of Russia in the first half of the 1990s, and the trend is still positive. But the migration-induced warming rate has slowed dramatically. In 1999 Russia's TPC rose by 12/1000 of a degree. In 2000 the increase was 6/1000 of a degree, and as of fall 2001 it is even slightly less. At the current rate, it will take about 150 years for Russia to get back to its 1926 TPC.

In a speech in September 2001 in Germany, Putin bragged of Russia's "highly dynamic" economy, alluding to its recorded GDP growth in 2000 and 2001. In fact, it is apparent from the cost of the cold exercise that in an important sense Russia is not at all dynamic. There is not enough mobility. Not enough Russians are moving, and when they do, it is not to warm enough places.

A Missed Opportunity?

The preceding discussion might suggest that the past couple of years represented an opportunity that was missed. But that assumes that the top

Figure 7.12 Temperature Per Capita of Russia

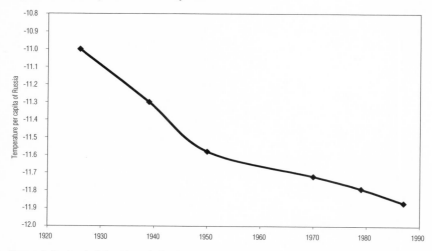

Source: Author's calculations from the Brookings Institution project on "The Cost of the Cold," Brookings Institution, Washington, D.C.

Figure 7.13 Temperature Per Capita of Canada

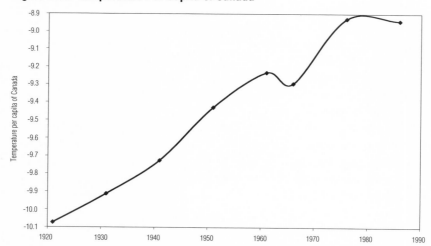

Source: Author's calculations from the Brookings Institution project on "The Cost of the Cold," Brookings Institution, Washington, D.C.

priority should have been and was fundamental economic reform. In Russia in 1999 and after, such reform has not been the priority. Rather, President Vladimir Putin has sought to use his period in office to consolidate political control of the country and strengthen the state (that is, the central government). For Putin the windfall was an opportunity to ensure political and social stability.

This does not mean that there was no economic reform; there was. But it is important to distinguish between two kinds of economic reform measures in Russia. The first category includes measures that are consistent with market reform, but which were not undertaken primarily for the purpose of furthering a market economy. They were done to strengthen the state. An example is tax reform. The second category of reform measures includes those that are essential to Russia's market transformation but that—in the short run at least—are regarded as a threat to social stability and the power of the state. Examples would include the closure of large "dinosaur" enterprises or land reform in the agricultural sector. Putin has implemented the first kinds of reforms but explicitly refrained from undertaking the second. He has stated, repeatedly, that the "time of revolution is over." Reforms of the second kind are revolutionary. But they are also the only type of reforms that can lead to fundamental change in the structure of the economy, thus allowing it to become globally competitive and thereby achieve long-term sustainable economic growth.

Perhaps the single most telling fact about what has and what has not been accomplished in the past three years is that despite extraordinarily favorable recent conditions, a staggeringly high proportion of Russia's industries remains unprofitable. As figure 7.14 shows, the 1998 devaluation did reduce the number of loss-making enterprises, but the improvement stopped at that point, leaving 40 percent of the companies still in the red. Russia thus remains burdened by tens of thousands of nonviable enterprises that cannot compete and yet live on year after year, no matter what the macroeconomic and policy environment. Whether high inflation or low, cheap ruble or dear, high world commodity prices or low, these enterprises do not change and yet do not—are not allowed to—die.

Changing management practices and reducing technical inefficiency will not solve these enterprises' problem. In most cases, efforts to reform them would simply be a further waste of precious resources. Russia needs to produce new and different goods and services in different places. The country's enduring dilemma is that the massive restructuring required—

Figure 7.14 Percentage of Loss-Making Industrial Enterprises, 1992–First Half 2001

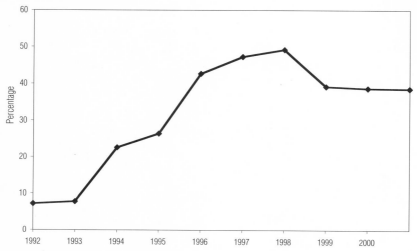

Sources: Data for 1992–1999 from *Rossiyskiy statisticheskiy yezhegodnik* (2000), table 21.31; data for 2000 from *Interfax Statistical Report*, no. 22 (2001); and data for 2001 from *Interfax Statistical Report*, no. 47 (2002).

that is, reallocation of capital and labor (including migration)—would entail vast dislocation; yet for perceived political, social, and security reasons, such dislocation is impermissible—even in the short term.

The interesting question now is: What will be the leadership's approach to economic policy as the windfall disappears and there are no compensating new sources of wealth creation to replace it? The answer can be only one: more efficient utilization of what is there, where it is. But efficiency has to be understood in relation to the overriding strategic goal of the current leadership: strengthening the state. The first priority therefore will be to ensure that more of the existing resources of society are channeled into directions deemed strategically important.

The role of government in resource allocation will continue to grow, as it has throughout the Putin tenure. For the leadership, this will in turn require ever-increasing effort in terms of national economic management. While the projected increase of the government role may seem reminiscent of Soviet central planning, the idea is quite different. Putin has long since realized that all attempts to micromanage an economy in the way the Soviets did are thoroughly counterproductive. For him, the key principle has been to establish priorities for where the state should act and where it cannot afford to. In this regard, the central government has to perform a balancing act. Putin realizes that he of necessity must rely on other agents to accomplish his overall goals. These others encompass the entire range of Russian society, from the private owners of strategically important industries (the so-called oligarchs) to regional government leaders to ordinary Russian households. All of them, in Putin's design, need to work together for a common goal.

Putin is asking two things of the oligarchs who control the vital sources of wealth creation such as the natural gas monopoly, Gazprom, the oil companies, and the metals and chemicals conglomerates. First, they must reduce—though not eliminate—their looting of the flows of wealth that they control. Second, they need to demonstrate that they, mainly in decentralized fashion, can channel resources to help support the socially and strategically important heavy manufacturing sector and other areas deemed critical, such as scientific institutes and defense research laboratories.

Regional government leaders—who, after all, are in many ways just a different variety of oligarch—will find themselves in a similar situation. They will be reined in like the oligarchs when it comes to excessive looting. They will be expected to ensure that the center receives its due in the form of cash tax deliveries. They may paradoxically receive more freedom. The key is to understand the concept of efficiency. Putin knows that he simply cannot afford to concern himself with micromanaging local (municipal) government or marginal enterprises. He will not bother reforming them. Such entities will be allowed to, and probably encouraged to, survive on their own. This could likely mean a revival of some old-fashioned mechanisms such as tax offsets and barter operations at the local level. It would be counterproductive to prevent local governments from using these virtual economy mechanisms when the cash runs out. They are mechanisms for coping at the local level (much like the garden plots at the household level). The enlightened Putin has to concentrate on the big picture. Russians at the bottom will be left to manage themselves.

This approach to the regions will involve a balancing act. The center cannot allow the regions to go so far in their coping and self-protection that they threaten the integrity of the country. Putin is not primarily interested in integrating Russian economic space horizontally. He stresses the vertical, in which the highest priority is the center. Nevertheless, excessive localism is a threat to national stability.

This is not an exhaustive list of important features of the new phase of Russia's economic evolution. Moreover, these are only likely trends, not a definite agenda. The new economic system appears more consistent and more stable than the Russian economy of the 1990s. But it is ultimately not sustainable because it continues to be based not on value creation but on value redistribution—albeit *more efficient* redistribution.

Notes

1. *Interfax Statistical Report*, no. 35 (2001).
2. *Interfax Statistical Report*, no. 36 (2001).

Part Three

Russian Society

8

What Has Happened to Russian Society?

Judyth L. Twigg

The human costs of the Soviet regime were unquestionably and unbearably high. Few would argue for a return to the political repression, pervasive economic and bureaucratic inefficiency, corruption, and general malaise that plagued late Soviet society. From the perspective of the Russian people, however, not everything about the Soviet Union was bad. In particular, an extensive and universal social safety net was an important positive element of Soviet rule. Free education and health care, a comprehensive and diverse system of pensions and social benefits, job security, extensively subsidized housing, basic foodstuffs, public transportation, child care, and vacations all contributed to a meager but reliable floor of living standards for the vast majority of the Soviet people. Upward social and economic mobility may have been severely limited, but there was little reason to worry about slipping down the socioeconomic ladder.

Despite ubiquitous and sarcastic undercurrents about the flaws in the safety net and the inadequate labor incentives provided by the command economy ("we pretend to work, they pretend to pay us" being the most popular expression of a common sentiment), the implied social contract of the Soviet era was a critical thread in the fabric of Soviet society. People accepted a low standard of living in exchange for economic and social security and equity. While economic inequalities did indeed exist in the form of an extensive network of perks and privileges for the politically powerful and well connected, they were carefully and mostly successfully hidden. To the extent, therefore, that Soviet consumers were aware of and craved unavailable luxury or convenience items—or even basic essentials of decent quality—there was a sense that the lack of consumer goods affected everyone equally. Everyone enjoyed the security of a rudimentary but all-encompassing social welfare network. On the flip side, living standards were not high, and the routine inconveniences born of material shortages were a constant irritant, but these too were a universally shared fate.

This common economic and social circumstance, together with a slow but gradual improvement in living standards during the late Soviet period, was a critical source of societal cohesion. A significant portion of the Soviet Union's national identity and political legitimacy derived from its provision of social benefits. As long as everyone viewed the state as the guarantor of some basic level of material comfort and survival, and to the degree that this guarantee extended universally to all segments of the population, the Soviet people could "buy in" to at least some portion of the regime's propaganda about the success of the socialist experiment.

Over the last decade, the stress of market reform has ripped apart the Soviet safety net. The jolt of the sudden transition to capitalism has left the state unable to maintain the bulk of the social benefit package that generations took for granted, producing unprecedented poverty, material inequities, and socioeconomic schisms. As a result, Russian society has become unanchored. One of its major sources of national identity and cohesiveness—the perception of socialist equity—has been fractured. The high expectations engendered by the early promises of reform have been devastated by a decade's worth of suffering and hardship. The Russian people's well-documented yearning for order and stability derives at least in part from nostalgia for the days when the social safety net was intact, and when life for many was not consumed by a daily struggle for basic survival.

Collapse of the Safety Net and Its Social Implications

The Russian government's acceptance of fiscal responsibility in the early 1990s forced it to slash social spending. Budgets for schools, kindergartens, health facilities, sanatoria, day care, and myriad other formerly state-provided services plummeted. At the same time, workplace-based social benefits, substantial during the Soviet era, were also eroded by the sudden demand for enterprises to either become profitable or go out of business. Inflation decimated savings, and wage and benefit increases could not keep up with even more rapidly rising prices. The state could no longer afford to subsidize a basic floor of material living standards for the entire population.

As a result, a significant percentage of the Russian people has sunk into poverty. Anecdotal horror stories surrounding this phenomenon abound: the grandmother arrested in Ryazan in October 2000 for trying to sell her grandson for $90,000 so that his organs could be removed and sold in the West, or patients in Omsk with multi-drug-resistant tuberculosis marketing their disease-saturated phlegm to desperate customers anxious to infect themselves so that they can buy food with the money from a disability pension. But these sensationalist accounts should not mask the larger and more important fact that 30 to 40 percent of Russians now grind out a living below the poverty line, with those estimates varying depending on how poverty is defined. Most analysts agree, however, that the government's definition of a "minimum subsistence" income—the amount of money required to purchase a basket of basic food and other consumer goods, and the figure on which pensions, child allowances, and other post-Soviet-era benefits are based—is woefully meager. In other words, these poverty levels, at monthly incomes of around $30 to $45, or the equivalent of less than a dollar a day, represent real hardship. One analysis in early 2001 showed that the minimum monthly income in Novgorod oblast could barely feed five cats. Bread production in Russia continues to increase each year, since it remains one of the few affordable staples as the overall purchasing capacity of the population dwindles. For the average Russian citizen, consumption levels have fallen by half since 1992, and only one family in six is better off now than it was then.

The root causes of poverty in today's Russia are unemployment and low-paying jobs. Although official unemployment figures hover around 2 percent, these statistics are notoriously difficult to interpret. On the one hand, they mask a significant level of underemployment among workers still officially categorized as enterprise employees but who actually perform little or no work and therefore receive few or no wages. These "unpaid vacations" may encompass as much as another 7 to 8 percent of the workforce. On the other hand, the official statistics also miss what may be a significantly larger phenomenon, the substantial number of people working in the shadow economy, with wages paid off the books (largely for purposes of tax evasion). But these workers' unreported incomes most often involve unskilled labor, poor work conditions, and low pay. Both reported and unreported wage rates in Russian industrial enterprises and business offices remain frequently at levels comparable to developing countries, meaning that getting a job is no security against poverty.

Poverty in today's Russia is also largely a female phenomenon. In the late 1990s, nearly 80 percent of Russia's unemployed people were women. The vast majority of single parents are women, and more than 80 percent of them have no job at all. The Russian labor code guarantees that a new mother can take a three-year unpaid leave without losing her job, but employers almost never comply, and many employers hesitate to hire a woman with small children for fear that she will take frequent sick leave. Few single mothers receive child support, and the alimony law is rarely enforced. Bureaucratic red tape has prevented many of the neediest single parents from claiming the scanty, traditionally untargeted child benefit offered by the state; only 30 percent of the poorest families claim their monthly child stipend.

Although Russian culture still prides itself on cherishing its children as a precious national asset, the declining material and social position of children has been one of the most alarming consequences of the post-Soviet transition. The single most potent predictor of poverty during the transition period has been the birth of an additional child to a family. The poverty rate among families rises steadily with the number of children, to the point where nearly three-fourths of families with four or more children are poor. Thanks to these economic trends, well over a million children in Russia aged fourteen to eighteen have been unable to finish high school in the last decade.

Substandard living conditions are taking their toll on children's health, starting at the very beginning of life. According to the Russian Academy of Medical Sciences, because of an overall decline in the health of the population, poor prenatal care, and other factors, only 30 percent of Russian births can now be classified as "normal." Leading Russian physicians speak of the "deceleration," or the mental and physical deterioration, of children and teenagers. More than 70 percent of Russian young people aged ten to fifteen suffer from chronic diseases, the number of disabled persons in that age group is growing at an alarming rate, and the incidence of mental disorders among teenagers has increased fourfold in the last decade. These statistics are troubling in and of themselves, but when put into sociodemographic context—this is the post-Soviet generation that is supposed to transform Russia into an energized, market democracy—they are genuinely alarming.

The most extreme manifestation of these negative trends is the problem of abandoned and orphaned children. In the words of one orphanage director, "I can tell how bad things are by the way families are starting to ask us to take their children. Families in Russia are falling apart." Networks of foster care and adoption services are still underdeveloped, and therefore almost 700,000 children must live in orphanages. Having been raised in an institutional environment, these children do not have positive long-term prospects. According to recent Russian government estimates, 40 percent of them will end up in prison, and another 30 percent will become alcoholics. Even more striking, the country is now home to between one and four million homeless children, with that number largely dependent on the weather; more kids take to the streets in the summer months and return home when the cold becomes unbearable. This seasonal variation hints at the peculiar nature of this "social orphanhood"—more than 90 percent of these street children have one or more living parents who have simply lost the psychological or material wherewithal to raise their offspring (usually due to alcoholism or unemployment). Either they have voluntarily abandoned their sons or daughters, or the state has stripped them of parental rights. The number of these social orphans at present is higher than that at any point in Russia's history, including any postwar period.

The plight of parentless children is but one manifestation of the breakdown of the Russian family. Elderly Russians are increasingly neglected, becoming known as the new *bezprizorniki* (unsupervised ones) because their adult children are too busy with their own lives to attend to the needs of their parents. On the whole, however, elders are generally better off than children and single parents, since the pension system is one of the few elements of the social safety net that has remained a political priority. Divorce, while remaining at about the same rate as in Soviet times, is increasingly costly for women and children. The number of weddings has declined over the last decade. More and more children are being born out of wedlock. An increasing number of intact families are opting not to have children at all, or to have just one child. In the last ten years, the number of children in Russia has dropped by over four million, a manifestation of declining birth and fertility rates. While some of this drop stems from medical infertility, much is due to conscious choice. Low birthrates are a direct message from people who have lost faith in their society and who have little confidence that their social and economic circumstance is likely to improve. A recent survey of new mothers in one Russian region showed that 14 percent had reacted with horrified, suicidal feelings upon learning that they were pregnant, wondering how they would possibly support a new, dependent life. Little wonder that there are two abortions for every child born in Russia.

Women's degraded economic positions have caused them to suffer in other ways as well. Hundreds of thousands of women have voluntarily turned to a life of prostitution, and tens of thousands more have been duped into sex slavery through an extensive European and Asian network of trafficking in women. At home, Russian women are now, even more than in Soviet times, routinely the victims of domestic violence. Between 12,000 and 16,000 Russian women each year are killed by their spouses, and another 50,000 suffer severe injuries—ten times the comparable U.S. figures. Only six shelters for abused women exist in the entire country, all the result of private or local initiatives. Russian culture still sees victims as somehow "deserving" their fate, and a lack of legal protection follows those cultural assumptions.

This view of women is unsurprising, given the blatant sex discrimination and sexualization of women that have accompanied the market reform process. The ideological doctrine of socialist gender equity has given way to a routine of overtly sexist remarks during parliamentary debates, job advertisements that specify positions for "attractive" females under age thirty *bez komplexov* (without complexes, or willing to perform sexual favors), and open street vendor sales of sexually explicit publications. One mid-1990s survey indicated that over half of Russian women had been the recipient of sexual advances by their job supervisors.

Not surprisingly, breakdown at the societal and family level is producing individual-level pathologies as well. One in three Russians now has psychological problems, a 50 percent increase in the last decade, and the country's suicide rate is among the highest in the world (and four times the U.S. rate). Work hours lost to psychological problems have significantly affected the country's economic productivity. Over the last ten years, disability certification for mental health reasons has grown more dramatically than for any other kind of illness. Meanwhile, Russia's mental health care infrastructure can accommodate only about 200,000 people, far below the capacity needed to cope with this growing problem, and even that network of facilities is rapidly decaying for lack of resources and investment.

Of course, the most well-known and visible manifestation of Russians' inability to cope with the stresses of the post-Soviet transition is the vodka bottle. The average Russian man now drinks three half-liter bottles of vodka each week, and consumption levels appear to be steadily increasing. Alcohol is clearly a major contributor to the country's demographic crisis, accounting as it does for the growing rate of traffic and industrial accidents and cardiovascular disease in middle-aged men. Alcoholic parents produce many, if not most, of the country's abandoned children. If the country had a functioning network of battered women's shelters, it would be filled with victims of domestic violence perpetrated by drunken boyfriends and husbands. Yet vodka remains cheaper than milk, supported by a state that relies on almost $500 million in annual revenues from alcohol duties. Despite efforts by the health ministry to call attention to this problem, the government continues programs such as rewarding a few select oblasts over the May 2001 holidays with additional vodka allocations as a prize for "good work" carried out during the preceding twelve months. A draft law that would limit advertising for alcoholic beverages and promote public health campaigns about alcohol consumption has remained stalled for several years.

Illegal drug use is also a growing problem, to the point where the health ministry refers to it as an epidemic. Between three and five million Russians are regular drug users. One-third of the country's urban population has tried illegal substances at least once. The rate of drug addiction has increased more than sevenfold in the last decade, with an even greater explosion among children and teenagers and a pattern of usage in which Russian young people abandon "light drugs" for heroin and other more dangerous narcotics far more quickly than is the norm in other countries. Russian specialists are also concerned about a recent drop in the age threshold for drug use, from sixteen or seventeen a few years ago to twelve and thirteen today. Injectable drug use is the almost exclusive transmission vector for Russia's growing HIV/AIDS problem.

Illicit drugs have also been a major factor in the country's surge in violent crime. Although crime rates fell slightly in the late 1990s, current levels still represent a significant increase over the Soviet period. Coupled with an unwieldy, often arbitrary judicial system, these crime levels have bestowed Russia with the world's largest prison population. One out of every four Russian adults has either been in one of the country's overcrowded, brutality-ridden prisons or has had a family member there. The government's attempts to reform its penal system have generally involved mass amnesties, with the unfortunate result that tens of thousands of actively infected tuberculosis patients—Russia's jails are the main breeding grounds for a sweeping tuberculosis epidemic—have been released into the general population.

Inequity and the Search for a Unifying Idea

Perhaps most important in terms of societal cohesiveness, the stratification of society according to income level has increased dramatically during the post-Soviet period. The gap between rich and poor is steadily growing, as is the absolute number of both very rich and very poor. At the end of the year 2000, salaries for the 10 percent of households with the highest income in Russia were thirty-two times those in the lowest income decile, and the richest households' total incomes were forty-four times higher. The new rich, or "New Russians"—former Communist Party leaders, bureaucrats, and others who had the skills, connections, and good fortune to take advantage of the opportunities presented by the transition—rapidly became objects of considerable scorn in the early and mid-1990s. Their combination of garish displays of excessive wealth and lack of education and manners made them the butts of a whole new genre of jokes. (Two New Russians meet on the street. "Hey, Vasya, where'd you get your nice tie?" "At the Valentino store. Cost me $2,000." "That's nothing, I know where you can get the same tie for $5,000!") But their profligate spending, particularly in Moscow and other major cities, drove up the price of new housing, public entertainment, and other goods to the point that ordinary people suddenly found those things out of reach. The new poor, by contrast, are those who work for the government or other still-public industries, including a wide array of skilled workers and former intelligentsia. They have suffered through the humiliation of meager and often late wage payments, or in-kind compensation in the form of goods like bras, caskets, and manure, and the need to supplement the scientific or technical positions that continue to harness their intellectual capacities with second and sometimes third jobs as taxi drivers, cooks, or janitors.

One of the Russian government's economic development strategy reports of late 2000 described the situation in these terms: Socioculturally and economically, two unequal social layers have formed over the last decade. About one-fifth of the population has maintained or improved its standard of living since the Soviet era, and a minority of those, about 5 to 7 percent of the population, have been able to adopt an essentially Western lifestyle, complete with modern spending and consumption habits. These people have been able to transcend Soviet assumptions and mind-sets regarding the personal work ethic and the appropriate role of the state. To them, the free market rewards those with skills, tenacity, and ingenuity. Their post-Soviet success has rendered the collapse of the old safety net irrelevant to them; they no longer need its protections. By contrast, the almost half of Russians who are subject to persistent poverty have become jealous and indignant over the new inequities. In their world, growing inequities have little to do with the natural results of free market competition. Instead, success for the few has stemmed not from hard work but from dishonesty and *blat* (political and social connections). The gap between expectations and reality for these people has been psychologically as well as economically devastating. The disappointment and resentment among those who mistakenly thought they would benefit from the marketization of the economy have been profound, particularly when success seems often to stem from criminal behavior and financial speculation rather than the production of legitimate goods and services. Surveys have repeatedly shown that most Russians view the primary beneficiaries of the transition period as "swindlers and manipulators," while few agree that ordinary, honest people have reasonable opportunities to increase their incomes and living standards. Hard work and a good education do not necessarily translate into a better life, and to the limited extent that they do, the latter is increasingly difficult to obtain. Declining public support for education and the rise of expensive private schools at all levels have seriously diminished one of the few remaining channels of social mobility.

The dynamic of this new, very public division of society into the haves and have-nots has exacerbated centuries-old Russian anger at the separation and exploitation of the masses by their masters. The well-known mantra about what the Russian people currently crave—order and stability—encompasses not just social and economic stability but also a fundamental sense of social justice. The gap between winners and losers in post-Soviet Russia still may not match the level of inequality in the United States, but the rate of explosion of inequality in Russia has been so rapid that people indoctrinated in the socialist mind-set have had little time to adjust. As a result, Russia has lost all sense of a common national identity. In the midst of socioeconomic chaos, no common set of unifying principles has emerged to replace the ideal, flawed as it was, of Soviet socialism. Gorbachev's perestroika undermined much of Russian tradition, forcing society to question its history, its political culture, its achievements as a superpower, the essence of its national dignity. For over a decade since then, the Russian people have been struggling with questions that cut to the core of their identity. What values do we hold? What values do we want to transmit to our next generation? How can we regain a sense of pride and patriotism? For a few, the answer has been found in Western-style individualism born of the free market and of liberal political democracy. For the majority, however, that path has been tainted by the stain of crass commercialism and materialism and the gross inequities produced by shock therapy.

Those people have struggled to find alternative social moorings. They feel isolated and abandoned. Most say that they can now count only on themselves in times of trouble; only a small minority claim they can rely even on family and friends. Only 30 percent are able to recall anything positive that has happened to them recently. Moscow's most popular radio station airs catchy tunes with lyrics that reflect the pessimism of post-Soviet life, songs about war, death from hepatitis, and, most strikingly, a number one single from early 2000 called "You Have AIDS (and That Means We Will Die)." This national malaise indicates that Russia continues to suffer a wrenching psychological upheaval. The symptoms of its discontent extend far beyond what would be considered "normal" for a country undergoing the pangs of economic development, or even the sacrifices now routine for a postsocialist transition. Almost nobody has had confidence in the ability of public authorities to put the country back on the right track.

A dramatic cultural sea change has formed an integral part of this national identity crisis. Even factory workers and taxi drivers in the Soviet era could recite Pushkin, wax lyrical about the latest achievements of the Kirov ballet and the Chekhov theater, or discuss the finer philosophical nuances of Tolstoy and Dostoyevsky. Stagnant as life may have been under Brezhnev, it afforded people time and energy to think private thoughts and to place those ideas within a rich cultural context. The transition to the market swept away this luxury. Pushkin and Tolstoy have been replaced with the most base and commercial representations of Western popular culture, with billboards sporting half-naked women advertising Levi-Strauss *dzhinsy* (jeans) or Marlboro cigarettes. The television and film industries have become similarly dominated by American imports. Only 10 percent of the movies shown in Russian theaters in the mid-1990s were actually produced in Russia. And the domestic Russian media have responded by sinking to the lowest common denominator. Representatives of the Russian Orthodox

Church have blamed Russian television and cinema for many of the pathologies currently plaguing Russian society, and one of Russia's leading film directors has accused Russian television of turning today's children into a "generation of monsters."

In practical terms, the most common response to the last decade's social and economic upheaval has been apathy, spiced with a generous dose of hopelessness. Cynicism reigns. There are no longer "honest" or "dishonest" ways to make money—just "easy" or "hard."[1] There have been practically no mass, public displays of discontent over the initial economic contraction in 1992, the financial crash in 1998, and the months' and years' worth of non-payment of salaries. Instead, only a small minority of people express an interest in protest actions. Most Russians avoid reading about or discussing politics at all.

Those few who do seek political expression of discontent are increasingly turning to extremist outlets. A small but expanding number of young people, even those with good jobs and higher educations, are joining radical communist and socialist groups to protest wage inequalities and economic dislocations. Even more disturbing are the growing ranks of neo-Nazi youth groups across Russia that have been violently targeting non-Russians, particularly those from the Caucasus and Asia. Of the distinct minority of Russian youth who express a strong interest in politics—no more than 5 or 6 percent of the total—over half claim to favor fascism. The two Chechen wars have provided more than ample fuel to this fire. Although it would be inappropriate to exaggerate the scope of these trends at the present time, it is a situation likely to be exacerbated if the Russian government pursues its currently proposed policy of increased immigration as a solution to its demographic problems.

Russian youth, although more individualistic, entrepreneurial, and adaptable than their parents, may be the most severely impacted by this crisis of values. Society has not offered them the *vospitanie* (the process of deliberate instilling of society's positive values) that their parents enjoyed, primarily because society has been uncertain about what those values are. Their formative years have been ones of turbulence and upheaval. Unable to derive meaning from society as a whole, lacking crucial societal anchors, many of them seem to believe in nothing larger than themselves. While this may bode well for their ability to survive in a competitive market economy, it also has led a significant number of them into a life of crime; well over half of Russia's racketeers are under thirty years old, and the crime rate for juveniles under eighteen is higher than that for adults. The country desperately needs a mechanism to reengage its young people and harness their considerable energies in a productive direction.

Sources of Societal Cohesion and Identity

How has Russian society survived this assault on its most basic structure and principles? Russian people and families have relied on a variety of coping mechanisms. Some involve social structures held over from the Soviet past; others have newly emerged from the chaos of market reform. Primary among the former are informal interpersonal networks. These "kitchen table" groups are close circles of family and friends that, during the Soviet era, served not only as trusted confidants but also as networks of mutual provision of scarce consumer goods. Now, in many cases, these informal circles continue to provide material and psychological support, serving as the primary or only remaining source of cohesion and stability for many people. A similar psychological and economic impact is being engendered by intergenerational transfers of wealth. It is well known that some young adults who have navigated the transition period relatively successfully have financially supported their less adaptable middle-aged parents throughout the last decade. Recent studies have further indicated that family survival in many other instances is being maintained almost entirely by older Russians "giving until it hurts" to their adult children and grandchildren, particularly in rural areas—food from the dacha, money, whatever they have.[2] The importance of these informal, uneven patterns of exchange, particularly in the villages, should not be underestimated. They have prevented famine in a country that has indeed known famine in the last century. They render a significant number of Russia's poor less so than they might appear on the surface and provide an important source of social "glue" that holds families and rural communities together.

In addition, many Russians are returning to the symbols, if not fully to the substance, of the Russian Orthodox Church. Well over half of Russians now call themselves Orthodox, and millions of baptisms were performed in the aftermath of the Soviet collapse. The Church has deliberately tried to place itself at the center of a post-Soviet Russian national identity, referring repeatedly to a uniquely Orthodox "Russian idea" or "Russian soul." But over the last decade, while successful in opening new parishes and monasteries, the Church has been less effective in bringing its essence to the center of people's lives. Basic knowledge of Orthodox doctrine and theology remains low. As a result, many Russians have turned to other faiths, a phenomenon to which the Orthodox Church has responded jealously. It has master-minded a law that restricts, and may ban, the activity of many of the thou-sands of non-Orthodox religious groupings in Russia, excepting only those deemed "traditional," such as Islam and Judaism. Officially sanctioned dis-crimination against religious minorities, to the extent that it fosters a climate of divisiveness and intolerance, may undermine spirituality and religion as a sustainable source of family stability and societal cohesion.

Russia is also now home to a burgeoning network of over 300,000 non-governmental organizations (NGOs), with many designed to provide fami-lies and individuals with social services and support. The obstacles these groups face are substantial, from ridiculous bureaucratic registration requirements to monitoring of their activities by the FSB. Fundraising also remains problematic for these groups, although some are now beginning to navigate the waters of public-private partnership, and others have been blessed by the largesse of well-known tycoons like Vladimir Potanin and Boris Berezovsky anxious to create positive public images for themselves through philanthropy. And many of them still suffer from public suspicion based on the fact that corrupt businessmen and politicians often set up ille-gitimate NGOs for purposes of money laundering. Nevertheless, some of Russia's most talented people are choosing careers in this "third sector." To the extent that they grow and thrive, these networks of NGOs may prove instrumental in progress toward a climate of self-generated social welfare to replace the paternalistic model of state provision. Even more important, to the extent that they can link their efforts through regional and national associations, they can provide the foundation for a genuine civil society, creating a sense of "common good" and perhaps also the foundation of a sta-ble, liberal democracy.

Government authorities have also recently attempted quite deliberately to reestablish a positive, distinctively Russian national identity. In a trans-parent effort to build a new foundation for political legitimacy, President Putin is overtly cultivating a new patriotism, a new national pride—a sense that the country's past and present are nothing to be ashamed of and an attempt to step out of the shadow of a decade of socioeconomic turmoil and more recent disasters such as the sinking of the *Kursk*. The restoration of the old national anthem was the first step; the second was the return of basic military training and patriotism classes to the public schools. In March 2001, the government announced a full-blown, $6 million "patriotic education" program designed to counter a wave of "indifference, individualism, cynicism, unmotivated aggression, and disrespect for the state" evident since the collapse of the Soviet Union. Over the next five years, the project will attempt to reshape the education system through new history and other textbooks, influence the mass media (with prizes offered to journalists, writers, and filmmakers whose work exemplifies the goals of the program), and create a network of "military-patriotic youth clubs" around the country. Whether these efforts are intended to foster positively directed Russian nationalism or a cult of personality around Putin himself is debatable, but in many ways they are clearly falling on fertile ground. Recent consumption patterns—Russian products are now preferred over Western brands, and not just because of the price differentials with imported goods resulting from the August 1998 ruble devaluation—and numerous public opinion polls are now revealing a rejection of things Western. Consumer nationalism is leading advertisers to stress the "Russian-ness" of their products, even if those products are made by Western firms. A newly launched candy bar from U.S. confectioner Mars, for example, is called "Derzhava"—the Russian word for "power" and an unofficial slogan of the strong Russian state.

One important constituency for this new, positive Russian nationalism is the emergent middle class. Significant evidence suggests that this new middle class has energetically arisen from the rubble of the 1998 financial crisis—middle class not only in income and wealth but also in outlook and behavior. They vacation abroad. They frequent cinemas and theaters and the country's most recent craze, bowling alleys. On average, they hold a significantly more optimistic view of the future than the rest of the population. Many of them are young professionals who believe in the virtue—and in the possibilities—of hard work, and they are determined to build a Russia within which they and their children can succeed. They manage to save some money, and they purchase major durables such as cars and houses. They typically invest whatever profit they make back into their ventures, creating jobs and the foundation for a stable economic base. Although it constitutes no more than 10 to 15 percent of the population, remains vulnerable to shifts in the economy, and is located primarily in Moscow and a handful of other major cities, this emergent social stratum, plugging the gap between rich and poor, could serve as a powerful foundation of the necessary context for stability and cohesiveness. It is a significant cause for optimism.

Conclusion: Looking to the Future

The Russian people have been subjected to seemingly unbearable humiliation and hardship over the last decade. It is hard not to ask why they have tolerated it. Why are masses of impoverished, disaffected, alienated Russians not marching in the streets, demanding an improvement in their living conditions and in their social environment? Some Russian analysts cynically— but perhaps with a grain of truth—claim that the history of the Russian masses demonstrates a love of suffering, a craving for martyrdom. Others observe that many Russians have quite evidently chosen a more individualistic form of protest through withdrawal to the vodka bottle or the heroin needle or, more broadly, through withdrawal from active participation in society as a whole. Still others might cite a fear of disorder, of even more disruptive and destructive chaos if significant demands for change are made. And many observe that most Russians have been too preoccupied and exhausted by the daily struggle for survival to muster up the necessary energy to complain. Centuries-old Russian stoicism certainly goes a long way toward explaining the Russian people's acceptance of their fate; for example, an older Russian looking back on her life might observe that the last decade represents just one of many ups and downs for Soviet and Russian society.

Perhaps the cultivation of symbols and slogans can serve as a rallying point around which people can restore the national identity they so desperately need. But resurgent patriotism, no matter how heartfelt, will not erase the grinding poverty and gross inequities that continue to plague the Russian socioeconomic landscape. The most important social questions for Russia today cannot be solved by surface propaganda. They can be addressed only by moving a large number of the truly depressed people and places throughout the Russian Federation stably into that new middle class. Putin's call to patriotism will ring hollow—or hypocritical—unless supported by successfully implemented policy to achieve noticeable improvements in the lives of the majority of the Russian people.

Notes

1. Vladimir Chuprov and Julia Zubok, "Youth and Social Change," in *Russian Society in Transition*, ed. Christopher Williams, Vladimir Chuprov, and Vladimir Staroverov (Aldershot, U.K.: Dartmouth Publishing Group, 1996), p. 132.

2. Cynthia Buckley, "Family Matters: Intergenerational Wealth Transfers and Survival Networks," paper presented as part of the conference *From Red to Gray: Aging in the Russian Federation* at the University of Texas, Austin, April 6, 2001.

9

Human Capital and Russian Security in the Twenty-First Century

Harley Balzer

Human capital is increasingly crucial to the national security of all countries, and this does not bode well for Russia in the twenty-first century. At a time when global economic integration offers new opportunities and poses new challenges and threats, the size and health of Russia's population, the performance of its education system, the nation's scientific-technical capabilities, and the competition among these and other claimants on limited resources portend a Russia less capable of competing effectively in the international system.

Russia's human capital crisis is not simply a temporary product of the transition from communism or an ill-advised reform program. The negative trends are rooted in the Soviet Union's inability to respond to broad changes affecting all industrial societies in the final third of the twentieth century. The Soviet Union achieved significant gains in public health, education, and science and technology, but these accomplishments—like Soviet economic growth—were based on extensive development. The system never adjusted to the more nuanced demands of intensive development. The exit from

The author is grateful for enormous assistance from Murray Feshbach and for valuable comments on earlier versions of this chapter by Georgetown colleagues Joe Lepgold, Mike Brown, and John McNeil.

communism was itself a response to an environment of profound socio-economic change, in which the Soviet model was increasingly unable to compete.

In Russia's case, the difficulties are exacerbated by a syndrome characteristic of nations where the economy is heavily based on exporting natural resources. Russia is becoming a "post-industrial petro-state" in which state capacity is being diminished in key areas. Russia's new elites derive their wealth overwhelmingly from natural resources, and few of them appreciate the connection between expenditures for human capital and overall national well-being. It is unlikely that they will provide adequate resources for health and education simply because these are worthwhile endeavors. Perhaps if the correlation between national security and maintaining a vibrant base of human capital is stated in the starkest terms, it could have some influence on policy.

Introduction: Human Capital and Russian Security after Communism

The increasing importance of human capital for national security presents the type of challenge Russia has historically been least equipped to meet. Russia's population is declining in numbers, aging, and becoming less healthy, while the medical and education systems are rapidly becoming stratified into for-fee sectors serving the elite and distinctly inferior public sectors serving the majority. Population decline magnifies the effects of a system less able to tap talent on the basis of merit, fewer students physically and emotionally capable of rigorous study, and education programs that do not prepare Russia's youth for work in a modern economy. Russia faces the prospect of being unable to field a modern military force in terms of physical or intellectual talent. Yet Russian elites believe they must fix their economy before addressing these crises, failing to understand that human capital and economic performance are intricately interrelated.

If the negative trends are not reversed, Russia faces a lengthy period of decline (not necessarily collapse) and is unlikely to reassume its "traditional" great-power status. What influence Russia retains in international affairs stems from a decaying nuclear arsenal, the weakness of neighboring states, and institutional legacies such as the UN Security Council veto. All are of limited and diminishing utility. The nuclear arsenal will continue to decay; the cost of replacing it is beyond the nation's economic capabilities, and nuclear weapons are of little value in meeting most post–Cold War security challenges. Although the weakness of Russia's neighbors may change over time, for now, Russian intervention in conflict-ridden places such as the Abkhazia region in Georgia and Transdneistria in Moldova permits Russia to exploit and perpetuate its neighbors' weaknesses. Weak neighbors cannot contribute much to regional economic or security systems. The UN Security Council may be reformed or expanded to reflect changes in the balance of power, or it may be bypassed as in the case of Kosovo. Real influence in the international arena is measured in terms of economic performance, the ability to project military power, and status as a role model. In all of these realms, Russia's performance is dismal.

This chapter addresses five interrelated areas: (1) Russia's declining population, a long-term demographic trend exacerbated by psychological and physical shocks in the 1990s; (2) the possibility that migration will offset the population loss, but also pose new challenges; (3) worsening health combined with a catastrophic decline in medical services for most of the population and in the system of public health; (4) reduced coverage, uneven quality, and radical stratification in the education system, magnifying the demographic challenge; and (5) the demise of the Soviet system of science and technology, exacerbated by Russia's limited participation in the knowledge economy.

The challenges in each of these realms increase the importance of the others, while undermining the capacity to address them. The result is a threat to Russian national security much greater than the inability to fund the military-industrial complex. There are not enough healthy recruits to maintain an army of the size or quality that Russia's generals claim to need. Qualified officers are harder to find and to keep. The officer-heavy Russian Army represents an increasing burden on an economy heavily dependent on commodities, a sector notorious for price fluctuations. As the population becomes older and frailer, social programs require a greater share of the nation's resources, while a smaller, less well trained, and less healthy labor force is less able to increase the resources available. Training not provided in schools requires remedial efforts by the military, diverting resources from other uses. The declining scientific-technical complex is less competitive in developing modern weapons systems. Uneven participation in the global knowledge economy increases the costs in all sectors.

Where Have All the Russians Gone? Russia's Demographic Disaster

In his first inaugural address in March 2000, President Putin identified Russia's demographic crisis as the greatest threat facing the nation. In October 2001, Duma Speaker Gennady Seleznev stated that the demographic situation had become a national security issue. Any effort to remedy the situation requires a nuanced understanding of its complex and interrelated causes.

Russia's demographic crisis stems from the interplay of multiple related processes that are long term and not easily reversible: declining life expectancy, especially for males; declining fertility; increased infant mortality through the 1990s; an aging and increasingly fragile population; and population movements.[1] Several million Russians, overwhelmingly young and frequently among the most talented, have left the country. The ethnic Russian population of the Russian Federation has declined in relative terms since the 1970s and in absolute numbers since 1989. The net decline in Russia's population in the 1990s (births minus deaths plus or minus net migration) was about 750,000 per year. In the first eleven months of 2001, net decline was 781,500. Goskomstat projections put the Russian population at between 77 million and 126 million by 2050. Murray Feshbach projects that Russia's population will shrink by one-third to around 100 million by that date. A more pessimistic assessment by researchers at the Russian Academy of Sciences projects a figure between 70 and 90 million by 2045. Nicholas Eberstadt cautions that the most pessimistic projections are extreme, based on worst-case scenarios in which current trends continue to "snowball" and nothing is done to alleviate the medical or fertility crises.[2] However, even the most optimistic projections are based on rates of mortality, disease, and accidental death unprecedented in industrialized countries since World War II.

Adult life expectancy in the USSR, particularly for males, began to decline in the 1970s. Following a brief improvement correlated to Mikhail Gorbachev's anti-alcohol campaign, male life expectancy plunged at an unprecedented rate between 1987 and 1994, recovered somewhat, and fell again beginning in 1998. The situation may have improved slightly in 2000, but data for 2001 look worse. The important point is that Russian men, particularly those in the peak years of labor productivity and parenting, are perishing at a rate difficult to comprehend in a society with high levels of literacy and large numbers of physicians and hospital beds per person. The crisis has been attributed to a damaged gene pool, increased poverty, the psychological stress of massive social dislocations, recrudescence of diseases, and alcohol abuse. Journalists and Russian politicians frequently lump all the causes together, making it impossible to formulate appropriate policy responses.

More careful analysis indicates that two-thirds of Russian adult mortality is due to cardiovascular disease (CVD) and injuries, accidents, and poisoning.[3] Substance abuse and lifestyle play a major role in these causes, making it unlikely that short-term solutions are possible. Injury prevention requires significant behavior modification, including expensive safety equipment and extensive programs to combat substance abuse. CVD generally results from a lifetime pattern of poor diet, substance abuse, lack of exercise, stress, and other long-term factors.

The increase in mortality has occurred overwhelmingly among the working-age population. As the Russian population shrinks, the age pyramid is becoming a more extreme variant of the pattern in Japan and many European nations. Deaths exceed births in a growing number of European countries. Germany and Italy have about 1.1 deaths per birth—a number that can be compensated for by immigration. In Russia in 1999 there were 1.8 deaths per birth, and the ratio could reach 2:1 if the trend is not reversed. Because the decline in adult life expectancy is such an anomaly, some observers believe that it can be reversed if the nation stabilizes its economy and improves health care. There is evidence that some better-educated Russians are adopting a healthier lifestyle, but alcohol consumption remains high and smoking continues to increase among younger age cohorts.

Even as some steps are being taken to address the most serious causes of mortality, the nature of the challenge may be changing. CVD and injury/poisoning may not remain the leading causes of death in the coming decade. The impact of HIV/AIDS and tuberculosis is expected to hit full force in Russia by 2005 or 2006. V. V. Pokrovskii, head of the Federal HIV/AIDS Prevention and Treatment Center of the Russian Ministry of Health, projects that up to ten million males aged fifteen to twenty-nine could die of AIDS beginning between 2005 and 2010. Deaths from tuberculosis, already increasing by about 30 percent in 1999 and 2000, will accompany the increase in AIDS due to its effects on the immune system. AIDS occurs overwhelmingly among the young, economically and reproductively active groups in a population, markedly exacerbating the burden of the disease on a society.[4]

The devastating increase in adult mortality has diverted attention from a longer-term issue of declining fertility. In the Russian case the lower birthrates characteristic of industrial societies are exacerbated by poor health among the declining number of women of childbearing age and economic factors. Many Russians have made a decision to have fewer children—rational behavior given that the birth of an additional child is the single strongest indicator of poverty in Russia. The combination of a decline in the female population of childbearing age, a rise in infertility (in part attributable to excessive use of abortion as a means of birth control), inadequate pre- and postnatal care for most women, and poor general health and nutrition results in markedly lower fertility. Official Russian projections of the twenty- to twenty-nine-year-old female population indicate that there will be a decline from 12.7 million women in these age cohorts to 7.2 million by the year 2022.

The smaller number of women of childbearing age are less healthy, and so are their children. Infant mortality, considered by demographers to be the most reliable indicator of social collapse in a society, began to rise in the USSR in the 1970s. While it appears to have stabilized in some regions of Russia in the late 1990s, infant mortality remains quite high in rural areas, Siberia, the Far East, and economically troubled regions. The latter, for example, Tuva, are also the areas of Russia with the highest birthrates.

To reverse the population decline, some Russian politicians have gone so far as to propose allowing polygamy. Pronatalist policies, however, are enormously difficult under the best of conditions. Russia has already experienced the "demographic revolution" to smaller family size, and thus far this transformation has not been reversed in other countries.

Migration: A Challenge, Not an Answer

President Putin has proposed that Russia offset its population losses by attracting more Russians living in former Soviet republics to return to Russia, bringing with them needed skills and increasing the ethnic Russian population. In-migration did offset much of the population loss in the 1990s, but it is not a viable long-term answer to demographic decline. Suggestions that Russia might attract one to two million immigrants each year in the coming decades are unrealistic. According to Goskomstat data, immigration peaked at 1,147,000 in 1994 but has declined each year thereafter, shrinking to 350,900 by 2000. Many of the Russians who wanted to leave Central Asia and the Caucasus have done so, and this certainly includes most of those with the means to immigrate and skills suited to the Russian labor market. Improving economic conditions in Russia could attract additional immigrants, but it is more likely to be on the order of tens of thousands rather than millions. There are also millions of illegal migrants in Russia, and this raises other issues.

All indicators—at least prior to September 11, 2001—show global migration increasing markedly. Yet thus far in Russia migration has been a source of problems rather than a source of population growth.[5] Russia is hardly alone in experiencing difficulties with immigrants: In the spring of 2002 immigration was viewed as a major reason for a turn to the right in many European elections. This also points up the growing global competition for migrants with high human capital.

Several million Russians have returned from former Soviet republics, often specialists with advanced training, but they have not been welcomed in major urban centers where housing markets are tight and well-paying jobs are scarce. Returning Russians represent a classic NIMBY (not in my back yard) issue. Most Russians agree that their co-nationals should be given opportunities to return "home," but they are equally firm in expressing the view that this should not be realized at the expense of their own housing standards, social services, or employment opportunities. In a nation where low-cost housing remains overwhelmingly in deficit, even for those who have served with honor in the military, accommodating the returnees constitutes a major challenge (a challenge exacerbated by the program encouraging internal migration from the Far North). The largest labor market in Russia, Moscow, enforces residence permit requirements in violation of the Russian Constitution.

Rather than a continuing return of Russian speakers, opening the country to more immigration will result in a greater influx of people fleeing political and economic difficulties and non-Russians willing to take the low-status jobs that Russians tend to eschew even if the alternative is unemployment or work in the informal sector. A significant but unknown number of illegal workers from neighboring countries are employed in construction and other forms of manual labor. Much of this work is seasonal, making the numbers difficult to track.

In some Russian regions authorities are worried about a large influx of non-Russians. In Krasnodar and Rostov, local leaders have sought to expel both legal and illegal migrants. Cities like Norilsk have demanded Soviet-style "closed" status. In the Far East, Chinese migration is a highly sensitive issue. Given the population density east of the Ural Mountains, poorly managed Chinese migration represents a genuine long-term security concern. The image of tens of millions of Chinese flooding across the border is an exaggeration—the Chinese regions bordering Russia are heavily populated compared to Russia, but not compared to other Chinese regions, while the most mobile Chinese are in coastal areas and are oriented toward less daunting climates. No one knows how many of the Chinese in Russia are temporary workers rather than settlers, and the experience of other nations suggests that the answer may depend on how economic and political conditions evolve in both countries.[6]

The departure of many talented Russians—the "brain drain"—is an obsession for some Russian nationalists. Much of the movement in the 1990s represented suppressed demand from the Soviet era, when emigration was permitted only for particular groups (primarily Jews and Germans). It now resembles the situation in most nations participating in global labor markets; for example, many leading Canadian and British scientists want to work in the United States. Far more extensive than the flow of Russians abroad has been the internal brain drain—the enormous shift of personnel out of the jobs they held in Soviet times. There are no good statistics on this phenomenon, particularly since many people retained their formal positions while relying on some other activity for their major source of income. Much of this turnover was inevitable. Everyone in the USSR essentially was a state employee. The Soviet system built up education and research systems, publishing and media enterprises, and sports and cultural facilities that were out of all proportion to the "real" economy. That much of this would come crashing down in the transition could have been predicted from the Latin American experience with neoliberal reforms.

Migration within the country showed a pattern of an initial burst representing suppressed demand, followed by slowing due to economic and housing obstacles. A large number of people lived in places that are not economically viable without massive subsidies. Much internal migration is from the north and east to the south and west, in addition to continuing movement from rural to urban areas.

Immigration to Russia in the coming decades will most likely involve populations that are neither Slavic nor Orthodox. Official data put the number of Muslims in Russia at fourteen million; other sources cite twenty million, perhaps reflecting their generally higher birthrate. Asians will continue to move to the Far East. Large numbers of Central Asian and other migrants will seek to use Russia as a transit route to Europe. When they fail to gain entry to European Union nations, many will stay. Most will be individuals with low human capital, while Russians with high human capital increasingly are joining the global labor market and spending at least some of their working years outside Russia.

In the unlikely event that Russia manages to achieve a net gain in population, it will represent a net decline in human capital, posing new challenges for Russia's crumbling public health and education systems. This underscores that the crucial issue is not the number of people but their quality—the human and intellectual capital available for economic, scientific, technical, and military activity, along with conditions that permit them to realize their potential. The amount of dead weight is increasingly important. The greater the proportion of the dependent population unable to contribute to the economy, the greater the burden is on those who are economically active. This adds a premium to each individual's health, educational level, and potential to contribute in the science- and technology-based knowledge economy.

Even Soviet Medicine Was Better Than This: A Health Care System in Crisis

Soviet medicine manifested the quantitative achievements and qualitative shortcomings characteristic of socialism. By the 1980s the USSR was affected by more extreme variants of the aging population and rising costs of health care that characterized all industrial nations. Russia's economic and social shocks in the 1990s reduced most medical providers to penury and put quality medical care beyond the reach of most Russians. Those with sufficient resources are able to afford medical services close to the level of European nations, while the majority of the population is forced to rely on aging medical personnel and deteriorating facilities. Medicines and supplies are scarce and costly.

The decomposition of medical services for most Russians has coincided with a deterioration in health indicators unlike anything witnessed in a nation not involved in war or suffering from major natural disasters. The list of diseases that have reemerged in Russia is daunting: cholera, typhoid, diphtheria, hepatitis B, whooping cough, measles, and all varieties of sexually transmitted diseases (STDs). While these are not yet claiming many lives, the growth trajectories suggest that without a vigorous response, they represent a serious threat to labor productivity and life expectancy. Diseases that were relatively under control now threaten to reach epidemic proportions. In 1985 tuberculosis resulted in 7.7 deaths per 100 cases; in 1999, the figure was 25.5 per 100 cases. Increasingly, the varieties of tuberculosis found in Russia are resistant to multiple antibiotics, making it an international public health hazard. The increase in STDs threatens reproductive health and increases susceptibility to HIV/AIDS. In both Russia and China, unchecked expansion of HIV/AIDS could reach the levels of crisis seen in Africa. AIDS overwhelmingly strikes the young, productive, and reproductive groups in a population—older people are less likely to use intravenous drugs or to have multiple sexual partners. It has a disproportionate impact on the labor force and future population growth.[7]

Some of the poor health is self-inflicted, the result of old and new patterns of substance abuse. Most demographers put alcohol at the top of the list of causes of premature death in Russia, and the 1990s featured an epidemic of both excessive vodka consumption and alcohol poisoning. One in seven Russians is an alcoholic. There were 35,000 deaths from alcohol poisoning in 2000, a figure not including alcohol-related accidents on the job and the roads or alcohol-induced violence. Smoking represented a major health problem in the Soviet Union and became more common among all but the best-educated groups of the Russian population in the 1990s. The World Health Organization attributes 14 percent of deaths in the USSR and Eastern Europe in 1990 to smoking-related illnesses and projects this will rise to 22 percent by 2006, making deaths from smoking-related illnesses the second greatest source of premature mortality. Inevitably, intravenous drug use has led to the problem of shared needles. Criminalization of both drug addiction and STDs contracted from drug use may make the official statistics look better (people cease seeking treatment, or physicians falsify reports), but it will not reduce the problem; it will only exacerbate it.

Before 1917 Russia had a strong tradition of locally oriented public health (*zemstvo* medicine). Soviet public health programs built on this tradition, and by the 1960s it could be argued that the system was performing credibly. Since then, the record is more dubious. The system has not adjusted to changing needs. Russian conditions require a vigorous program of public health, far beyond what the government has been able to organize. In part, this is a global problem: All nations are struggling to cope with higher costs and the challenges presented by larger and more rapid flows of people and goods.[8]

Not only are costly medical facilities and products unavailable to most Russians, but the provision of basic medical care and preventive medicine has declined dangerously. Vaccinations are no longer routinely offered. Iodine is no longer regularly available in salt. Many people are eating less healthy diets than they did before 1990. The number of invalids in Russia increased from four to ten million in the 1990s. This figure certainly includes many individuals who have benefitted from the kindness (or avarice) of physicians who provided certification of a disability to enable them to get a pension or evade the draft.[9] But even allowing for falsification, the numbers are enormous.

The physical condition of young people deteriorated significantly during the decade of the 1990s. By the end of the decade, the Military Medical Administration reported that 300,000 (one out of three) of the young men conscripted into the military were underweight and unfit for service. The average child in Russia in 1999 was 5 to 8 centimeters shorter than a decade earlier, and average chest size had diminished by 5 to 6 centimeters. Approximately 50 percent of secondary school graduates have at least one chronic ailment. In the Soviet era, 75 percent of children were fed meals at school. By 1999 the number had declined to 25 percent, and in some cases the food itself is a health hazard. Young people who are hungry, cold, or ill are not likely to perform well in school.

Education: Dissipating an Imperfect Legacy

In both the Soviet Union and the United States, literacy and school coverage levels peaked in the 1970s. Since 1990 the portion of Russian children attending school has declined; they are staying in school for less time; fewer of those in school are physically, emotionally, and intellectually capable of studying; and the education system is being stratified into an elite sector serving the affluent and a generally inferior sector for the majority of young people. The latter development represents a Russian version of a pattern common in resource-based economies, where elites tend to seek quality education for their own offspring but pay less attention to more general issues of human capital. Recent research suggests that as these nations develop education and health systems serving the elites, the overall national health deteriorates. Nations with marked income differentials generally have less healthy populations than those with relative income equality, even when the nations with high differentials are wealthier overall.[10]

Russia's less healthy, less physically developed, and less well-nourished young people are entering an education system that is both highly stratified and starved for resources. Russian education, like the health system, was designed to storm the barricades of backwardness. It has never fully adjusted to subsequent challenges.[11] Russian education is characterized by positive developments producing unprecedented opportunities for a limited number of people, along with serious problems affecting the majority and jeopardizing the nation's long-term development. Impressive, innovative schools are experimenting with new models and programs, but these represent islands of creativity in a sea of decline. If compared to the United States, the real contrast is not the elite or the uneducated, but the "middle." In Russia, the drop-off from the elite institutions is much steeper, and the proportion of young people receiving no suitable training for the modern labor market is far larger.

Coverage (the proportion of young people in an age cohort attending school) has declined at all levels except higher education since 1991. Enrollment in preschool programs has dropped by nearly 50 percent, largely explained by poverty and the demise of enterprises that provided day care. While the value of preschool programs is intensely debated in the West, much developmental research suggests that the first three years of life are crucial in developing an individual's capacity to learn. Elementary school coverage (grades 1–4) in 2000 was close to 90 percent, but dropping. Russia now has hundreds of thousands of homeless children, most not attending school regularly. The phenomenon of "social orphans" (children who have at least one parent but avoid their homes due to substance abuse and/or physical abuse) has grown markedly. The number is estimated at between one and four million, in part because it fluctuates seasonally.[12]

Data on "incomplete" secondary education (grades 5–9, roughly equivalent to middle school) indicate declining coverage. In the 1990s, one in five children aged fifteen to nineteen did not complete secondary school. This translates into two million young people not attending school and missing vaccinations and meals (in the schools that still provide them). Overall, secondary education remains characterized by a less than optimal distribution of institutions. An excessive number of vocational-technical schools continue to function, even though this is generally the least effective type of education. Industrial education is successful only when closely tied to industry and does best when enterprises finance the training.

Teachers at all levels are underpaid, and local governments have frequently delayed paying salaries, using the funds for other purposes. Russian teachers are paid less per hour than teachers in Thailand. The result is high turnover and a marked aging of the teaching profession. During the year 2000, 97 percent of the strikes that took place in Russia were at educational institutions. Legislation in 2001 promised a doubling of teacher salaries, from an average of $34 per month to $68 per month, but many regions lack the resources to implement policies mandated in Moscow.

Some of the demand for teachers will be relieved as the number of students declines in the first two decades of the twenty-first century. But this will require much greater coordination in deciding which schools to close or consolidate. A large number of rural schools serve a small proportion of students. More than 70 percent of general secondary schools are in rural areas; they employ 41 percent of teachers but enroll only 29 percent of students. Eliminating them could leave the local population with no options for education.

Growing demand for higher education represents one of the positive indicators in Russia's human capital development. The number of higher education institutions and their enrollments have been increasing, but this is taking place at a time of serious resource stringency—the third time since 1917 that proliferation of higher education institutions has coincided with an economic crisis.[13] Along with expanded educational opportunities and increased social mobility, it has created a perpetual infrastructure crisis.

Higher education has become a global middle-class entitlement, even though higher education is among the most regressive forms of public expenditure and is clearly the most regressive type of education expenditure. As with subsidized housing, the preponderance of benefits accrues to the economically better-off groups. Some 58 percent of students in Russian higher education come from the 23 percent of the population considered well off.[14] Many nations are discovering that it is impossible to publicly finance a mass system of higher education. The recent boom in Russian higher education must be viewed in this context. The number of students increased by 50 percent between 1995 and 1999, and competition to enter desirable institutions and specialties became stiffer. Survey data suggest that perhaps a quarter of the increase is attributable to young men seeking to avoid military service, particularly since the beginning of the wars in Chechnya.

Corruption has become a serious problem at higher education institutions, threatening to limit access for some talented young people. In university classes, a portion of places is set aside for those who do well on exams; others must pay. Some administrators, however, juggle the numbers to increase the proportion of fee-paying students. "Tutoring" for the entrance exams has become such a well-established racket that the government is struggling to introduce a standardized national admission exam and is seeking ways to steer the funds spent on tutoring and side payments into the regular education system. Stories in the press about university administrators driving BMWs deflect attention from the extent to which these payments supplement low faculty salaries. Whatever the money is used for, higher education represents the largest realm of nonbusiness corruption in Russia.[15]

While new institutions have proliferated, there is no evidence of "creative destruction." Old institutions and programs do not disappear. In the late 1990s the engineering, transport, and construction institutes enrolled record numbers of students. Does Russia really need tens of thousands of new engineering graduates? As the number of young people declines in the coming two decades, these institutions will be able to maintain their enrollments only by competing to keep young people out of the military or the labor market.

The two significant positive trends in Russian education in the 1990s—increased numbers of diverse educational institutions and innovative pedagogy—are profoundly inegalitarian, representing ad hoc changes serving the elites rather than policies based on an assessment of how to utilize the limited resources available. As in many realms of public policy in Russia, much of the discussion of education focuses on fundamental principles—what the system was like, what it ought to be like, what the ideal would be—rather than confronting more pragmatic issues based on judgments of what is realistic. No one questions that a teacher-student ratio of 1:12 is highly desirable. But if this means that none of the teachers can be paid a living wage, would 1:18 be acceptable? If the result of providing low-cost university education to children from affluent families is to deprive low-income children of day care, is this a trade-off that promises a better society? The specific answers to these questions are probably less important than learning to frame the questions in terms of what may be accomplished using available resources.

In December 2000, President Putin announced plans to double spending for education in the context of improving military training. Most of the increase will be eaten up by mandated increases in salaries and pensions. Emphasis on federal support is a disincentive to finding resources elsewhere. Only 13 percent of education expenditures is from the federal government; the rest is from local and regional budgets, where (as in many countries) the available resources and the commitment to schooling vary widely.

The demographic, health, and education situation has had a profound impact on Russia's labor force, exacerbating the effects of economic decline. Russia overall has a less skilled workforce than a decade ago. Many schools are not teaching skills needed in the new economy. The Soviet-era lists of specialties have not been radically changed, and it appears that in the late 1990s many engineering and specialized technical schools markedly increased their enrollments (although it is not always clear what content is being offered under some of the broad rubrics).

Russia's current educational trajectory points toward a nation that will not have the human capital to support a globally competitive economy or a modern military establishment. At the same time, the system of science and technology inherited from the Soviet Union is rapidly decaying.

The End of Soviet Science?

In the history of science, the 1990s will likely be remembered as the decade when the particular model of organizing scientific activity known as "Soviet science" ceased to exist. Pressed to serve Soviet leaders' needs for prestige, legitimacy, and a vast military-industrial complex, Soviet science could not simultaneously contribute much to economic development. The bloated technostructure was badly in need of restructuring. Yet its elite group, the Academy of Sciences, proved to be among the institutions most resistant to reform, a stance that has increased the price of change in myriad ways.

The difficulties facing Russian science are long term, structural, and global in nature. But memories are short, encouraging tendencies to blame the crisis simply on funding, to ignore the social context and global processes, and to forget why perestroika was initiated in the first place. The dysfunctional attributes of the Soviet system were discussed quite frankly in scholarly journals in the 1970s and in the open press after 1985.[16] Most institutes were overstaffed and experienced financial constraints; scientific personnel were aging; equipment was increasingly outmoded (a particularly acute problem in computing); inhibited information flows exacted enormous costs; lack of horizontal linkages seriously hindered innovation; and contact with the international scientific community was limited and distorted.

The Soviet science system could not exist in a country with a market economy. Funding cuts are the most obvious manifestation of the crisis. Financing for basic research has declined by 80 percent since 1991, while spending on applied research and development has been reduced by fifteen to twenty times. The significance of these numbers is far greater when we recall that prior to 1991 prices did not provide an accurate reflection of resource allocations. Since 1999 funding has become more regular and predictable, although problems in paying salaries at the local level remain.

The absence of creative destruction is startling. Rather than scientific institutions developing new sources of funding, during 1990–1995 the federal budget share increased from 55.4 percent to more than 90 percent of all funding for science. Virtually all federal budget funds for most research institutes are devoted to salaries and utility costs, leaving no money to purchase equipment or finance research. Foreign support accounts for as much as 50 percent of the research and development being conducted, and many of the best scientists either work abroad or continue their work in Russia with foreign support. Putin's government has responded to this situation by increasing surveillance and reporting requirements and initiating several high-profile cases against scientists, but it does not have the resources to replace funding from foreign sources.

Despite abysmal economic conditions and the opportunities for higher incomes in other spheres, tens of thousands of scientists have managed to continue working actively in their specialties—perhaps 75,000 in civilian research and development and a similar number in military research and development. Although the economy appears to have achieved a rough stability, researchers face a crisis from having exhausted the inherited infrastructure in terms of both equipment and human capital. There has been little investment in new equipment since 1991, and the pipeline of young people into science is being choked off at the level of graduate students and post doctorates. As in other nations, the best young science and technology personnel seek to go abroad, first of all to the United States.

Conditions vary markedly both across sectors and among institutions within each sector. The Academy of Sciences began in the most privileged position, has insisted upon its qualitative preeminence, and has resisted reforms despite significant budget pressures. Industrial science (*otraslevaia nauka*, often translated as branch science) has suffered the most. The government initially believed that applied research and development would be financed by Russian industry. By the time government officials understood the fallacy in this proposition, it was too late to save most of the industrial research establishments. Some are now being partially reestablished, particularly in informatics and the life sciences, and as part of technology incubators, but the available anecdotal data suggest that salaries for researchers are the lowest priority for enterprises. Higher education has fared slightly better, in part because federal and local governments recognize the need for education, and in part because teaching has absorbed nearly half of the scientific personnel who have left research institutes.

Some positive changes have taken place in Russian science. The system has become more open and more integrated with international science and technology. Talent, rather than political rectitude, is more often the basis for opportunities. In some fields, particularly life sciences, new research organizations have developed, and an offshore software industry shows promise. For the most part, however, only younger people emphasize these positive aspects.[17]

There has been regression in a number of areas in the Putin era. There are indications of a retreat from peer review, as the Academy Presidium seeks to reassert its privileges, and there have been growing indications that security issues are being given a much higher priority. While few would question the need for a state to protect important security interests, the history of Soviet interference in science makes this a highly sensitive issue. Suggestions that the Russian government must play a role in protecting commercial information imply that businesses and individuals will not defend their own interests, and likely slows their learning curve. Putting bureaucrats in a position to control intellectual property is an invitation for rent seeking.

Russia is not being left entirely behind in the global knowledge economy, but the unevenness of Russian participation continues a characteristic feature of the Soviet era. The Academy of Sciences began the new millennium by announcing development of a new supercomputer, but only one prototype has been built. Internet penetration has grown substantially, as has the use of computers, but both remain limited to a narrow segment of the population.

Russia has developed a flourishing software industry that is achieving a good reputation in the global marketplace. Some observers suggest that this represents a genuine bright spot in Russia's science and technology economy and presages a return to world-class status. One American executive has suggested that while routine software development is cheaper in India, highly complex programming is done better in Russia. Certainly the talent is there, not only among the hordes of scientists and engineers left over from the Soviet military-industrial complex, but also among thousands of young people seeking to join the global marketplace.

The larger questions involve what this represents on a national or international scale, and what it says about the overall development of the society. India has had a thriving offshore software market for more than a decade, one that in 2001 earned ten times the amount earned in Russia. Yet India also has a literacy rate on the order of 50 to 55 percent and in 1999 ranked 132nd in the UN Development Program's Human Development Index (Russia ranked seventy-first). The lesson is not that an offshore software industry is unimportant, but rather that it is not necessarily a bootstrap for the rest of the economy or society.

Press coverage of the Russian software industry suggests that management skills are in short supply, as are the talents needed for marketing and integration with international businesses. One Russian company drawing on the talent of mathematicians and programmers from the Academy of Sciences has done quite well marketing software and control systems and has a client base consisting almost entirely of the major Russian oil companies. This lucrative niche provides opportunities to learn skills for growth, but it is not easily replicable on a wide scale.

None of the initiatives adopted during the 1990s succeeded in placing scientific institutions or individual researchers in a position of long-term sustainability. The real problem is not money, although few would admit this. Certainly, money is needed, but it will be wasted without changes in institutional structures. Russian commentators still compare their scientific establishment with Europe and America, rather than focusing on their own capabilities and needs.

There is scant evidence that leaders of the Russian scientific community are developing the skills needed to convince the public and politicians of the importance of their work, a sharp contrast with Central European countries where the prospect of membership in the European Union is encouraging reform. Hunger strikes (Vladimir Strakhov) or even suicides (Vladimir Nechai) are tragic and dramatic but are not viable long-term strategies. Rather than embracing or at least grudgingly accepting inevitable changes, many leaders of the Russian scientific community continue to look to the state to bail out and preserve their decaying institutional structures.

Eventually Russia will have no choice but to put the bulk of its available resources into the higher education system. The Russian system will never be like the U.S. system; it is likely to more closely resemble the systems in France or Germany, where similar battles are being waged between researchers trying to defend elite, pure research institutions and universities insisting on the importance of the Humboldtian combination of research and education.

The lion's share of Soviet expenditures for science and technology was devoted to a costly military-industrial complex. A decade after the end of the Soviet Union, Russian military research and development has been significantly deconstructed, but what remains is mostly unreconstructed, despite the development of a few new weapons systems. The talk of conversion in the Soviet era produced no visible results, and Yeltsin's government wisely ignored the blandishments of those who asserted the virtues of Russia's "science-intensive" technology potential.[18] The Soviet Union did have a lot of technology, some of it quite good, but little of it was embedded in cost-effective systems that could be competitive in global markets. Recent proposals to revive military industry by organizing the enterprises into large holding companies may generate some improvements, but innovation generally comes from smaller firms. Rather than integrating with the global economy, Russia's large energy and defense conglomerates have sought to sell things in global markets while continuing to operate in nonmarket ways in Russia.[19]

Russia's Role in Eurasian Security in the Twenty-First Century

The evidence adds up to a devastating picture of increased disease and mortality, environmental degradation, an overall decline in education and science, and the demise of social services. Yet this is not the entire story. One of the big questions remains: Why, if so many people are reporting alarming data and horrendous stories, do things look to be so "normal"? The most striking feature of what is happening in Russian education and health is radical differentiation and stratification. There were always elite schools and medical facilities in Soviet days, but now the differences are both more public and more extreme. In these trends Russia may not be so different from the United States, where there is a growing chorus of alarm about the increasing cost of education and expansion of elite health care.[20] But as always in Russia, the drop-off below the elite sector is much steeper.

Some of the maladies in general health and in the education system take a long time to become visible. It is a slow cancer, not a stroke. Or, to use a different analogy, the damage done by termites may not show outward signs for decades. To judge by the reports of some educators, decline is now becoming evident, although there could well be a subjective element in these accounts ("things were better in our day"). There is no standardized testing to measure results over decades.

Implications for the Russian military are more imminent. The smaller pool of less well-educated and less healthy recruits will require inducting more young men who do not meet mental and physical standards. In the fall of 2001 only 14 percent of young men of conscription age actually went to the army. There have been recent reports of illiterate draftees, and some units in Chechnya are operating remedial reading programs. It will be increasingly difficult for the military to find needed skills. Officers already staff many specialized services, creating a de facto professional army, while draftees are consigned to a privatized version of Soviet construction battalions or become cannon and kidnap fodder in Chechnya.

Russia cannot afford the science and technology base needed for a modern military. The USSR perpetrated a myth that it was possible to maintain military systems of research and production at a higher level than what prevailed in the civilian sector. The growing prevalence of dual-use technologies makes this increasingly unrealistic. The idea that Russia might leap ahead in the "Revolution in Military Affairs" is based on an unrealistic assessment of both the situation in science and technology and the possibilities of the Russian economy. It is not only the size but also the character of the economy that matters. Natural resources may generate positive statistics without fostering the human capital needed in the post-industrial world. The struggle with a rentier elite is now Russia's greatest challenge.

By the year 2020, Russia's major southern and eastern neighbors likely will include Iran, Pakistan, India, China, Japan, and Korea. All will have larger populations. All but Pakistan will probably have larger economies. All except perhaps Japan will have nuclear weapons. One does not need to be an American chauvinist to conclude that the rational course for Russian leaders would be to follow the path of France, exchanging old myths of national greatness for a place in the Euro–Atlantic community. If Russia's elite can shelve great-power aspirations and rent seeking in favor of policies to rebuild the medical and education infrastructure, they could still manage to play an important role in the world. This will require overcoming daunting demographic trends, great-power psychosis, and the resource curse.

Notes

1. The coincidence of declining life expectancy and aging strikes some people as a contradiction. It is better understood as evidence that Russians, and Russian men in particular, are dying at unusually high rates between the ages of eighteen and sixty, and particularly between forty and sixty.

2. Nicholas Eberstadt, "Too Sick to Matter," *Heritage Policy Review*, no. 95 (June/July 1999), available at http:// www.policyreview.com/jun99/eberstadt.html. Murray Feshbach, "Russia's Population Meltdown," *The Wilson Quarterly* (Winter 2001); Alexei Cherniak, "Analysis of the Demographic Situation in Russia," *Vremia Novostei*, no. 54, April 2002.

3. Eberstadt, "Too Sick to Matter"; Julie S. Davanzo and Clifford Grammich, *Dire Demographics: Population Trends in the Russian Federation* (Santa Monica, Calif.: RAND, 2001); also available at http:// www.rand.org/publications/MR/MR1273.

4. Pokrovskii's estimates differ significantly from official Russian government data. Official data on HIV/AIDS report only the registered cases. Legislation criminalizing sexually transmitted diseases has exacerbated an already serious problem of underreporting. By 2002 AIDS was listed among the five leading causes of death in Russia.

5. See Kevin H. O'Rourke and Jeffrey G. Williamson, *Globalization and History: The Evolution of a Nineteenth-Century Atlantic Alliance* (Cambridge, Mass.: MIT Press, 2000), and Williamson's recent articles, online at http://www.harvard.edu/economics. On Russians returning to Russia, see Hilary Pilkington, *Migration, Displacement and Identity in Post-Soviet Russia* (London and New York: Routledge, 1998).

6. In April 2002 a Russian government official told me that "officially" there are 140,000 Chinese living in Russia, whereas unofficially there are about four million.

7. Before September 11, 2001, Richard Holbrooke called AIDS the greatest threat to international security, and he still may be correct. In South Africa, AIDS is now the leading cause of death. See *New York Times*, October 17, 2001, p. A10.

8. Laurie Garrett, *Betrayal of Trust: The Collapse of Global Public Health* (New York: Hyperion, 2000); Helen Epstein, "Time of Indifference," *New York Review*, April 12, 2001, pp. 33–8.

9. In spring 2002 the Russian press reported the cost of a false certification of a lung or stomach ailment at $2,000 to $5,000. A less certain psychological deferment cost $1,000. Certification as an alcoholic or drug addict could be had for $300 to $500, but this could have a negative impact on one's employment prospects. Robert Cottrell, "Russian Army Starts Spring Draft," *Financial Times*, April 2, 2002.

10. Epstein, "Time of Indifference," and the edited volumes cited in her review.

11. Each of the major achievements of Soviet education policy involved a trade-off. The campaign for adult literacy in the 1920s was politically important, but for every adult who

learned to read there was a child growing up illiterate. The overall result was to delay universal literacy for a generation. The enormous expansion of higher education in 1930–1931 was accomplished by subdividing existing institutions, creating an enormous number of resource-starved universities and institutes.

12. See Judyth Twigg's chapter in this volume.

13. The two earlier bursts of expansion were in 1918–1921 and 1930–1931. See Harley Balzer, "Engineers: The Rise and Decline of a Social Myth," in *Science and the Soviet Social Order*, ed. Loren R. Graham (Cambridge, Mass.: Harvard University Press, 1990), pp. 52–3.

14. A. Osviannikov in *Trud*, July 9, 1999, p. 1.

15. *Izvestiya*, August 29, 2001, p. 3.

16. See the discussion in Harley D. Balzer, *Soviet Science on the Edge of Reform* (Boulder, Colo.: Westview Press, 1989).

17. *KPD*, no. 4 (1996), pp. 1–2.

18. Balzer, "Engineers."

19. See the contributions to Klaus Segbers, ed., *Explaining Post-Soviet Patchworks: Volume 1, Actors and Sectors in Russia between Accommodation and Resistance to Globalization* (Aldershot, U.K.: Ashgate, 2001).

20. Ceci Connolly, "Healers Go for the Well-Heeled," *Washington Post*, May 28, 2002, p. 1.

Part Four

Foreign and
Security Policy Challenges

10

From Pragmatism to Strategic Choice: Is Russia's Security Policy Finally Becoming Realistic?

Dmitri Trenin

During his first twenty months in office, President Vladimir Putin's most celebrated hallmark was his hard-headed pragmatism. On the eve of assuming the presidency, he started with a frank analysis of the state of Russia and its prospects. He appointed a largely liberal team to pursue the policy of economic reform, and the reform policy was set out in the first two annual presidential messages to the Federal Assembly. In his first year at the Kremlin, Putin initiated very liberal tax reform legislation. Land reform bills have passed in the Duma, and legal reform is also high on Putin's agenda. The stated purpose of these efforts is to make Russia attractive to foreign investment and technology flows, which are deemed critical for sustained growth. Meanwhile, Moscow has intensified efforts to gain accession to the World Trade Organization (WTO). These steps have been accompanied by Putin's drive to reassert the power of the state: some of it necessary (curbing the political influence of business tycoons); some clearly excessive (expanding state control over the media). The main tenets of the Kremlin's economic policy under Putin—liberal reform at home plus integration into the world economy—are essentially sound.

By contrast, Putin's national security and defense policy was neither as clearly defined nor as pragmatic as his economic policy. In his first year Putin signed several important documents apparently amounting to a comprehensive foreign, security, and defense policy doctrine. Rather than taking a step forward and adjusting to the realities of the twenty-first century, they registered a partial return to a traditional late nineteenth century geopolitical view of the world, with some Cold War–era overtones. The military doctrine implicitly designated the United States as Russia's principal potential adversary. The pattern of Russian military exercises such as Zapad-99, the new emphasis on air defenses, and military procurement practices gave credence to this doctrinal proposition. It is clear that the North Atlantic Treaty Organization (NATO) air campaign against Yugoslavia was the defining moment for this reassessment, but this was not the only reason.

The Russian national leadership has found it extremely difficult to devise a new and credible concept of security relations with the West. The partnership rhetoric of the early 1990s died down because it was not backed up by bold but necessary deeds. While Russia was too weak for condominium with the United States, it was also too big and too unreformed to be integrated with the West. As a result, the Russian elites retreated some hundred years to embrace the maxim of Tsar Alexander III: "Russia has only two true friends in the world. One is the Russian army. The other one is the Russian navy." That meant the restoration of the principle of balance, or more precisely the correlation of forces, as the foundation of the national security policy. This was fine in principle. The problem was the discrepancy between means and ends. Resources for grandstanding were lacking; both the army and the navy continued to deteriorate. This created an impossible situation in terms of national security. Russia could not balance the West even if it had to. But it did not have to because the ideological divide of the Cold War was absent and there existed a broad commonality of interests. Yet Russia could not integrate successfully due to misgivings and wide skepticism in the West. This mutual frustration led to the increasing alienation of Russia.

Certain Western actions played a provocative role. NATO's enlargement to the east and its military intervention in the Balkans were seen as proof of Russia's strategic isolation, if not outright Western hostility. This feeling was enhanced by the perceived breach of faith in NATO, first caused by the withdrawal of private pledges not to advance the alliance beyond the Cold War confrontation line and later by the offensive operation against Slobodan

Milosevic's Yugoslavia. It needs to be remembered that the Russian security and military community, unlike its economic and financial elites, is largely composed of old faces with even older ideas. Consequently, traditional geopolitics in the 1990s organically replaced international class struggle as both the general conceptual framework and the main analytical tool.

This trend was further aggravated by the second Chechen war that broke the self-imposed taboo on large-scale use of military force observed after the 1996 Khasavyurt truce.[1] In a way, this was a war of Russia's liberation from the perceived political dependence on the West during the Gorbachev and Yeltsin administrations. The new Russian leadership palpably enjoyed defying the international condemnation of its crude methods of "fighting terrorism." Ever since, and until September 11, 2001, there had been recurring fears of a new cold war, as a result either of America's missile defense deployments or Russia's actions in the Caucasus and its new policy of demonstratively reaching out to those labeled by Washington as the "states of concern"—Iran, Iraq, Libya, Cuba, and North Korea.

For the supporters of Russia's "special way," there was no fundamental conflict between the objectives of Moscow's economic policy and its security policy orientation. Theories were advanced whereby Russia could become a market economy without becoming politically engaged in the Western world. China, with its massive foreign investments and a booming trade relationship with the United States, was cited as a prime example. In practice this was translated into treating NATO as an adversary while treating the European Union (EU) as a strategic partner. This was absurd, of course, but there was logic to this absurdity. The collapse of communism and the USSR was brought about by the eagerness of the late Soviet elites to "exchange ideology for property." Later on, the fusion of political power and private property inside Russia and the vestiges of great-power mentality in international relations emerged as the principal hindrances to the course of the country's transformation.

This led to a peculiar blend of myth and reality driving Russia's security policy. Even as the Russian conventional forces were being reconfigured to repel a Balkans-type aggression by NATO following the Kosovo crisis, Russia had to concentrate its meager military resources in the south (the Caucasus), while wondering what to do about the southeast (Central Asia), where shooting wars were also becoming a reality.[2] In July 2001 Russia signed a new treaty with China and upgraded its arms transfers to Asia's rising colossus, but at the same time Putin and other leaders were becoming increasingly worried about the fate of the Russian Far East and Siberia.[3] Moscow reestablished or intensified top-level contacts with the "states of concern" while the dangers of missile proliferation were increasing.

This conflict was being managed by means of careful tactical maneuvering. For Putin, the economic agenda took precedence. In his first state of the nation address, despite the considerable cooling of relations with the United States, he barely mentioned traditional security issues but highlighted instead the appalling state of health of the Russian population, its high mortality rate, and the resultant annual net loss of three-quarters of a million people. His second address, delivered against the background of harsh rhetoric from Washington over Chechnya, was again mostly about economics. Putin, in fact, announced military reform as a necessary by-product of his economic reform agenda. The reform entails a 30 percent reduction of the military establishment's personnel. The Russian strategic nuclear forces, the country's unique international power asset, are being reduced in size and downgraded, even as Moscow protests against Washington's national missile defense (NMD) plans.

At the same time, the central question of Russian military reform remained not only unanswered but even unasked: Should the United States be treated as a potential enemy in the twenty-first century? The shape and structure of Russia's military establishment fully depend on the answer to this question. A failure to answer it means that the remnants of the defense system Russia inherited from the Soviet Union will substitute for a genuine threat assessment. A failure to ask the hard question testifies to the lack of political will. Through September 2001 President Putin was rather successful tactically, but he remained strategically uncommitted, which threatened to undermine his successes in the long term. A possible explanation, based on his background, could be that he had already made the choice, but being cautious by nature and secretive by training, he did not see fit to share his vision with the nation as yet.

The Russian president made the choice in favor of the West within two weeks after the terrorist attack of September 11, 2001. His decision to side with the United States and join the antiterrorist coalition was likely motivated by a combination of factors. At the emotional level, his visceral public statements and actions against Chechen separatists made an antiterrorist position a natural one for him to adopt. Further, given that the United States would have likely acquired access rights to Central Asian bases regardless of Russia's feelings on the matter, Putin's decision can be considered pragmatic. The underlying reason for Putin's decision, however, was his desire to lead Russia to Europe.

Not everyone among his associates—not to speak of the bulk of the Russian political class—shares Putin's vision of a European Russia. Many appear to be standing at a crossroads. Like medieval Russian knights, they temporize in front of three possible options. The Russian tales usually and very conveniently provided the traveling knight with a milestone at the crossroads point succinctly describing the expected outcome of taking each choice. This chapter will lay out the options and the likely results of exercising each option.

Three Options

The first option, so obvious to most Russians as to be often seen as the only one available, is to take an equidistant position vis-à-vis the major power centers. In terms of military security, this calls for a defense *tous azimuts* (in all directions). This option rests on a very long and solid historical tradition. Indeed, this is the Russian tradition. For centuries, the Russians thought of their country as a great power. And a great power, they always knew, differed from the smaller ones in that it was able to stand alone, and if need be defend itself and protect its clients. To proclaim such an option today would thus be comforting to the national psyche. Problems start when one proceeds to implement such a declaration.

To pursue this path seriously under the current set of circumstances, Russia would at minimum need to engage in constant and risky maneuvering. The country is still very big in spatial terms but relatively small and weak in economic, political, and military ones. Like a vast but weak object whose outlying parts fall within the gravitation zones of several much more powerful poles, it risks being torn among them. There is also the need to commit huge resources to national defense along the world's longest land border. Russia would have to continue to maintain a strategic force capable of deterring the United States and China, as well as the smaller nuclear powers, and conventional forces capable of keeping NATO and China at bay, in addition to fighting shooting wars in the Caucasus and Central Asia. Moscow would also need to regard the former Soviet republics as its security glacis and be prepared to go to great lengths to create its own military-political alliance within the Commonwealth of Independent States (CIS).

Russia's gross domestic product (GDP), meanwhile, is roughly 5 to 10 percent of that of the United States and two-fifths or approximately 40 percent of China's; Russia's defense budget is $8 billion, compared with the United States' $300 billion. Even if adjusted to purchasing power realities, the gap is only insignificantly reduced.[4] Russian conventional forces, though still just over one million strong, are numerically inferior to NATO's in Europe by a factor of 1:3. The qualitative imbalance is much more striking. Also, Russia is both heavily dependent on Western trade and indebted to Western creditors.[5] Reintegrating the CIS states is beyond Russia's means, and in any case the former republics are more of a liability than an asset in security terms. That said, there are no resources to support the isolationist course. Russia may still be a pole, but a relatively small one, inferior to its neighbors in the west and the east and thus placed in a very precarious position in any balance-of-power game. There can be no balance that would suit a Russia that stands alone. Strategic isolationism is anything but splendid for present-day Russia.

The second option is proposed by those who are not content with "passive" isolationism. They want action and strive to reduce what they view as U.S. world hegemony. Thus they are looking for a power constellation capable of counterbalancing U.S. power. These people usually come out in favor of an "Eastern bloc" consisting of China, India, Iran, and possibly also of Iraq and Libya. Actually, this construction follows the political logic of the multipolarity concept approved at the start of Yeltsin's second presidential term and still formally in place. The problems with this obviously chimerical project are too many to be discussed here. Suffice it to say that in the highly improbable case of such an alliance actually emerging, Russia is likely to play a subordinate role. The supreme but bitter irony could be that having refused to be a junior partner of the United States, Moscow would end up as Beijing's "little brother" and "ammunition bearer."

Since neither option would work, at least not to Russia's benefit, one must look for a third way that could be a viable alternative. The search for such an alternative might have lasted a long time, had it not been for the terrorist attack against the United States on September 11, 2001. President Putin, in his first "strategic" foreign and security move, made it clear that Russia would side with the West and become its ally in the fight against international terrorism.[6] In Putin's case, early pragmatism eventually led him to realism. He has concluded that the presence of a common enemy for the first time since 1945, and the U.S. need for Russia as an ally in its struggle against terrorism, opened a window of opportunity to achieve Russia's integration with the West on far better terms than anything that could have been contemplated since the early 1990s.

However, this strategic choice needs to be consolidated both internally and internationally. Not all of Putin's associates are enthusiastic about the emerging relationship. There are vested interests who self-servingly pursue anti-American agendas. Thus, there are many aspects to policy consolidation, but one is truly indispensable. There is a clear need for a general strategy encompassing the entire range of security issues that Russia faces. The key, of course, is the formation of a solid alliance between Russia and the West, leading to Russia's integration within the new West (or "North"), that is, a security community embracing North America, Europe, and Russia. As regards Russia's two other geostrategic facades, the key words there should be stabilization of the south and a balancing policy in the east.

The Hard Part: West Plus East Equals North

The point of departure in Russia's relations with the West is that even before the terrorist attack on America, "objectively," as they used to say in Soviet times, the Russian and Western security interests largely overlapped. The Balkans were actually a good test case. Once Slobodan Milosevic lost the Yugoslav presidential election in 2000, the major irritant in Russian–Western relations was gone. In Macedonia in 2001, Russian and Western positions were very close. The Contact Group for the former Yugoslavia resumed its work to mutual satisfaction. NATO enlargement may be psychologically unpalatable, but, as Poland's example has demonstrated, it is also nonthreatening militarily and even stabilizing politically. Whatever the unstated reasons behind the U.S. NMD plans and their strategic implications, nothing the Americans can deploy in the foreseeable future would undermine Russia's deterrence capability vis-à-vis the United States.

Meanwhile, Russia's relations with the EU are becoming increasingly important. Half of Russian foreign trade is with the EU members and candidates. Russia supplies over one-fifth of Europe's oil needs and two-fifths of its gas requirements. The EU enlargement basically will force Russia to adopt norms and standards that would match those of Europe. Conversely, from the EU perspective, contributing to Russia's stability and prosperity and engaging it as a partner are essential. Europe will not be fully at ease with itself until it solves its "Russia problem."

As old defense worries are becoming ever less relevant, new security concerns work to bring Russia and the West together. Terrorism is the principal danger present, but it is not the only one. Proliferation of weapons of mass destruction and missiles as well as terrorism affect the Russians as much as, if not more than, the West. Even though their security interests and priorities are not wholly identical—due, among other things, to the differences in the geostrategic position and the resultant perceptions, and the politico-economic competition—this does not constitute an insurmountable obstacle to working toward a security community.

What stands in the way are the surviving Cold War–era mutual perceptions, the more recent historical experience, and the reluctance of dealing with both, often based on the vested sectoral interests. Parts of the military establishments and defense industries still find it prosperous and prestigious to "keep old enemies." It is important that new myths are not added to that list, including the one of the "Balkan-type aggression" against Russia or Belarus. This scenario was based on an improbable generalization of a unique NATO experience in the Balkans, and the assumption that the West would be contemplating an attack against a nuclear power. The supreme example of paranoia being conveniently blended with reality to serve the vested interests was the *Boevoe Sodruzhestvo* (Battlefield Friendship) exercise held in early September 2001. Days before the attack against the World Trade Center and the Pentagon, the Russian and CIS air defense forces were training to repel a coordinated air attack from NATO in the west and the Taliban in the south. It would be fair to add that, at the same time, the U.S. Joint Chiefs of Staff in their own contingency planning were most reluctant to reduce the number of targets for nuclear attack in the Russian territory.

The Osama bin Laden factor changed the pattern of security alignments. In September 2001, Russia became a de facto ally of the United States. The challenge today is to turn this antiterrorist alliance into a permanent security relationship firmly binding Russia to the West. Otherwise, the new friendship will remain fragile and vulnerable to the twists and turns of international developments and domestic politics. It must be remembered that not a single security issue is off the table following September 11. It would also be wrong to overestimate Russia's new importance to the United States. Immediately demanding a quid pro quo is also wrongheaded. What needs to be done without delay is to devise a strategy for Russia's stage-by-stage integration within the West's security structures. Such a strategy would entail several major directions:

- There needs to be strategic accommodation on both sides, involving the problems of missile defense, offensive arms reductions, and postparity, postdeterrence strategic posture. In particular, missile defense should be made an area of cooperation, not confrontation. With Russia dropping its objections to missile defense in principle, the Russian military-industrial complex could be offered participation in the U.S. NMD program. The program itself needs to be harmonized with Putin's European theater defense initiative, which has to be fleshed out. Eventually, the goal is a common system of weapons of mass destruction/missile proliferation monitoring, prevention of accidental launch, and defense.

- Russia–NATO relations have been revived on the basis of the Founding Act. The 2002 Rome declaration paves the way for creating an *alliance with the alliance* (in the words of Alexander Vershbow, the U.S. ambassador to Moscow). Eventually, this could lead to Russia's membership in a new U.S.-led security arrangement stretching from the Atlantic to the Pacific. Such an evolution would entail forging an inclusive rather than exclusive relationship between NATO and Russia (that is, "at 20" instead of "19+1") and endowing the new council with all the necessary mechanisms for close interaction in the new strategic environment. Cooperation with NATO and the United States, not the least in Central Asia, could and should be turned into a vehicle for military reform in Russia.

- For the domestic Russian skeptics, an organic relationship with the EU would be the unassailable guarantee that NATO would never be a threat to Russia. Here, Russia's long-term objective should be associate membership in the EU, complete with a free trade area and membership in Europe's "Schengen zone" of free cross-border travel. That involves implementing the EU's Northern Dimension Initiative. In particular, Russia and the EU should seize upon the opportunities offered by the "Baltic chance" and turn Kaliningrad into a laboratory for Euro–Russian cooperation, not a rampart against NATO. Furthermore, Russia should be ready for security cooperation with the EU in peacekeeping on the basis of the Petersberg tasks,[7] including in the Balkans, Moldova, and the Caucasus.

- With regard to the Balkans, Russia and the West could join efforts with the moderate forces in the region to prevent further destabilization of the situation and assist in economic and social reconstruction such as in the Caucasus and Central Asia. The Contact Group would be the prime working instrument to accomplish this.

- One particularly important area is Euro–Russian defense industrial cooperation, with a special emphasis on the aircraft industry. This would include coproduction of weapons systems and joint ventures in the international armaments market. More broadly, making room for Russia in the arms markets controlled by the United States and Western Europe would reduce the power of the Iranian, Iraqi, and Chinese lobbies in the Russian establishment.

As these measures are implemented and confidence increases, trust will begin to form between the former antagonists. The main tangible benefit for Russia would be much reduced requirements in both nuclear and conventional areas, allowing the country to concentrate on the areas where genuine security concerns demand attention, such as the creation of effective rapid deployment forces.

Such a breakthrough in the relations with the West will not be cost-free, however. The Russian elites must drop the old and by now unsustainable pretenses, such as insisting on equality with NATO and the United States. The plan calls for Russia aligning itself with the West and eventually becoming part of the West, not the formation of yet another unworkable bipolar structure. One logical consequence will be that a Russia enjoying close relations with NATO as an ally of the alliance would have no reason to object to NATO's enlargement. Another logical consequence, now for NATO, would be its willingness to work out a plan for the alliance's third wave of enlargement that would include Russia in the foreseeable future.

What are the assurances for Russia in the difficult transition period? Actually, the world's second nuclear power with a still formidable army does not need many, at least in the traditional way. Deterrence will work for some time to come, even if there is a guaranteed delivery to the United States of only a handful of Russian nuclear warheads. The security regime established by the Conventional Armed Forces in Europe Treaty (CFE) continues to make any large-scale attack against any country in Europe highly improbable. In addition, Belarus has been acting as Russia's security cushion in the west, and Ukraine is a de facto buffer in the southwest. Belarus is so closely integrated into the Russian security and defense system already that a formal military alliance is unnecessary and even harmful. No formal alliance is needed with Kiev either. Defense–industrial cooperation, which the Ukrainians want badly and the Russians might find beneficial, would serve as the basis for continued friendly relations in the security area.

As regards the northwest, Russia's only exposed flank in Europe, the assurances would lie not so much in the Baltic states staying outside NATO or in the alliance's disavowal of specific intentions. Rather, Moscow's confidence would be bolstered by the Baltic countries' integration into the EU, coupled with an active pursuit of the EU's Northern Dimension Initiative with Russia, and by an invitation for them to join NATO, followed by a similar one addressed to Russia in the next round.

Stabilization of the South

To the south and southeast of Moscow, Russia's main security problem highlighted by the attacks by international terrorists is twofold. First, the more immediate threat is rooted in the weakness of its new—and some old—neighbors. All the newly independent states of the CIS are weak. Some of them are failing. Afghanistan, rocked by the Soviet invasion over twenty years ago, has been the regional generator of tension ever since and a global center of drug trafficking, arms smuggling, and terrorist operations. This presents Russia with a long-term security challenge. No military involvement in the Caucasus or Central Asia can again be thought of as a "diversion from the main (Western) front" or a quick adventure.

The second security threat is obviously terrorism and religious extremism, but its underlying cause is the instability produced by the prolonged economic crisis, the growing disparity in wealth, and the propensity of the largely corrupt ruling cliques to quell all dissent, outlawing political opposition. This helps channel all opposition to the "fundamentalist" camp. In this way, the regimes create more detractors. These policy failures are exploited by the terrorists whose ultimate goal appears to be overturning the existing status quo in the strategically vital region from the Gulf to Pakistan to the Caspian and imposing upon it an extremist and expansionist regime.

Under these conditions, for Russia to concentrate only on boosting its own military presence in the region, deepening alliance relationships, and fighting terrorists would be insufficient. Russia's own resources are limited.

Early in 2001, it had to abandon plans for reinforcing the 201st division in Tajikistan with some 3,000 paratroopers. A 50,000-strong rapid reaction corps to be based at Omsk is a long way off in terms of Russia's capacity to implement this plan. Even when the corps is formed, it will find it difficult to get to its likely destination. In the 1990s, Russia's power projection capabilities were severely curtailed. The guerrilla war in Chechnya still calls for a major force on the ground there. To protect its exposed southern flank, Russia will need to work closely with the CIS states, China, anti-Taliban Afghans, and now with the United States and its allies.

The risks of these engagements are high. For the past twenty years, almost without interruption, Russian soldiers have been exclusively fighting Muslim rebels in Afghanistan, Tajikistan, Chechnya, and Dagestan. Most of the "international terrorists" Russia has taken on likewise come from the Islamic world. It is extremely hard to draw a distinction among Islamists, fundamentalists, separatists, and plain terrorists. This fact has clear implications for a country whose own Muslim population is estimated to be between 12 and 15 percent of the total and growing, and which counts a half-dozen Islamic republics among its eighty-nine regions. Demographically and politically, the Islamic element in Russia and on its immediate periphery will continue to grow.

A realistic security policy would complement any antiterrorist effort with a political dimension. Moscow should work with governments, private companies, and international organizations to promote development strategies for the regions that serve as hotbeds of new conflict. Stability building in the region would also include an alliance with moderate Muslim political forces and mainstream Islamic clergy, as well as the isolation of militant groups using Islamic slogans, something that will be very difficult to implement. Russia would also help others and itself if it persuaded the governments that rely on it for protection to allow a measure of political pluralism that would cement a community of interests favoring peace and stability. In any case, Russia will not be able to underwrite the Central Asian regimes' security if they are seriously challenged from within. Last, but very important, the Russian and local forces will need to adopt counterterrorist warfare tactics that would, to the maximum possible, spare the population and reduce "collateral damage." Accepting such an approach requires abandoning the "Great Game" mentality, which views international relations in the energy-rich region as a zero-sum exercise. Because Russia will not be able to impose its imperial control or even to stabilize the region single-handedly, it will need to reach out to the United States, the EU, China, and India, as well as Turkey and Iran, in an effort to consolidate regional order.

In the special case of Chechnya, the new approach means seriously revising the previous policies. Moscow used its military power almost without restrictions in Chechnya and still cannot pacify the republic. It now needs to emphasize political means over military ones. Reaching out to the leaders of the Chechen separatists and drawing a distinction between them and the terrorists and bandits, Moscow needs to work out a credible power-sharing formula for the republic. It must give its present-day enemies a stake in the postwar administration. The federal authorities will also need to promote an intra-Chechen dialogue on the republic's future constitution. This should precede the Russian–Chechen negotiations on the republic's future relations with the Russian Federation. Whatever the terms of the final settlement, Russia's main concern should be the security of its southern flank rather than Chechnya's formal status.

The looming challenges to Russia's security are weapons of mass destruction and missile proliferation along its southern borders. The coming of the second nuclear age is being felt most acutely in South Asia and the Middle East. At present, India, Pakistan, and Israel are nuclear powers. Iraq had reportedly come close to acquiring its own nuclear weapons before the process was cut short by the Gulf War. Within the next two decades, however, Iran may join the group of second-tier nuclear powers, and Iraq, under certain circumstances, may restart its programs. Pakistan is inherently unstable, challenged by religious radicals. Should the radicals come to power in Saudi Arabia and the Gulf states, this would amount to a strategic earthquake.

To meet this challenge effectively, Russia needs to act with its partners in the group of permanent members (P-5) of the UN Security Council, which comprises all the declared nuclear powers, in an effort to limit the damage to regional and world security. This effort includes stabilizing the nuclear relationship in South Asia, as well as between India and China; implementing an effective monitoring regime in Iraq; and preventing leakage of nuclear and missile components to Afghanistan. On the issue of Iraq, in preparation for a post-Saddam era, Russia needs to reach accommodation with the West on the practical issues (such as Iraqi debt to Moscow, the oil agreements signed by the Russian companies, and so on). On Iran, Russia should proceed with special caution. The willingness in some Russian quarters to embrace a future missile-armed and nuclear-capable Iran—all in the name of multipolarity—is dangerous. Even if the cash flow from Tehran were much more significant than it is now, such an outcome could be detrimental to Russia's security. Any attempt to stem it, however, would impinge on well-entrenched interests.

It would be particularly useful for Russia to engage in a dialogue with the United States and Europe about the nature and scale of the likely missile and nuclear threats from the greater Middle East region, with a view to exploring the feasibility of a joint missile defense.

At the same time, Russia needs to help maintain the regional balance of power with its many players. Its own policy, though necessarily formulated with a dose of ambiguity, would need to set priorities. In Central Asia, the only vitally important country in terms of Russia's own security is Kazakhstan. It is the ultimate line of defense if the security situation in Central Asia deteriorates, and it is Russia's principal ally in ensuring it does not. Kazakhstan also has the most natural resources in Central Asia and the greatest capacity for economic cooperation with Russia. The ethnic composition of the Kazakhstani population makes it virtually certain that Russia will get involved if serious internal tensions develop. By contrast, Uzbekistan, the most populous nation of the region, remains critical for the future fate of Central Asia as a whole. It is an important security partner for Russia.

No amount of Russian military assistance will be able to save the Tashkent or other Central Asian regimes, however, if they do not change their ways. Across Central Asia and in Afghanistan, Russia should avoid overextension and, wherever possible, direct involvement. Moscow's security policy must always be wary of deepening Muslim–Christian, North–South fault lines, let alone turning them into front lines. Russia has found it both necessary and useful to cooperate with China in providing stability to Central Asia. The interests of Moscow and Beijing are in many ways parallel when it comes to opposing instability and extremism. However, Russia should realize that the establishment of the Shanghai Cooperation Organization already makes China a Central Asian power on virtually equal terms with Russia.

The force structure for antiterrorist and counterinsurgency operations in Central Asia needs to include several elements. The first echelon, composed of Russia's allies and friends, would enjoy Russian logistical and technical support. The second echelon would include Russian forces on the ground that would provide support when necessary. Russia would also need some form of coordination with Western—especially U.S.—forces deployed in Central Asia. Russia's own military presence in the region needs to be optimized. What military functions can the 201st division really perform, besides being the political support base for the present Dushanbe government? The Russian-led border troops in Tajikistan used to provide a fire-break between the civil war in Afghanistan and the situation in Central Asia. With the war over, at least for now, what is their new role? How effective can stopping drug trafficking at the border be in the atmosphere of pervasive corruption all the way from the border into Central Asia and beyond? The Afghan Northern Alliance forces, which played a substantial role in the defeat of the Taliban in 2001 and which had acted as a buffer zone between the Taliban and the CIS countries for several years before that, will continue as important regional formations unless Afghanistan is tightly centralized— an unlikely outcome. It is important that Russia acts as a force for stability and national unity in that country and continues to resist the temptation to engage in geopolitical competition there.

The configuration of forces will be different in the Caucasus region. In the South Caucasus, where security challenges are different from those in Central Asia, Russian military forces are effective only when they are welcomed by the host countries. That leaves Armenia as the only place for a Russian base whose role assures the regional balance. As for Georgia, the political role of the Russian forces there is diminishing. They would need to leave, except for the peacekeeping contingents in Abkhazia and South Ossetia until the final settlement of the two conflicts. In the North Caucasus, Russian forces would be deployed in the zones of conflict. However, bombing the Chechen camps in Georgia's Pankisi Gorge or engaging the rebels in hot pursuit across the border would lead to a strong reaction by the United States and condemnation by the EU.

Balancing in the East

The main security problem in Russia's east is the uncertain fate of the Far East and Siberia. This will be the principal geopolitical challenge to Russia in the new century. Accordingly, Russia's security policy in Asia must start immediately east of the Urals. Its key element is a new regional development strategy, giving the region a viable alternative to the previous colonial (Tsarist) and mobilization (Soviet) models. If Russia should lose its Asian territories, it would most likely come as a result of neglect or inability to develop them rather than an outside invasion.

For the moment, there are relatively few outside military threats to Russian security in the east. The outlook, however, is uncertain because the regional situation remains volatile. The most important international factor shaping the regional security environment will be the rise of China to the position of the world's second most powerful nation after the United States, and the concurrent rise of India. The medium-term risks include the potential outbreak of war on the Korean peninsula, a military conflict in the Taiwan Straits (with possible U.S. involvement), and the clashes in the South China Sea. In the longer term, China's relations with the major Asia Pacific countries, including Russia, are a cause for concern.

In the Asia Pacific region, collective security mechanisms have a subordinate role. The raw balance of power continues to be of central importance. Russia is mercifully not in the center of regional struggles, but it is the weakest of the major powers and is trending down. To be able to win back some confidence in the east, Russia needs to integrate closely with the West (the EU and the United States)—economically, politically, and also in security terms.

Russia's strategy needs to include political and military responses. On the political side, Russia must maintain a balance in its relations with Asia Pacific countries. Friendly relations with China remain of critical importance and need to be developed, but also better balanced to escape Moscow's one-sided dependence on Beijing. In particular, this strategy would mean securing and expanding niches on the Chinese domestic civilian goods market. Such a strategy also relates to energy supplies to an increasingly import-dependent China. Russia would need to take the Chinese market seriously and prepare for hard competition there instead of relying on political decisions. Also required is a forward-looking immigration policy designed to integrate foreign workers—Chinese, but also Koreans and others—in the sparsely populated Russian Far East and Siberia. In foreign policy terms, Russia needs strong and healthy relations with its other neighbors in Asia as well—above all Japan, Korea, and India. In its relations with Japan, Russia would need to combine geopolitics with geoeconomics. When it is ready to absorb Japan's investment and technology, Russia would be wise to be generous on the territorial issue regarding the Kuril Islands. Helping to manage a soft landing for the regime in Pyongyang, Moscow needs to look ahead to the time when Korea unifies. As to the United States, it is in Russia's interest to cultivate it as an ally of last resort. The military component of the Russian security strategy in Asia entails continuing nuclear deterrence at strategic and tactical levels and building up a strategic redeployment capability so that forces stationed in the European part of Russia could be rapidly deployed to the Far East.

Realistic But Not Real?

For Russia's foreign policy to be realistic, it must match its generally liberal economic policy in accepting the current realities and dropping long-held views. This is not easy, nor is it coming soon. Russia—and above all the Russian elites—must unlearn old-fashioned pretensions that claim Russia as a great power and embrace a policy of integration with the West. This requires complementing promarket, prodemocracy reforms with the full demilitarization of Russian–Western relations. Such a bold move is the only realistic way of solving the Russian security conundrum. Keeping alive the Cold War–era security and defense policy continues to divert scarce resources from addressing the more pressing security concerns. Unless this is understood and acted upon, assuring Russia's external security will soon become a mission impossible. The two other components of the three-part security policy formula could be summarized as stability building in the south and balancing in the east.

Tactics are useful also in the field of national security, but they do not suffice. One can play a European with the EU, a Eurasianist with China, and a fellow post-Soviet with the CIS states, but not for long. Caution has its uses, but it is only a means to an end. There is a clear need for a strategy. Putin may have made his choice, but Russia as a whole has not as yet. There are difficult tests down the road and many disappointments, even backsliding. Nothing is guaranteed. But if Russian leaders decide to orient the nation's policy toward realities rather than relics, here is a raw blueprint.

Notes

1. The agreement signed by General Aleksandr Lebed, then secretary of Russia's Security Council, and Aslan Maskhadov, then commander of the Chechen rebel forces, which led to Russian withdrawal from Chechnya and the republic's de facto independence, which lasted through 1999.

2. Since 1999, the combined strength of the Russian military contingent in Chechnya has been about 80,000, of which half are Ministry of Defense personnel.

3. Compare, for example, the president's July 2000 remark in Blagoveschensk (on the Amur River) in which he publicly wondered what language the population of the Russian Far East and Siberia will speak in the future.

4. This is the exchange rate equivalent; in purchasing parity terms, Russia's defense budget is estimated to be about $30 billion. See International Institute for Strategic Studies, *The Military Balance 2000–2001* (London: Oxford University Press, 2000), p. 120.

5. Nearly half of Russia's total trade is with the advanced Western economies. Russia's total debt stands at about $148 billion. See International Monetary Fund (IMF), *Direction of Trade Yearbook 2001* (Washington, D.C.: IMF, 2001), p. 922.

6. In a televised address on September 24, 2001, and his speech to the German Bundestag on September 26, 2001.

7. In EU parlance, *Petersberg tasks* refers to conflict prevention and peacekeeping. Petersberg, a suburb of Bonn, was the venue of a meeting at which these tasks were formulated and agreed upon.

11

Limits of the Sino–Russian Strategic Partnership

Andrew C. Kuchins

Against the backdrop of deteriorating relations between Russia and the West, the specter of a spurned Russia seeking solace in an antihegemonic alliance with China, India, Iran, and perhaps others spread through both Russian and Western commentary during the latter 1990s. Some Russians offered up this alternative alliance structure as a thinly veiled threat, intimating that Russia could look elsewhere for its partners if the West did not treat it with proper respect. A resurrected Sino–Russian alliance typically served as the crux of this threat. Some U.S. critics of Clinton administration policy cited the improvement in Sino–Russian relations as proof of misguided policy decisions that were eroding U.S. geopolitical advantages. These critics argued that unlike the successful Nixon-Kissinger era triangular diplomacy of the 1970s, when the United States developed better relations with the Soviet Union and China than the communist giants had with each other, the growing collaboration between Russia and China in the 1990s was making the United States the "odd man out."[1] Both the Russian threats and the U.S. critiques, however, failed to appreciate the structural constraints faced by Russia as well as the enduring advantages and allure of U.S. power. Not only is Russia too weak to realistically balance the United States, it is not a sufficiently attractive partner for other major players in the international system to join Moscow in a balancing game.

Russia is, of course, not alone in its discomfiture with the overwhelming U.S. global power after the Cold War. Even the European allies of the United States are increasingly concerned about U.S. power unbridled by unilateralism. What former secretary of state Madeleine Albright called the indispensable country, French Defense Minister Hubert Vedrine dubbed the hyperpuissance. Russia, China, and India all regularly express support for a multipolar international system. When Russians and others advance the establishment of a multipolar world as a goal, they are expressing the sense that unconstrained U.S. power is not healthy for world affairs. They understandably seek a voice in making the key decisions that define the international system.

When, in December 1998 during a trip to New Delhi, former Russian foreign minister Yevgeny Primakov broached the vague notion of a "strategic triangle" among Russia, China, and India to serve as a stabilizing force in international security, he did not mean the establishment of a military alliance. The proposal itself had the air of an emotional improvisation formed in response to the anger and frustration that Primakov felt about the U.S.–British bombing of Iraq that had just taken place and the growing perception by Russia of overbearing and sometimes irresponsible U.S. power. Primakov's frustration resonated deeply among Russian political elites who agonized over Russia's abrupt and traumatic deprivation of status in the 1990s. Sergei Karaganov, head of the influential Council on Foreign and Defense Policy, enthusiastically endorsed Primakov's proposal, suggesting that "we [Russia] like to use our cooperation to counterbalance the excessive power of the United States."[2] Pavel Felgenhauer, a leading Russian journalist specializing in security issues, went further by noting in February 1999 that "a growing convergence of basic interest is bringing the major Asian landmass countries together in opposing the Western sea nations. Maybe one day relentless pressure will force these countries to sign a formal alliance."[3]

A formal alliance among Russia, China, and India was hardly imminent in 1998–1999, and it is even less so after the terrorist acts of September 11, 2001. Nonetheless, Russia's relations with China and India are, and will remain, important for several reasons. First, although, as argued by Dmitri Trenin and James Goldgeier in this volume, Russia's principal foreign policy orientation will be toward the West, Russia remains a huge continental Eurasian landmass that simply by virtue of geography will continue to have significant interests from East Asia to South and Central Asia to the Middle

East. Second, despite the recent economic upswing, Russia's greatly weakened international position will put a premium on maintaining constructive relations with all the major powers on its periphery to concentrate the energy of the nation on domestic recovery. In addition to the accustomed power of the West, for the first time in its history Russia faces a number of rising powers on its southern and eastern peripheries, most notably China. Third, Russia has no formal alliance partners of note, something that is not likely to change anytime soon.[4]

Russia's unique geography and daunting domestic challenges have shaped the incentives and constraints on Russian foreign policy during the 1990s and will continue to do so for the foreseeable future. Since Moscow's relationship with China has sometimes been identified by Russians and U.S. observers, mistakenly in my view, as an alternative to the West, the task of this essay is to examine the common interests and cross-cutting issues that will set the parameters for bilateral relations between the Russian Federation and the People's Republic of China.

The Sino–Russian relationship has steadily improved since 1989, when relations were officially normalized during Gorbachev's historic visit to Beijing. The agreements of 1996 and 1997 that resolved nearly all contested territories along the old Soviet–Chinese border and demilitarized border regions are major achievements. The border agreement signed by China, Kazakhstan, Kyrgyzstan, Russia, and Tajikistan launched the Shanghai Five Group that was formally institutionalized with the addition of Uzbekistan in 2001 as the Shanghai Cooperation Organization. Also, in July 2001, Russia and China signed a twenty-year Friendship Treaty that calls for further deepening of economic and security cooperation. Undoubtedly, Sino–Russian ties are more positive and constructive than at any time since the Sino–Soviet alliance of the 1950s.

Despite these positive developments and the expansive official rhetoric about strategic partnership with Beijing, the growing power of China evokes deep concern among Russian analysts and strategic thinkers. The striking juxtaposition of Russia's fall and China's rise in the last twenty years is perhaps unparalleled among major powers during peacetime in modern history. According to official calculations, in 1980 the Soviet gross domestic product (GDP) was about five times that of China, whereas in 1999 Chinese GDP was two and a half times that of Russia at fixed exchange rates and four times adjusted for purchasing power parity.[5] This dramatic fall, coupled with the fragmentation of state power, adverse demographic trends, and the deterioration of Russian conventional military forces, helps us better understand the sources of Russia's sense of vulnerability.

These Russian pathologies of the 1990s are accentuated in the Russian Far East, a vast region rich in resources but thin in population and infrastructure. Russian historians and political analysts are acutely aware of Chairman Mao's claim on more than 1.5 million square kilometers of territory acquired by the Russian Empire in the nineteenth century during a period of Chinese weakness. Now the table has turned, and in the coming decades Russians fear either a Chinese revanche or, more likely, increasing Chinese economic influence, along with large numbers of legal and illegal migrants. It is telling that in the 1990s, in both the regional and the central press, one could repeatedly find exaggerated estimations of up to several million Chinese migrants in the Russian Far East. Official statistics are striking enough as they indicate the Chinese population in Russia growing by nearly a factor of twenty in the 1990s, from the very low base of about 11,000 to over 200,000.[6]

As noted by Harley Balzer in this volume, leading Russian and international demographers anticipate a continuing contraction of the population of the Russian Federation for the first half of this century. One of Russia's leading demographers, Zhanna Zaionchkovskaia, predicts that by 2050 the Chinese population of Russia will number between seven and ten million, making it the largest national minority in Russia—possibly 10 percent of the Russian population.[7] Such a demographic shift would pose very significant social, economic, and political challenges to Russian federal and regional officials. Russian analysts are less concerned about a possible military annexation of formerly Chinese territories and more concerned about a gradual increase of Chinese influence. Many recognize the powerful role that Chinese "overseas" communities play in other Asian states. Given such adverse demographic projections, Russia will likely increasingly depend on migrant workers to help fill the labor gap and fuel economic recovery. Managing an effective migration policy will be a large challenge for Russia, but it will also pose a growing challenge in bilateral relations with China as each country deals with growing nationalist sentiments. In the 1990s this was evidenced by how the "China card," played by nationalist politicians in the Russian Far East, added an irritant to bilateral negotiations.[8]

Although the conventional wisdom of China as a rising hegemonic power in Asia, together with a near visceral stereotype of "yellow peril," unnerves many Russians, more thoughtful observers are at least as concerned about the more dangerous implications for Russia of a social, economic, or political collapse in China. From this perspective, that the unemployed and underemployed in China outnumber the entire population of Russia is more worrisome than China's two-decade-long economic boom. The breakdown of central government authority over China's periphery, especially the already economically strapped northeastern territories of Manchuria, could stimulate increasing and uncontrolled numbers of Chinese migrants.

Fairly recent history, however, suggests a Russian predisposition to exaggerate the power of China. The Sino–Soviet split more or less became public knowledge at about the same time China exploded its first nuclear device in 1964, and the frequency of border incidents increased markedly, culminating in the major incident in 1969 on Damansky/Zhenbao Island.[9] The Soviet Union responded to these events in the 1960s with a massive and expensive military buildup on the Chinese border despite already having a huge military advantage over China at the outset. The Soviet threat assessment was colored by ideological differences and perhaps more importantly by the Soviet leadership's perception of Mao Tse Tung as an irrational, unpredictable leader who was prepared to sacrifice millions of Chinese lives for his megalomaniacal visions.

The Chinese response to the Soviet buildup, however, was textbook realism; the Chinese allied with the powerful adversary of their adversary, the United States (as well as with Japan). In retrospect, despite the deep dysfunction in China brought on by the Cultural Revolution, it was not Chinese international behavior that appears illogical and miscalculated, but rather Russian behavior. Anybody with an elementary understanding of the security dilemma could have predicted that a huge military buildup and thinly veiled threats of preemptive nuclear strikes would drive China to the United States. This history of deep-seated hostility (that nearly led to nuclear conflict), coupled with a sense of Chinese betrayal, remains etched in the Russian psyche and will mitigate against the current Sino–Russian partnership developing into a full-blown military alliance against the West.

Contemporary Russian political elites, among whom realism is the dominant paradigm for interpreting international relations and security trends, appreciate the link between economic and military power. Although Russian military power remains superior to that of China, it is only a matter of time before China will surpass Russia, excepting a drastic reversal of economic growth in China. Russian strategic thinkers may take some solace from the likelihood that for the next ten to twenty years Chinese interests will focus on expanding influence, if not recovering disputed territories, south and east, with Taiwan being the main prize. But after issues of disputed territories in the southeast are resolved, Chinese attention may turn to its northern neighbor to redress disputes, perhaps after the twenty-year period of the current Sino–Russian Friendship Treaty has elapsed. Russians hold a high regard for China's long-term strategic vision that, from the perspective of Moscow, calls for restoring national power after a nearly two-century anomalous period of international weakness. For a country with at least several thousand years of history, twenty years is but the blink of an eye. It is also not lost on Russian sinologists that the socialist ideological underpinning of the Communist Party of China is being replaced with nationalism.

Nuclear Security and Stability

Russia's nuclear deterrent should guarantee its security from conflict with China for the foreseeable future, but here too, the trend is disconcerting. The consensus among Russian and U.S. strategic analysts is that Russia's strategic forces will decline due to aging and economic constraints to a level of about 1,000 to 1,500 warheads by 2010 and are likely to continue to fall beyond that unless significant funds are reallocated for modernization. Chinese nuclear forces already number around four hundred. Russian opposition to the U.S. decision to withdraw from the Anti-Ballistic Missile (ABM) Treaty to pursue deployment of a national missile defense system has many rationales. One less noted in U.S. discussions is that withdrawal could force China to modernize and expand its nuclear forces more rapidly. Russia certainly does not want to hasten the day when China reaches nuclear parity or superiority.

Although both Russia and China oppose the U.S. decision to withdraw from the ABM Treaty, one would expect the Russian government to be leery of extensive technical assistance to China's nuclear and ballistic missile programs. But the problem of weapons and weapons technologies transfer from Russia (and not just to China) is the degree of control the Russian government has over scientists, designers, and various enterprises. In addition, corruption of government officials may compromise Russia's capacity to restrict the transfer of sensitive technologies. Finally, there are figures in the military and political elite who support strengthening Russia's strategic relationship with China and would encourage such transfers. This all goes to say that it is very difficult to get a clear picture of the proliferation and technology transfer problem, including what is taking place with or without the connivance of the government. And here I am referring not so much to the sales of conventional systems that we know about, but rather to the murkier world of possible cooperation and transfers that could bolster China's nuclear weapons program, including delivery systems. Since March 1999, perhaps not so coincidentally when North Atlantic Treaty Organization (NATO) forces began bombing Serbia, Chinese and Russian military officials have held talks about possible joint measures to respond to U.S. missile defense plans. It is also stipulated in the new Sino–Russian Friendship Treaty that Moscow and Beijing would consult about addressing new common threats. One could imagine Russian assistance to China in developing penetration aids to enable Chinese missiles to evade U.S. defenses, but for now this kind of cooperation remains speculation.

Since at least the spring and summer of 2000, the Chinese had been nervous that the United States and Russia would reach a compromise agreement to allow for a modification of the ABM Treaty. The Chinese were seriously concerned about the U.S.–Russian agreement at the June 2000 Clinton–Putin summit to explore cooperation on missile defense and to monitor jointly missile launches, as well as by Putin's proposal to the Europeans in Rome in the same month to cooperate on the development of a joint European theater missile defense (TMD) system. The failure of the United States and Russia to officially reach an agreement on the future of the ABM Treaty can possibly be explained in part by Moscow's concern about the impact of such an agreement on its relations with China. But the possible engagement of Russian enterprises in developing components for theater defenses that Russians have several times proposed for Europe—and possibly, although quite unlikely, for U.S. homeland defense—will continue to be of concern to China because technologies for a European theater system may have some utility for TMD systems in Asia as well. Cooperation on missile defense systems between Russia and Europe has been promoted by Alexei Arbatov, one of Russia's leading liberal politicians and strategic analysts, as a stepping-stone to a broad Russian alliance with the West.[10]

The old U.S.–Chinese–Soviet/Russian triangle has far less explanatory power today than during its heyday in the 1970s, but on issues of nuclear security this triangular relationship is becoming more relevant. As suggested above, the future of the ABM Treaty and future deployments of missile defenses have catalyzed a triangular dynamic. In fact, as part of the improving

Sino–Russian relationship, after each bilateral U.S.–Russian discussion in 2001 on strategic issues, Putin briefed Chinese President Ziang Zemin. With the new arms treaty calling for reductions on the part of the United States and the Russian Federation to levels of possibly less than 2,000 warheads each and the likely expansion of the Chinese arsenal in the future, the gap between offensive forces will narrow. The Russian proposal made by President Putin to French President Jacques Chirac in June 2001 that the nuclear powers recognized by the Nuclear Non-Proliferation Treaty (NPT)—the United States, Russia, China, France, and Great Britain—agree to bring down their arsenals to a total level of 4,000 weapons was probably inspired as much by the desire to spur U.S. reductions as to curb a Chinese buildup.

Conventional Arms Sales and Technology Transfers

Russian sales of conventional weapons systems in recent years have been controversial in Moscow and a source of concern for U.S. policy makers. China is the largest client of the Russian military-industrial complex, and sales are estimated to be between $1 and $2 billion of a total $4 billion, with India and Iran the next two largest clients. These sales have particularly bolstered the People's Liberation Army (PLA) Air Force and Navy, improving China's capacity to project power in the Taiwan Straits and the South China Sea. U.S. analysts view Russian arms sales as increasing China's capacity to damage, but certainly not defeat, U.S. forces in a possible conflict over Taiwan.

Many Russian military and security analysts have questioned the wisdom of the weapons sales because they view China as a potential long-term security threat. Indeed, former defense minister Rodionov referred to China as a "potential threat" in a speech in December 1996.[11] Russian commanders in Transbaikal have complained that China is purchasing Russian-made aircraft in their theater in better repair than their own. Those defending the sales argue that these transferred technologies are not on the cutting edge because SU-27s and Kilo-class submarines, for example, have been in production for over a decade. The problem for Russia is that many of the newer generation designs remain on the drawing board or in experimental samples that have never gone into serial production. In addition, Russia sold most of the off-the-shelf systems during the 1990s. If the arms relationship is to grow as each side seemingly desires, then Russia will be increasingly forced to sell state-of-the-art systems and technologies. There is also discussion about future collaboration at the research and development stage, although except for money it is hard to see what the Chinese have to offer in this regard to Russian efforts that will eventually support indigenous Chinese industry.

Regional Security

China and Russia share deep reservations about U.S. military interventions that have occurred since the end of the Cold War. The Gulf War, Kosovo, and now Afghanistan have graphically illustrated the extraordinary gap in military capabilities between the United States and the rest of the world. Part of their opposition to missile defense stems from the view that this additional capability will enhance U.S. perception of invulnerability and thus even further encourage the deployment of U.S. military power around the world. And despite the fact that the primary motivator behind the establishment of a U.S.-led alliance system in Europe and Asia—the Soviet Union—has ceased to exist, Moscow and Beijing face alliances from the West (NATO) and the East (the U.S.–Japanese Alliance) that are expanding membership and missions.

China and Russia in the 1990s were united in their opposition to the expansion of NATO's membership and mission. The war in Kosovo highlighted the sensitivities of Moscow and Beijing to international (read U.S.) intervention into conflict zones that violate norms of national sovereignty. For China, of course, the reinvigoration and broadening of the geographical purview of the U.S.–Japanese Security Alliance are far more immediate security concerns than NATO. Still, the current rapprochement between NATO and Russia sparked by U.S.–Russian cooperation in the war on terrorism in Afghanistan and President Putin's more positive policy toward NATO, including efforts to more closely integrate Russia into NATO decision-making structures, are viewed with considerable concern by Beijing.

China's darkest security future would involve the emergence of a quasi-alliance system including the United States, Japan, India, and Russia that would amount to virtual encirclement. It should not be lost on Chinese strategic thinkers that the perception of aggressive Soviet international behavior in the 1970s led to an encircling alliance and quasi-alliance system including the United States, Western Europe, Japan, and China; and that high military expenditures for deployments west and east were a major factor in the stagnation of the Soviet economy and ultimately its collapse. Since the initial pro-Western orientation of the Yeltsin regime dissipated in the early 1990s, Moscow has tried to calibrate a more balanced foreign policy between China and the West. But there have been increasing indications, especially after September 11, that Putin's preferences are for a Russian orientation that "leans to one side"—the West—and the rapprochement between NATO and Russia is symbolic of this. In the fall of 2001, Putin announced that Russia was prepared to go as far as NATO was in integrating Russia. Russia has also expressed interest in participating in the development of the European Union rapid reaction force that is slated to be operational by 2003. Still, it is quite unlikely that in the near term Russia's rapprochement with NATO will involve membership, and the China factor influences thinking for both NATO and Russia in this regard. NATO would be leery of making security guarantees that would take it to the Chinese border in Russia's east. Unless Russia felt directly threatened by China, it is unlikely to seek membership that may be viewed as provocative by China.

Central Asia is another area where Russian and Chinese interests coincided to a considerable extent throughout the 1990s. Russia and China both have viewed secular and stable regimes in Central Asia as an important bulwark against religious extremism, separatism, and terrorism, and they shared concerns about Afghanistan's Taliban government. For Russia, the threat of radical Islam was more acute because of the Chechen conflict, the view of Central Asia as a traditional Russian sphere of influence, and the growing Muslim population in the Russian Federation itself. China's Muslim population is relatively smaller—primarily Uighurs in Sinkiang Province bordering Kazakhstan and Kyrgyzstan—and Beijing has aggressively moved to stamp out separatist groups there.

The mutually perceived threat of the new "isms"—terrorism, separatism, and religious extremism—inspired the formal institutionalization of the Shanghai Five grouping into the Shanghai Cooperation Organization in summer 2001, coupled with the entrance of Uzbekistan into the organization. Some U.S. observers viewed this development, along with the Sino–Russian Friendship Treaty, as the emergence of an anti-Western coalition. More significantly, however, the Shanghai Cooperation Organization symbolized the expanding interest of China in Central Asia. The charter of the organization provides for the introduction of military forces from one member at the invitation of another member. In other words, the charter approves the possible introduction of Chinese military forces into Central Asia, or even Russia for that matter. This fairly remarkable development, unimaginable only a short time ago, in effect codifies a shifting regional balance of power in Eurasia. Establishment of the organization marked a considerable diplomatic achievement for China, as shown by its very name; it is the Shanghai—not the Moscow or Tashkent—Cooperation Organization. Throughout the 1990s Beijing was content for Russia to flex its now flabby muscles on security issues in Central Asia while Chinese economic interests and influence grew considerably, but that may not be the case in the future. Still, for both Russia and China, Central Asia is at best a secondary theater of concern, so the perception of lower stakes may alleviate the possibility of future tension.

The terrorist attacks on the United States and the resounding U.S.-led military defeat of the Taliban in Afghanistan in the fall of 2001 raise questions about the future utility of the Shanghai Cooperation Organization. The Central Asian member states are ambivalent about Russian and Chinese power and would to a greater or lesser extent welcome an enduring U.S. military presence in the region. The U.S. government had reportedly requested observer status in the Shanghai grouping in the past but was denied. It is possible that the defeat of the Taliban will create a more felicitous environment for durable multilateral cooperation in the region. But already during the Afghan campaign, an effort that both Russia and China supported to various degrees, differences over the definition of what constitutes terrorism surfaced. U.S. recognition of the role of international terrorists in Chechnya was viewed by Moscow as a symbolic concession. After the bombing of Afghanistan commenced, China urged the United States to officially support its war on Sinkiang terrorists and Tibetan and Taiwanese separatists. China's accusations that the United States practices double standards on terrorism were supported by Moscow. Although international leaders agreed on a joint statement at the Asia Pacific Economic Cooperation forum (APEC) summit meeting in October 2001 that condemned the September 11 attacks, press reports indicated that no agreement was reached on a definition of terrorism and that there were lively discussions on the topic.[12]

Similar to their shared sensitivities about encroachment on national sovereignty raised by international humanitarian interventions, Russia and China are both generally more inclined to broaden the category of terrorism to safeguard national sovereignty. Because of the Kashmir conflict on its territory, India is also exceedingly sensitive about terrorism and what it perceives as U.S. double standards. Despite the fact that Russia, China, and India support the toppling of the Taliban and the weakening of al Qaeda, officials in Moscow, Beijing, and New Delhi tire of U.S. admonishments about the need to use political solutions rather than military force to deal with local separatist and terrorist groups when the United States does not seem shy about using military force itself.

South Asia presents perhaps the gravest threat of nuclear conflict, and it is a region where Russian and Chinese interests traditionally have not coincided—at least since the Soviet war in Afghanistan when the Chinese supported the Mujahadeen and provided considerable assistance to the Pakistani nuclear program. India was the major partner for the Soviet Union in South Asia. After a brief flirtation with Pakistan in the early 1990s, the Russian Federation once again sought to strengthen ties with India, an endeavor that culminated in the signing of the strategic partnership agreement during Putin's trip to India in October 2000. India is the second largest client after China for the Russian military-industrial complex, and the ongoing Indian military modernization is directed at both China and Pakistan. If Primakov's notion of a Russo–Sino–Indian strategic triangle could prove of some use in helping India and Pakistan resolve their long-standing differences (which have produced three wars since the late 1940s and ongoing fighting in Kashmir for the last decade), then the former foreign minister should be awarded the Nobel Peace Prize! But Russia does not bring much to the table to serve as a broker for peace, and neither Russia nor China can be considered a disinterested party.

After South Asia, Taiwan may be the next most dangerous flash point for major power conflict, in this case between the United States and China. Russia has steadfastly promoted a one-China policy, which was confirmed in the new Sino–Russian Friendship Treaty. Beneath the rhetorical unanimity lies a more complex reality, however. If an actual conflict were to erupt over Taiwan, Russia would find itself in an awkward position with possibly a very difficult choice.[13] It would seem that continued simmering of the Taiwan conflict would be in Russia's best interest because it could marginally increase Moscow's leverage with both Washington and Beijing while ensuring that Chinese strategic attention and potential expansionism are diverted away from Russia.

China and Russia view the U.S. military presence in Asia, and the U.S.–Japanese Security Alliance in particular, quite differently in the wake of the Cold War. In the 1990s, Russia tended to view the U.S. military presence reasonably positively as a hedge first of all on growing Chinese power and secondarily on Japan from assuming a more independent security stance, including more rapid militarization and possible development of nuclear weapons. Given its bloody history with Japan, the Chinese leadership may be inclined tacitly to recognize the utility of the U.S. presence to rein in Japan. But the U.S. military presence at large is now viewed in Beijing as primarily designed to contain China.

Chinese and Russian regional interests also do not fully coincide on the Korean peninsula, where Russia is intent on regaining some of its lost influence. Russia seems ambivalent if not resigned to eventual reunification of the Korean peninsula. China, on the other hand, seems quite satisfied that Russia is no longer a major player on the peninsula and, to put it lightly, is not enthusiastic about reunification.

Energy and Economic Ties

Sino–Russian trade has grown rapidly in the past two years after stagnating at a disappointingly low level throughout the 1990s. In 2000 bilateral trade grew about 40 percent to $8 billion and in 2001 reached about $10 billion. For China, though, trade with Russia accounts for only 2 percent of overall trade and is less than 10 percent of its trade level with the United States.[14] Those who argue that the United States is somehow the "odd man out" in a triangular format vastly underestimate the geostrategic importance of economic relationships in a rapidly globalizing world. It is not surprising that Russia's economic relations with China have not blossomed during a decade of economic collapse, dislocation, and trauma in Russia.

But the future of Sino–Russian trade and economic cooperation may not be so grim, and the foundation for this brighter future will be energy. Barring any cataclysmic events that could significantly disrupt its economic growth, some projections have Chinese energy consumption growing between five- and sevenfold by the year 2050.[15] Chinese dependence on imported oil will grow considerably, and imports of Russian oil will play an increasingly important role, as will those from Central Asia. In September 2001 Russia and China signed their first joint agreement to explore and develop oil resources in eastern Siberia, about 1,000 kilometers from the Chinese border, an effort that will partner Russian firms Rosneft and Yukos with the Chinese Daqing Oil Field Corporation. Officials also agreed to build a 2,400-kilometer pipeline with a capacity of about 20 million tons of oil annually by 2005.

Russia's vast natural gas resources should also become an increasingly important part of China's overall energy consumption picture. Currently China is far too dependent on burning dirty coal, and it will need to incorporate much cleaner natural gas to alleviate already alarming environmental problems. Discussions have been ongoing about the development of the Kovykhta gas field near Irkutsk, but the vast Siberian gas fields near Yamal hold even greater promise. In 1998 Gazprom proposed a project to build a gas pipeline from Yamal to Shanghai, the longest in the world at about 7,100 kilometers, at a cost of $15 billion.

The question of increasing Russian energy supplies to China seems to be when, not whether. The kinds of projects under consideration in most cases would also necessitate multilateral cooperation and sources of financing, and these discussions have been well under way for several years with Japan, South Korea, the United States, Kazakhstan, and others. Sino–Russian energy cooperation will have to be embedded in a broader Northeast Asia energy community that will give regional major powers a far greater investment in security cooperation. The more quickly the Russian Federation develops the legal and financial infrastructure to handle and guarantee foreign investment, the more rapidly these large-scale energy projects will come to fruition. In the case of Sino–Russian economic relations, an optimistic scenario would have the returns to Russia from energy cooperation dwarfing those from the weapons trade ten years from now.

Conclusion

The predictions and scenarios that Sino–Russian relations are leading either to military alliance or to a heightened danger of conflict are premised too heavily on geopolitical considerations that ignore the increasing importance of geoeconomics in today's world. Undoubtedly, China and Russia will continue to share common concerns about the deployment of U.S. power in the world, but it is exceedingly difficult to envision these security concerns developing into the foundation of an alliance directed against the United States. There is simply too much to lose and too little to gain for Moscow as well as for Beijing. Similarly, while Russia will continue to face tremendous development challenges in the Russian Far East and Siberia for years to come, it would be senseless for China to risk nuclear conflict to redress territorial grievances from the nineteenth century. This territory does not hold the same emotional value for China as Taiwan does today.

Like Deng Xiaoping, who initiated successful Chinese economic reforms in the late 1970s after a chaotic decade or so that included the misnamed Great Leap Forward and the debilitating Cultural Revolution, Vladimir Putin recognizes that economic recovery is essential for Russia's future after years of Soviet stagnation and then economic collapse for most of the 1990s. And like Deng, he appreciates the long-term nature of this project as well as the importance of dramatically increased integration of Russia into the world economy for the project ultimately to be successful. Russia and China can both play a useful but limited role for each other in facilitating modernization and development efforts. But the role of Western (including Japanese) trade, investment, and technology will be far more significant for both countries, and this will prevent any rational leaders in Beijing and Moscow from fundamentally turning away from the West to resurrect a new Sino–Russian alliance. The first experience was distinctly unpleasant for both the Russians and the Chinese, and the costs of such a step are far higher in 2001 than they were in 1949. "Strategic partnership" is the appropriate designation for this important bilateral relationship today, and that would likely also be the case if we were to gather in another ten years to assess "Russia—Twenty Years After."

Notes

1. For the fullest statement of the Republican Party critique of Clinton administration policy on this point, see the chapter on Sino–Russian relations in *Russia's Road to Corruption: How the Clinton Administration Exported Government Instead of Free Enterprise and Failed the Russian People* (Washington, D.C.: Speaker's Advisory Group on Russia, 2000).

2. See *Radio Liberty Daily Report*, December 23, 1998.

3. Pavel Felgenhauer, "Defense Dossier: Asian Triangle Shapes Up," *Moscow Times*, February 25, 1999.

4. While falling short of alliances, Russia's security relations with its former Soviet neighbors in the Commonwealth of Independent States (CIS) are manifold. Armenia, Belarus, Kazakhstan, Kyrgyzstan, and Tajikistan are all members of the CIS Collective Security Treaty, and Russia maintains a variety of bilateral ties and agreements with these and other CIS states. These agreements range from training exercises to joint air defense to border guard assistance to military basing.

5. The 1980 figures are taken from Paul Kennedy, *The Rise and Fall of the Great Powers* (New York: Random House, 1987), p. 436; the 1999 figures are from World Bank, *World Development Indicators 2001* (Washington, D.C.: World Bank, 2001). There are myriad reasons to question the accuracy of these figures, but they are the best available, and they do reflect popular impressions of China's economic success and Russia's difficulties. One should also keep in mind that although China is outpacing Russia in GDP, the per capita income of Russia is still at least twice that of China.

6. Dmitri Trenin, *The End of Eurasia* (Washington, D.C.: Brookings Institution Press, 2002), pp. 216–7.

7. Viliam Gdalivich, *Kitaiskaia Real'nost' Rossii* (The Chinse Reality for Russia) (Moscow: Muravai, 2001), p. 19.

8. For a particularly vituperative example of this sentiment, see Liberal Democratic Party of Russia (LDPR) leader Vladimir Zhironovsky's rant against Chinese immigrants in *Itar–Tass*, August 11, 1999, published in FBIS-SOV-1999-0811.

9. On March 2 and March 15, 1969, this island along the Russian–Chinese border was the site of border clashes between Soviet and Chinese troops. The military clashes and ensuing casualties created a major crisis between China and Russia and contributed to further military buildup along the border.

10. "Press Conference with State Duma Committee for Defense Vice Chairman Alexei Arbatov on Vladimir Putin's Foreign Policy," Federal News Service, March 5, 2001.

11. Yuri Savenkov, [China decides not to take offense at Rodionov], *Izvestiya*, December 28, 1996, in *Current Digest of the Post-Soviet Press*, vol. 48, no. 52 (1996).

12. See Amit Baruah, "No Double Standards on Terrorism, Warns China," *The Hindu*, October 21, 2001; and "China's APEC Spokeswoman Comments on China's Anti-terrorist Stance," Zhongguo Tongxun She news agency (from BBC Worldwide Monitoring), October 21, 2001.

13. Rumors circulated in Asia just before Putin's trip to Beijing in the summer of 2000 that the Russian president offered the Chinese direct military assistance in the event of a crisis in the Taiwan Straits. Supposedly the Russians would send their Pacific Fleet to cut off U.S. naval access. It is hard to believe the Russians would make such an offer and also hard to believe the Chinese would find it credible, given the deplorable condition of Russia's Pacific Fleet. Still, neither Russian nor Chinese officials denied the story, and there was no comment on the rumor either by top U.S. officials or by major media. For more, see Yu Bin, "Putin's Ostpolitik and Sino-Russian Relations," *Comparative Connections: E-Journal on East Asia*, Third Quarter (2000).

14. "Politics Continue to Haunt Russian-Chinese Trade Ties," *Prime-Tass*, September 17, 2001.

15. Michael May, *Energy and Security in East Asia* (Stanford, Calif.: Asia/Pacific Research Center, Stanford University, 1998), pp. 5–9.

12

State Building and Security Threats in Central Asia

Martha Brill Olcott

While most of the papers in this volume address the process of political, economic, and social transformation taking place in Russia over the past decade, this essay offers an overview of these same state-building processes as they have been unfolding in the five Central Asian states. It focuses more on the failures of state building than on its successes. These failures of state building are creating the security risks that emanate from the region and are magnified by developments in Afghanistan.

Central Asian security challenges are increasingly problems in which Russia must engage; in the past, Russia saw security issues in the region as a means for manipulation or expansion of its power in what it considered its "near abroad" or sphere of influence. But this was the case before the terrorist attacks of September 11 and the subsequent increased U.S. military presence in the region to support its war effort in Afghanistan. Russia's rather quiet acquiescence to the U.S. decision to establish military bases in Uzbekistan, Tajikistan, and Kyrgyzstan (the latter two states are still part of a collective security agreement with Russia) indicates a relative distancing of Moscow from these countries.

This is a major change from a decade or even seven or eight years ago, when Russia still set much of the economic and political agenda for the Central Asian states and dominated their security relations. It is also a sharp contrast from Russian behavior in the south Caucasus. Today, the agenda of state building is being developed much more in the region itself than by outside actors. In Kazakhstan and Kyrgyzstan state building occurs in dialogue with Western financial institutions, and in Kazakhstan in particular through serious engagement with Western foreign investors.

The shift in decision making from Moscow to the region is potentially good news, because it puts the burden of choice on the leaders of these states themselves. The people of Central Asia have been relatively generous toward their leaders, tempering expectations of the benefits of independence with some realization of how difficult the transition process is. But the honeymoon period associated with independence may be coming to an end (and particularly in contrast with the states of the south Caucasus, it truly has been a honeymoon period in Central Asia). Notwithstanding the civil war in Tajikistan and the decade of continued fighting in Afghanistan, the situation in Central Asia has been far more peaceful over the past decade than many observers initially anticipated.

However, the relative calm of Central Asia's recent past may not be indicative of its future. As this author and others have pointed out in a number of works, the region faces major security risks that have been fueled in part by the instability in neighboring Afghanistan, the Islamic terrorist networks that took refuge there, and the drug trade that thrived under the instabilities.[1] These dangers will not immediately evaporate with the early efforts of the international community to reconstruct the situation in Afghanistan.[2]

The real danger that these states face comes from within. Advocates of democracy building may be frustrated by some of the changes occurring in Russia, but compared to Central Asia's democracy-building efforts, the Russian situation must clearly be judged as positive. The governments of Kazakhstan and Kyrgyzstan, which had initially given at least limited endorsement to the ideals of democratic reform, began reversing themselves in the mid-1990s, restricting the freedom of action of their citizens and sharply reducing the role that political opposition groups could play. As a result, the elite and the masses in the region are growing more frustrated by the increasing social and economic inequalities that now characterize their societies and by the diminishing opportunities to express their dissatisfaction by legal channels in the existing political system.

Political institution building is faltering in the region, and in many countries there, so is economic reform. The blame should be placed squarely on the region's leaders because of the assumptions that they make about the nature of the challenges they face and their strategies for facing them. This essay explores eight of these assumptions and shows how they are each increasing the risks of instability in the region.

Assumption 1: *Independence in and of itself is a political solution.*

In reality, independence is simply a change in juridical status, albeit a critical one, especially for the ruling elite. But in the absence of institutional development, the only difference for the masses is a psychological change, and the benefits or hardships that it provides are ephemeral. The titular nationalities, those after whom these new nations are named, may have initially believed that they gained status from independence by simply having the name of their ethnic community join the list of sovereign states. But this perception of psychological empowerment is diminishing with time. Those who live in a country should feel some sort of stake in its future, or failing that, feel some hope for their own future or that of their children.

When these states became independent, their governments gained some breathing room to solve the problems that helped bring down the Soviet Union as well as a host of new symbolic weapons to use in their efforts to appease their populations. Central to this was the myth that independence in and of itself would be a source of a better life for the citizens of the newly independent states of Central Asia. However, after ten years of independence, the poor are growing poorer and recovery seems beyond their reach.[3] The memory of the last years of the Soviet Union is still vivid for most of the region's citizens; they know firsthand that governments are brought down when thousands of people take to the streets. To some extent this has a salutary effect. Throughout the region, the old Soviet pessimism that things could get worse still prevails as well. But it is the tenuous nature of the current stability that makes the region's rulers nervous about democracy building—and rulers in Uzbekistan and Turkmenistan nervous about economic reform as well. Even limited economic reform increases popular demands for political empowerment.

The illusion of stability could be short lived. Uzbekistan, in some ways the most "natural" nation-state in all of Central Asia, could prove to be the most devastatingly fragile. Ethnic Uzbeks make up over 70 percent of the nation's population, and they rule over a landmass that seems neither too small nor too large and is resource-rich enough to more than provide for the country's growing population. However, ten years of erratic and ineffective economic reform, combined with a regime that is increasingly repressive politically, could lead the country to split eventually along regional lines. A more likely scenario is that growing popular unrest will turn violent—possibly organized by Islamic activists—and be sustained with popular support. The Central Asian states would not be the first to experience state collapse as a stage in the state-building process. There have been many failed states, particularly in Africa, that preserve their de jure independence but are lawless or chaotic societies in which anarchy or civil unrest prevails.

Assumption 2: *Regional organizations can help solve common problems.*

Weak states make weak partners, and organizations composed almost entirely of weak states are doomed to be ineffective. It is the very weakness of these states, however, that has been both pushing them to establish regional organizations to manage common threats and problems and hindering these organizations once they are established.

All five Central Asian states realize that they are still part of an interconnected regional system created by both geography and Soviet economic planners. These states share a common water system and have long shared a common energy grid and highway system; both the energy grid and the highway system are coming unraveled at considerable cost to all involved. Despite these common interests, for the foreseeable future the region's weaker states will continue to threaten the stability of their somewhat stronger neighbors. We already see this pattern developing in Central Asia, as armed Uzbek groups with bases in Afghanistan have taken refuge in Tajikistan (in particular, fighters of the Islamic Movement of Uzbekistan who are allied with Juman Namangani) and then have sneaked into the high mountains of Kyrgyzstan to get a better vantage point for forays into Uzbekistan's Ferghana Valley.[4] Although Namangani is reported to have been killed in Afghanistan, fighters tied to the Islamic Movement of Uzbekistan still have enclaves near Tavildaar in Tajikistan and will continue to pose a threat.

All of the region's leaders talk of the need for a regional approach to solve the seemingly unhampered movement of international terrorist groups across the new national boundaries, as well as other regional security problems, such as narcotrafficking. It is hoped that new international initiatives to combat international terrorism will have an impact in Central Asia. In the long run, however, water management is likely to prove to be the region's most deadly potential security problem, worse even than the consequences of the capture of the economy by narcobusiness or the impact of the increasingly popular Islamic groups.

Agriculture is a critical sector in all five countries, and the dominant one in the region's two principal cotton producers, Uzbekistan and Turkmenistan. Cotton is a water-intensive crop, and these countries are both downstream users. Central Asia's water originates in the mountain streams of Kyrgyzstan and Tajikistan. This water is still provided for free, while the upkeep of reservoirs is paid for by the country in which they are found. Efforts to create a new regional water-management system have been floundering, despite offers by both the United Kingdom and the United States to sponsor a regional dialogue. Plans for unilateral actions by states rich in water resources (Kyrgyzstan and Tajikistan) are potentially destabilizing.

The Central Asian states have turned to a number of regional configurations in an attempt to solve their problems. Initially the region's leaders hoped that their membership in the Commonwealth of Independent States (CIS) would provide the right forum for addressing issues like this, as well as the region's interconnected energy and transport system. But fearing that Russia would use this organization for its own neo-imperialist purposes, almost none of the region's rulers were willing to see the CIS develop an effective institutional framework. The one exception was Kazakhstan's Nursultan Nazarbayev, who advocated an even closer integration in the form of a Euro–Asian Union (EAU).[5]

One of the major problems that everyone hoped the CIS would address was the question of delineation of national borders, frozen by common consent of the CIS members. However, in 1999, after the incompetence of this organization became wholly apparent to all concerned, Uzbekistan began to delineate unilaterally its own borders, citing the security threat from the February 1999 bombings in Tashkent.[6]

This same action also dealt a serious blow to the Central Asian Economic Community established in 1994.[7] Fears that Russia would dominate the CIS led them to want to develop regional counterweights. But most of the same factors that undermined the CIS have also kept the Central Asian states from developing a viable regional organization. None of these states is willing to surrender sovereignty to a multilateral organization.

Nowhere is this more evident than in the area of trade and finance. Whereas Central Asia could have formed an attractive market of more than fifty million people, each of the countries has adopted some form of economic protectionism, except for World Trade Organization member Kyrgyzstan. In places such as Turkmenistan and Uzbekistan, these barriers support a weak and indefensible currency; in other places such as Kazakhstan, the barriers have been largely retaliatory. The net effect of all of these barriers is to introduce hardships on those millions of Central Asians whose livelihoods are somehow dependent upon cross-border trade and to further dampen the prospects for foreign investment in light industry throughout the region.

Regional cooperation within Central Asia has been further hindered by the sense of historic competition among the peoples of Central Asia, and although this is sometimes exaggerated, there truly is personal competition among the three leaders who once served together as Communist Party leaders under Soviet President Mikhail Gorbachev. Uzbekistan's Islam Karimov, Kazakhstan's Nursultan Nazarbayev, and Turkmenistan's Saparmurat Niyazov all want their country to be seen as the region's most important and to gain the respect and prestige that would accompany leading the region's most important state.[8]

One of the results of this competition is Turkmenistan's refusal to join the various regional organizations that have developed, in keeping with the country's formal posture of positive neutrality, which was formally recognized by the United Nations in 1995. As a result, Turkmenistan has never joined the Central Asian Economic Community and does not participate in the CIS Collective Security Treaty. This was initially called the Tashkent Collective Security Agreement, but the name was changed when Uzbekistan failed to renew its membership in 1999.[9] Current members of the treaty are Armenia, Belarus, Kazakhstan, Kyrgystan, Russia, and Tajikistan.

The Uzbeks, however, did join the Shanghai Cooperation Organization, which includes Russia, China, and four of the five Central Asian countries. It was initially established as the Shanghai Five in April 1996, as a confidence-building effort of former Sino–Soviet border states: China, Kazakhstan, Kyrgyzstan, Russia, and Tajikistan. Its functions were expanded in June 2001 when Uzbekistan became a member and the organization was reestablished to grant all six states equal status. It is too early to know whether this organization will become more than a consultative body, and it is highly unlikely to prove effective in keeping either Russia or China from pursuing its perceived national interests in the region.

Assumption 3: *Central Asian independence will be compromised by the actions of a hegemonic power.*

As a people living in a landlocked region, the Central Asians will always be particularly vulnerable to pressure from the two great powers just beyond their borders and susceptible to internal developments in Afghanistan, Iran, and Pakistan—their principal alternative routes to the sea. While China could turn out to be the regional hegemon of the future, Russia is the great power that all the states of the region fear most. Since independence, the region's leaders have been deeply concerned about Russian interference in their internal affairs. The speed with which independence was achieved led to exaggerated fears that forces external to the region might provoke instability. On the one hand, Russia became the center of their fears; Russian rulers had both dominated and guided some of these areas for more than two hundred years. On the other hand, Central Asia's leaders worry about who will guarantee their security if Russia should withdraw entirely from the region.

Before September 11, no one really expected the United States to replace Russia as a source of collective security guarantees, although all of the region's leaders wanted the United States to play a more active role as a means of keeping pressure on the Russians to respect the sovereignty of the Central Asian states. Kazakhstan, Kyrgyzstan, and Uzbekistan are all active participants in the North Atlantic Treaty Organization's (NATO's) Partnership for Peace (PfP) and have participated in a number of PfP-sponsored cooperative regional conflict-management exercises. All have strengthened bilateral military relations with the NATO countries, especially the United States and Turkey. Before the recent U.S. military engagement in Afghanistan, however, none of the Central Asian states harbored any illusions about forthcoming NATO membership.

The initial 1992 U.S. posture did not significantly improve the security situation in the region, although Washington's championship of alternative pipeline routes for the Caspian is helping to separate and insulate the economies of these countries from the economy of Russia. On the whole,

U.S. policy often had the opposite of its intended effect, serving as a source of pressure on Moscow to remain active in the region, but Russia itself has not completely decided on its future rule and how to accommodate its own diminished capacities.

Even before September 11, there was evidence that Russia was moderating its approach and choosing opportunities for engagement more carefully. Russian behavior in the south Caucasus should not be viewed as an indicator of likely actions in Central Asia, as the former borders on Russia's north Caucasus and is intricately tied to developments in warring Chechnya.

While Russian leaders believe that events in Central Asia could destabilize the situation in the Russian Federation, their priority seems to be dealing with this risk by better demarcating and fortifying their over three-thousand-mile-long border with Kazakhstan and by heightening security at transit points. Russia also is likely to continue to maintain a military base and some 12,000 troops in Tajikistan to help secure the Afghan border, at least through Afghanistan's long transition period.

The newly upgraded U.S. military presence in Central Asia will dampen the process of military cooperation between Russia and the Central Asian states. Russia had been offering technical assistance to the militaries of these countries (and charging for such services), in the hope that these armies would function better at home and be capable of being offensively deployed in neighboring nations. Russia had also been working to reinvigorate the CIS Collective Security Treaty and held joint exercises in Central Asia in 2001.[10] The future of this pact could be called into question if the United States remains an important military actor in the region, even if the U.S. military presence in Central Asia is a small one. Relations between Russia and Uzbekistan, which withdrew from the treaty in 1999, were being developed on a parallel track, and the two militaries were cooperating more closely in 2001 than at any time since the Tajik civil war of 1992, when the Uzbeks provided Russian ground troops with air cover.

Although some of the Central Asian states might like to trade military ties with Russia for a close partnership with the United States, there is little evidence to suggest that the United States will pursue this goal. The degree of future U.S. military engagement in Central Asia will not be decided until the situation in Afghanistan stabilizes. Moreover, the purpose of the bases seems certain to remain one of securing U.S. security interests and not of protecting the Central Asian states against their populations. It is even more unlikely that the United States will use its military presence to somehow bolster the Central Asian states against the potential of either Russian or Chinese aggression.

Nor is the U.S. presence likely to conflict with Russian policies designed to advance the cause of Russian military security. Increasingly Russia had been finding ways to respect the sovereignty of these states, and over time Russia's goals in the region are becoming commercial, and the Russian regime is becoming more interested in lessening security threats in cost-efficient ways. The Russian government under Putin has also become more concerned with placing its relationships with the Central Asian states on stable bilateral footings.

Probably the best example of this new approach is Russia's relationship with Kazakhstan. Kazakhstan's enormous economic potential, the long border that the two states share, and the large Russian community still living in Kazakhstan make it the most important Central Asian state for Russia. The nature of the relationship between the two states is steadily evolving. This is especially apparent since Vladimir Putin's rise to power, as he seems to recognize Nursultan Nazarbayev's greater international experience. It is becoming increasingly obvious that Russia no longer has the ability to dictate the terms of the Russian–Kazakh relationship. However, it is still too early to speak of a real partnership between the two countries.

Kazakhs are also no longer paralyzed by the fear that Russia will become a vigorous defender of the rights of its minority Russian population. The nature of Central Asia's "Russian problem" is evolving as the region's demographic makeup is transformed. Ethnic Russians who are able are likely to continue to leave the region, or at least to dream of doing so.[11] Over the past dozen years much of the able-bodied Russian (and other European) population has moved out of Central Asia, and in places such as Tajikistan, Turkmenistan, and Uzbekistan the Russian population is now largely composed of pensioners.

The decision to leave the region is a rational one. Ethnic Russians have realized that their future opportunities are limited. This is true even in Kazakhstan, where the fate of the Russian language is distinct from that of the Russian nationality—a situation analogous to what happened in postcolonial India and Pakistan, where English remained the leading language long after the departure of the English themselves.

Kazakhstan has steadily been losing its Russian population. With time and the quiet departure of over a million and a half Russians, the Kazakhs have become more confident, while Moscow saw the departure of ethnic

Russians from Kazakhstan as troubling. Because there is no natural geographic boundary between Russia and Kazakhstan, many of Kazakhstan's Russians perceived themselves as living in Russia. During the early years of independence, the Kazakhs feared that the Russians would stage some sort of political provocation to intervene in the name of their "stranded compatriots."

But the problem of abandoned conationals is still very much in evidence throughout the region and is not limited to Russians. All the Central Asian states have stranded conationals, but the Uzbeks have the largest irredentist population of all. Uzbeks are found in each of the other four Central Asian countries chiefly because Uzbekistan is the only country in the region to share borders with all four of its Central Asian neighbors.

In place of the preoccupation with the risk of Russian hegemony, fear of another potential hegemon has arisen—the fear of a Greater Uzbekistan that could alter the picture of Central Asia. Although Uzbekistan's neighbors often dramatically exaggerate Uzbekistan's capacities, it remains true that weak but militarized societies unquestionably make bad neighbors, and civil unrest in Uzbekistan might prove far more destabilizing in the long run to Kazakhstan, Kyrgyzstan, and Tajikistan than any deliberately aggressive policy that Tashkent might pursue. The Uzbeks have the region's largest army, and many in the region fear that the United States will now provide substantial assistance targeted for its modernization.[12] Uzbekistan's neighbors did not want the United States to be engaged exclusively with Tashkent, and Tajikistan and Kyrgyzstan have both provided bases to U.S. troops, and the Kazakhs have offered to do so as well. One reason for concern is that Islam Karimov already set his neighbors on edge by claiming Timur (Tamerlane), the fourteenth-century conqueror, as Uzbekistan's national hero.[13] Their fears were affirmed when the Uzbek leader ordered force to be used in setting the boundaries in disputed villages in Kyrgyzstan and Kazakhstan and then fortified its boundaries with landmines, which have been responsible for several civilian deaths in Kyrgyzstan and Tajikistan.[14]

Much of the Uzbek behavior seems to be imitating that of the Russians, a similarity of which everyone in the region is well aware. Uzbekistan is a major gas supplier, and the old Soviet pipeline system has left Kyrgyzstan and the southern part of Kazakhstan dependent on Uzbek resources. Like the Russians, the Uzbeks are quick to turn off the spigot when debts mount, and also like the Russians, they are not above using these energy supplies to extract other kinds of concessions. For example, at the height of the heating season in winter 2001, the Uzbeks coerced the Kyrgyz to agree in principle to a territorial exchange, where the Kyrgyz got some marginal pastureland and the Uzbeks a direct highway link to the previously isolated Uzbek enclave contained within Kyrgyzstan.[15]

Such actions also fed the desire of leaders in Kazakhstan, Kyrgyzstan, and Tajikistan to remain active members of collective security agreements that include Russia. In contrast to Uzbekistan, Russia is seen as a predictable partner, whose geopolitical interests seem to be diminishing rather than increasing. Russia is also a partner that shows little or no concern with how power is shared in the country, or whether the economy is becoming more transparent. For that reason, Russia could prove to be a helpful friend when power is finally transferred from the region's current leaders to their successors.

Assumption 4: *Political power need not be shared, and political succession can be successfully stage managed to protect the interests of a privileged circle.*

The region's leaders have begun to age and in some cases have become noticeably physically frailer. The seemingly sickest of these, Turkmenistan's Saparmurat Niyazov, is coping with the ravages of passing time by dying his hair and doctoring his portraits that blanket the capital city of Ashgabat and all of the outlying regions to depict a younger and more healthy looking man than in fact exists.[16]

The cult of personality developing around Niyazov—signified by the 120-foot gold-plated statue that sits atop a large tower in Ashgabat and rotates with the sun—is extreme even in the context of Central Asia. Even so, none of the region's leaders have encouraged the development of political institutions that would regulate political competition or attempted to integrate a new generation of potential political leaders into positions of responsibility.

Five years ago, there was still faint hope that two of the region's most popular leaders—Kyrgyzstan's President Akayev and Kazakhstan's President Nazarbayev—might consent to participate in free and fair presidential elections and that after their second terms they would accept existing constitutional limitations and step down from office, setting the precedent for a peaceful transfer of power founded on political institutions.[17] These hopes were short lived. In the mid-1990s Kazakhstan and Kyrgyzstan changed their constitutions and then in the late 1990s once again held presidential elections that fell far short of international norms.[18] Now many of the region's leaders have effectively set themselves up as presidents for life, with little formal planning for what comes after their deaths. Some of the constitutions provide for a formal succession process, but invariably the designated successor's post is filled by a political lightweight whose ambitions pose no threats to the country's incumbent strong-man. In fact, the Turkmen and Uzbek constitutions do not even recognize the possibility of the president dying while in office and provide only for his temporary incapacity.[19]

Everyone in the region is watching with interest efforts by Azerbaijan's President Heydar Aliev to have his son, Ilham, designated as his heir. There is also evidence to suggest that both Nazarbayev and Akayev may try to arrange a transfer of power to one of their children. President Akayev has promised to step down at the end of his current term, although he is also grooming his young son Aidan, who was educated in the United States, to play a prominent role in the country. For his part, Nazarbayev has an ambitious and prominent son-in-law (Timur Kulibayev, the de facto head of Kazakhstan's oil industry), a politically active daughter (Dariga, actually a child from his wife's first marriage), and a nephew who is rising in prominence.

Efforts to reinstate some sort of modern-day princely system are dangerous. Over the past five years, Central Asia's leaders have been honing their "winner-take-all" philosophy, but the societies they rule are complex, filled with populations reluctant to accept a loss of the benefits that they are used to enjoying, and replete with former political and economic stakeholders who are accustomed to accommodation. In every country in the region, members of the elite from disfavored wings (be they regions, hordes, clans, tribes, or families) have been sitting by, waiting for the opportunity to grab more economic and political power. Because institutions to ensure a peaceful transfer of power do not exist, there is no foundation on which people can rest their hopes. There is also no example of a voluntary resignation of power and little reason for optimism that any of the region's leaders will simply retire. Citing the difficulties of the transition process, the rulers of the region have become more interested in insulating themselves from the ruled than in dealing with their grievances, which also allows those in power to accumulate a disproportionate amount of assets.

The greatest retrenchment from democracy is in Kyrgyzstan, where the arrests of opposition leader Topchubek Turgunaliyev from the Erkindik opposition party and former vice president Feliks Kulov were designed to serve as a warning to any who might try to rock the state's boat in any way. Turgunaliyev, a mild-mannered former academic, was initially sentenced to sixteen years in jail but was released in 2001, and Kulov was initially given seven years of hard time and then an additional ten-year sentence was added on. The dampening of opposition has certainly worked to the benefit of the ruling Kyrgyz family, with President Akayev's close and distant relatives likely to have fewer roadblocks placed in their way as they seek to consolidate their economic holdings.

In Kazakhstan the gap between those who are "in" and those who are "out" of favor politically also appears to be broadening and has the potential to upset the delicate balance that has always been maintained among the leading Kazakh clans (and hence the three Kazakh *zhuzes* or hordes) as well as among the various regional elites.[20] Moving the capital to Astana has helped the "in" group consolidate its position. Hundreds of millions of dollars are reputed to have changed hands when Western companies bought rights to Kazakhstan's oil deposits.[21]

The vast differences between the official and unofficial currency rates in Uzbekistan and Turkmenistan have given both these governments a powerful tool to reward the few who are favored. During Soviet rule, leading Uzbek families in both Tashkent and the Ferghana Valley had been able to use the gray areas of Soviet law to function as entrepreneurs and even to accumulate capital. Some of these people became close to President Islam Karimov, who himself comes from Samarkand, but most of this elite has been kept at arm's length by the regime, and the slow pace of economic reform has given them little opportunity to accumulate more capital.

With every passing year the number of "winners" in Central Asia seems to grow smaller. Titular nationalities are being rewarded at the expense of other groups. In all five countries it has become more difficult for those outside of the ruling circles to share in the economic and political spoils, and the criteria for inclusion in the inner circles are growing ever more restrictive.

Assumption 5: *There is no popular support for democratic development.*

The region's leaders are quick to defend the political choices that they are making as natural and in keeping with the culture and history of the population they are ruling. But popular indifference is not to blame for the lack of progress in establishing democratic regimes in the Central Asian states so much as the change in strategies of the region's leaders. The region's leaders claim that democratic systems are too dangerous to introduce in the current social and security environment in Central Asia, and that the various peoples of Central Asia lack the cultural underpinnings necessary to support a democratic polity. It is easy to find nondemocratic or authoritarian episodes in the history of any people, and the histories of those living in Central Asia are no exception. But it is racist to claim that one people is more or less fit for democracy than another. Similarly racist is the assumption that the Central Asians somehow want rule by an "iron fist." Throughout Central Asia, a committed minority remains in place who is eager to see democratic development move forward, but the ruling powers feel confident that these groups can be isolated.

President Akayev's most prominent critic, Feliks Kulov, who is serving a lengthy term in a maximum security prison on charges that he was initially acquitted of, had ample opportunity to flee the country between the two arrests, but he chose to stay and become a political symbol instead. His fate continues to provoke small but regular public protests and demonstrations. Kazakhstan's Akezhan Kazhegeldin decided to put personal safety first and remains abroad, where he is regularly threatened with arrest by Kazakh law enforcement's use of international channels. But Kazhegeldin has become an active international lobbyist for the cause of democratic reform in Kazakhstan and maintains a well-funded and active organization in the country that tries to help sustain both an independent press and a labor movement.

Political consensus-building measures in the aftermath of Tajikistan's civil war are at least worthy of mention, because that country is the only one in the region in which the government has reached some accommodation with Islamic religious activists, and it has done so in a framework that supports democratic goals. Here, too, a strong and extralegal presidency is developing, and this, rather than Tajikistan's Islamist population, is the cause of the country's growing political abuses.

Initially, Uzbekistan had the best developed network of nongovernmental organizations at the time of independence, including two fledgling secular parties, Erk and Birlik.[22] The principal founders of both parties were driven into exile, minor figures were arrested, and the leadership's families have been persecuted. Nonetheless, there remains a core group of democratic activists in Uzbekistan, including local human rights monitors, who continue to pursue what are now clandestine activities, risking arrest and torture of themselves or close relatives. The nongovernmental organization movement in Turkmenistan was the least well established, and that country's political activists suffer a fate analogous to that of the Uzbeks. However, they received a real boost with the defection of former foreign minister Boris Sheikhmuradov in October 2001, who has formed the People's Democratic Movement of Turkmenistan.

Assumption 6: *Ethnonationalism can be the building block of patriotism.*

The regimes in power feel competent to deal with the threats from the new democratic groups, but they continue to be concerned about competing ideologies based on regional, subethnic, or supra-ethnic ties. To counter these ideologies, they are trying to use Soviet-style social-engineering techniques to create new political loyalties that use the Soviet-era ethnic divisions as the building blocks of a new national consensus. Some of these efforts, such as those of the Kazakhs and Kyrgyz, are more focused on tolerance for ethnic minorities, while others, such as the Uzbeks, are trying to recast ethnonationalism as civic patriotism.

Most Central Asians' understanding of nationality and ethnic identity is still shaped by the Stalin-era divisions of society that divided the Soviet population into well over a hundred ethnic communities, with each enjoying varying legal statuses based on size, history, economic capacity, and location. Central Asia's five principal nationalities—the Uzbeks, Kazakhs, Kyrgyz, Tajiks, and Turkmen—were all deemed worthy of union republic status and so received independence. However, it is proving difficult to sell political slogans to populations weary of ideological manipulation by the state. Independence has led to a growing sense of ethnic empowerment by the titular nationality, but this is not translating itself into political loyalty, in part because the state is doing such a poor job of meeting popular expectations in the social sphere.

At the same time, the process of postcolonial societal redefinition has already begun, although as in Soviet times, nationality continues to be recorded on passports and most other official documents. Assimilation is already taking place among those who are deemed "marginal" to the titular nationality—people who came from ethnically mixed families or were members of subethnic groups that are represented in two different national communities, such as the Kipchak, a tribal group found among Kazakhs, Kyrgyz, and Uzbeks. Consequently, it is not particularly difficult for an Uzbek of

Kipchak ancestry living in southern Kazakhstan to reidentify with the Kazakhs.

While the dominant nationalities in each country are consolidating, they are also breaking down. Both patterns are often observed in the same country, where in some areas new groups are coming to identify with the dominant nationality, while in other regions there is an increase in subethnic identity, be it clan, *zhuz*, or a local territory. It is still unclear in many cases whether the dominant political influence will be centripetal or centrifugal forces. Take the case of Bukhara, for example, where there is a very strong regional identity. In some ways this is good. In Bukhara it is not particularly important whether one is of Uzbek or Tajik background; rather, it is important that one is native to the region. Many people speak both languages freely, and this Bukharan identity could form the basis of an ethnically blind sense of Uzbek civic patriotism. Or, alternatively, it could be the basis of a serious separatist movement. Subethnic identities are strong enough in both Kyrgyzstan and Uzbekistan to successfully undermine either state, if the right preconditions were in place.

Assumption 7: *Islam is fundamentally dangerous and must be contained.*

In the absence of a civil society, there are few secular political institutions around which opposition can coalesce. Islam, especially the mosque and the medresseh, is about the only organizational center available to those in opposition to the regime, and it is very difficult to restrict popular access to it. As a result, the advocacy of Islamic goals can be useful for both the regime's supporters as well as its detractors. Everything depends on the rules of the game, and these are still in flux.

The challenge posed by Islam remains particularly acute in Uzbekistan. Islam is deeply rooted in many parts of the country, and the precedent of competition among Islamic fundamentalists, modernists, and Islamic conservatives is well established. All three traditions withstood the vicissitudes of Soviet rule. Some of today's radical groups have their roots in an anti-Russian uprising that occurred in the Ferghana Valley in 1898, and a few of the leaders have even studied with a "holy man" who witnessed the revolt as a young child and who, much to Soviet displeasure, survived to a very old age.

Uzbek President Islam Karimov believes that Islam can be managed, as do most of his colleagues. In fact, all of Central Asia's leaders still remain committed to the social-engineering approach that characterized Soviet rule. They believe strongly that religion can be managed by the state, as can the development of Islam, and that governments are competent enough to influence the social evolution of society. The Central Asian elite, of course, is not formally against Islam, but it is very wary of revivalist or fundamentalist Islam that teaches living by "the exact teachings of the book." Central Asia's leaders wish to keep their republics as secular states and prevent devout Muslims from forcing all of their co-religionists into the public observance of the faith. The relationship of religion to mass belief is much more complex and interactive than the region's leaders credit it. The governments of Central Asia are in no position to regulate the religious beliefs of the masses, but they may exert their influence on social processes. In trying to do so, however, they could inadvertently trigger social explosions.

Assumption 8: *Things must get better.*

So often it is argued that ten years is but a blink of an eye in the life of a newly independent nation and that things are certain to improve with time. The invocation of the colonial past is becoming a part of the litany used in explaining problems or insufficiencies in the process of political and economic development. It is a ready excuse offered up for any problem, be it a preexisting one or something that has been exacerbated by recent policies.

The bottom line is that the Russian and Soviet colonial past is offered up as an explanation for why the population of these regions should not expect too much of their governments. U.S. and other Western policy makers and pundits have not always played a helpful role. Competition with Russia for control of these countries' natural resources has increased U.S. willingness to "play the colonial card." The insufficiencies of the old Soviet system were legion—supporting a resource-based, export-oriented economy that placed "common" needs above the local ones—but it is also dangerous to oversimplify the Soviet past.

Ten years of independence has led to even deeper entrenchment of the export-oriented, export-based economy that the Soviets were so often criticized for creating. For oil- and gas-rich states such as Kazakhstan and Turkmenistan, this could someday lead to a filling of state coffers with money aplenty for downstream industrial projects. In the case of Uzbekistan, however, this has meant increased dependency on the production and export of raw cotton, a crop that damages the environment and is still grown on cooperatively owned plots and sold to the government at state-determined purchase prices.

Central Asia's population still shares the hopes and expectations that were produced by the political and economic thaw of the late Soviet years across all of the USSR. Independence further kindled these hopes, which were never uniformly expressed across society. Those living in cities had one set of expectations, particularly those living in republic capitals, and those living in the countryside had quite different hopes. The one shared belief they have is that ten years is a very short time in the life of a nation and that the transition to independence is by definition a difficult one. Naturally, it follows from this that the lives of most people have grown more difficult, but (as the myth goes) people can now take consolation from the fact that they are living as masters in their own country and that conditions are certain to improve with time.

Western observers may choose to accept this explanation, yet this myth is becoming increasingly harder for most people living in the region to believe. Anyone traveling throughout Central Asia cannot fail to notice worsening social conditions: growing illiteracy, deteriorating health conditions, rising unemployment, a growing gap between the city and the countryside, and so on. It is becoming harder for people to figure out what they have in fact become the masters of. In countries such as Uzbekistan, the state is more brutal today than at any time since the Stalin era, and their treatment of devout Muslims is almost indistinguishable from the punishments meted out to them during the "Great Terror." For those living on the ruined state and collective farms of rural Kazakhstan and Kyrgyzstan, gaining control of one's fate feels an awful lot like abandonment. Most of the farmers lack the resources to buy or work the land effectively, and neither national nor local authorities show interest in helping them cope with the economic challenges of transition.

Overall, people are simply losing confidence that things will improve anytime soon. Rumors of signing bonuses by foreign firms and billions of dollars of unaccounted-for international assistance circulate widely in each of the Central Asian countries. Although such rumors cannot be proven, there are enough visible signs of conspicuous consumption by a small new elite to give substance to the stories that these same people have vast fortunes hidden away abroad. Decolonization in Central Asia is becoming increasingly more reminiscent of what occurred in parts of Sub-Saharan Africa, where a number of states have spent the past forty years stepping backwards from the levels of development that characterized their countries and their populations at the time of independence or in the first decade after independence was achieved.

Truly, ten years is not a long time, and the negative trends described here could prove to be mere temporary glitches in the very difficult process of transition. But given the political and economic trajectories chosen by just about all of Central Asia's leaders, it is easier to imagine that conditions will continue to deteriorate. Perhaps when the ruling families have sated their ambitions for wealth and power, things might improve. But the rulers and the ruled seem to tell time in different ways, whether the international community wants to take note of this or not. Most people need the hope that things will improve in either their lifetimes or that of their children. Those born in the Soviet Union were raised on a diet of "deferred gratification," and all independence seems to have brought is a new version of the old dietary staple.

Notes

1. Martha Brill Olcott and Natalia Udalova Zwart, "Drug Trafficking on the Great Silk Road: The Security Environment in Central Asia," Working Paper no. 11 (Washington, D.C.: Carnegie Endowment for International Peace, Russia/Eurasia Program, 2000); International Crisis Group, *Central Asia: Crisis Conditions in Three States*, International Crisis Group Asia Report no. 7 (Brussels: International Crisis Group, August 2000); Nancy Lubin et al., *Calming the Ferghana Valley* (New York: Council on Foreign Relations, 1999).

2. Martha Brill Olcott, "Preventing New Afghanistans: A Regional Strategy for Reconstruction," Policy Brief no.11 (Washington, D.C.: Carnegie Endowment for International Peace, January 2002).

3. International Crisis Group, *Incubators of Conflict: Central Asia's Localised Poverty and Social Unrest*, International Crisis Group Asia Report no. 16 (Brussels/Osh: International Crisis Group, July 2001).

4. The Ferghana Valley, which spreads across part of the territory of Tajikistan, Kyrgyzstan, and Uzbekistan, was the location of the August 1999 incursion into Kyrgyzstan by Tajikistan-based terrorists.

5. In addition to convening an intergovernmental parliamentary assembly, the EAU member states were to share a common currency and common foreign economic policies. Highlights of Nazarbayev's plan for the EAU were published in *Izvestiya*, June 8, 1994, p. 2, as translated

in RusData DiaLine, *Russian Press Digest*. Additional information is available in *Itar-Tass*, April 21, 1994.

6. On February 16, 1999, a series of bomb blasts ripped through Uzbekistan's government headquarters, killing fifteen people and prompting waves of government action against the Islamic extremist groups considered responsible for the bombings as well as a security threat to the entire nation.

7. The Central Asian Union, the precursor to the Central Asian Economic Community, was created by the leaders of Uzbekistan, Kazakhstan, and Kyrgyzstan in July 1994 and was renamed in July 1998 when Tajikistan joined the organization. See Martha Brill Olcott, Anders Åslund, and Sherman Garnett, *Getting It Wrong: Regional Cooperation and the Commonwealth of Independent States* (Washington, D.C.: Carnegie Endowment for International Peace, 1999), pp. 157–66.

8. All three presidents—Karimov, Nazarbayev, and Niyazov—were heads of their respective Soviet Socialist Republics before the collapse of the USSR. Each went on to become the elected president of the resulting independent republic. Nazarbayev has since extended his term in 1995 and was reelected in 1999, after having disqualified the other candidates. Niyazov similarly was reelected after running unopposed in 1992 and then extended his term by a 1994 referendum before being voted "President for Life" by Turkmenistan's parliament in 1999.

9. The Tashkent Collective Security Treaty, signed in May 1992, established the heads of state as a Collective Security Council. The signatories were Armenia, Kazakhstan, Kyrgyzstan, Russia, Tajikistan, and Uzbekistan, later joined by Azerbaijan, Belarus, and Georgia. Azerbaijan, Georgia, and Uzbekistan formally withdrew from the Tashkent Treaty in April 1999. For more, see Olcott, Åslund, and Garnett, *Getting It Wrong*, pp. 77–108.

10. Joint command exercises called the "Southern Shield of the Commonwealth" were held in March 2000 and April 2001. During these exercises, troops from Kazakhstan, Kyrgyzstan, Russia, and Tajikistan, along with participants from Armenia and Belarus, were drilled and prepared for possible terrorist acts in the Central Asian theater of operations. See Vladimir Georgiyev, "Maneuvers in Moscow," *Defense and Security,* April 6, 2001, p. 5.

11. From 1998 to 2000 alone, the Federal Migration Service of the Russian Federation estimated that 927,000 former Soviet citizens emigrated to the Russian Federation; most of these were ethnic Russians. Note that these figures do not include people who have emigrated to other CIS states, Germany, Israel, or the United States—all of which have received sizeable numbers of former residents of Central Asia.

12. Although Uzbekistan still has the largest army in the region, the total size of Kazakhstan's armed forces (64,000) now exceeds that of Uzbekistan (59,100), in large part to better protect the Kazakh state against its southern neighbor. Kazakhstan has also created new border districts along its southern border. Uzbekistan's army consists of 50,000 troops, followed by Kazakhstan's 45,000, Turkmenistan's 14,500, Kyrgyzstan's 6,600, and Tajikistan's 6,000. See International Institute for Strategic Studies, *The Military Balance 2000–2001* (London: Oxford University Press, 2000).

13. Amir Timur (1336–1405) controlled a territory stretching from Asia Minor to India. Timur, who prided himself on being a descendant of Chinggis Khan, was a member of the Mongol White Horde and lived before the present-day Uzbek people were ethnically constituted.

See Edward A. Allworth, *The Modern Uzbeks* (Stanford, Calif.: Hoover Institution Press, 1990), pp. 242–8.

14. In August 2000, there was a border clash between Uzbek guards and Kyrgyz villagers, resulting in several serious injuries; there have also been exchanges of fire along the Kazakh–Uzbek border. There have been at least twelve reported deaths from landmines in Kyrgyzstan and thirty deaths in Tajikistan. See "OSCE Criticizes Mine Fields on Tajik-Uzbek Border," *The Times of India,* January 17, 2001, p. 3.

15. The enclave of Sokh was juridically part of Uzbekistan but fully physically contained within Kyrgyzstan. When word of this agreement, signed on February 26, 2001, leaked out in April, the Kyrgyz were quick to stress its provisional character, but members of Kyrgyzstan's parliament began to call for President Askar Akayev's resignation.

16. Niyazov suffers from respiratory problems and had an operation on his leg to remove a blood clot in 1994, heart surgery in 1997, and in February 2000 cancelled a meeting with Armenian President Robert Kocharian due to an unspecified illness.

17. Presidential elections were originally set for early 1996 in Kazakhstan and December 1995 in Kyrgyzstan. Constitutional provisions set term limits to two consecutive terms in both countries.

18. Presidential elections were again held in Kazakhstan in January 1999 and in October 2000 in Kyrgyzstan. In both elections the presidents' principal opponents were effectively barred from running. In Kazakhstan, former prime minister Akezhan Kazhegeldin was banned because he had a record of administrative arrest, earned by holding an unsanctioned political rally. In Kyrgyzstan, former vice president Feliks Kulov opted not to take a mandatory language test after other candidates who were native speakers of Kyrgyz had failed it. Kazhegeldin, who served as prime minister of Kazakhstan from 1994 to 1997, headed the Republican People's Party of Kazakhstan (RPPK). Lieutenant-General Feliks Kulov was Kyrgyzstan's former vice president, as well as former minister of defense, former governor of the Chui region, former mayor of Bishkek, and leader of the Ar-Namys (Dignity) political party.

19. Article 60 of Turkmenistan's constitution states that "the President may be prematurely relieved of office if incapable of meeting her or his obligations because of sickness." In such a case, power would be temporarily transferred to the Chair of Parliament. Likewise, Article 96 of Uzbekistan's constitution holds that "if, for reasons of health … the President of Uzbekistan is not able to meet her or his obligations … an acting President will be chosen by Parliament from among the deputies" to serve for three months until a general election.

20. The Kazakhs trace from three *zhuzes* or hordes: the Small Horde in western and central Kazakhstan, the Middle Horde in north-central and northeastern Kazakhstan, and the Great Horde in southern Kazakhstan.

21. See Steve LeVine and Bill Powell, "A President and His Counselor," *Newsweek,* July 2, 2000.

22. Noted Uzbek poet Muhammad Solih formed Erk (Freedom) in 1990, and Abdurahim Pulat and Timur Valiyev formed Birlik (Unity) in 1988.

13

What Is the Future of Chechnya?

Anatol Lieven

The reordering of U.S. security priorities in the wake of the terrorist attacks of September 11, 2001, has placed the Chechen war in a new international context. What effect if any this will have on the situation on the ground is still unclear and may not become apparent for a considerable time. From the 1999 invasion of Chechnya to the period immediately before September 11, U.S. rhetoric attacking Russian policy and actions had little visible effect on the course of the Chechen war but did succeed in infuriating the Russian government and army, as well as many ordinary Russians. This lack of U.S. influence was not surprising, because the United States did not back up its rhetoric with concrete threats or inducements.

Now that official U.S. language has become much more sympathetic to the Russian position, it would seem possible in principle that in the future the United States might play the role of an honest broker in persuading more moderate Chechen separatist leaders to abandon the radical Chechen and international Mujahedin forces and to surrender on reasonable terms, including a restoration of full Chechen autonomy under certain strict conditions.

However, for Russia to welcome or permit any such U.S. involvement, an entirely new U.S.–Russian relationship must develop. Essential elements of such a relationship would have to be full Russian cooperation with the United States in the struggle against terrorist groups across the Middle East; U.S. abandonment of attempts to "roll back" Russian influence in the southern Caucasus and elsewhere; and a Russian conviction of strong and unqualified U.S. commitment to Russian territorial integrity. Whether fulfillment of all or indeed any of these conditions is really possible will become apparent only in the course of the next several years.

In crafting U.S. policy toward Chechnya, U.S. leaders and officials should remember several sobering facts. It is probably true that the renewed Russian military intervention of October 1999 was a mistake from Russia's point of view. It is also true that the Russian campaign has involved numerous crimes and great human suffering. However, if Russia had not reoccupied Chechnya, then the U.S. government and media after September 11, 2001, would undoubtedly have identified that territory as a prime refuge for Osama bin Laden and his lieutenants if they were forced out of Afghanistan. They would have had no choice but to do so, given the openly acknowledged links of international Mujahedin fighting in Chechnya to bin Laden's al Qaeda organization.

Roots of the Chechen Conflict

The basic cause of the Chechen wars of the post-Soviet period is not complicated and does not require elaborate conspiracy theories to explain. In many parts of the world, national groups—or powerful forces within them—are seeking to remove their territories from the control of larger states and are meeting fierce resistance from those states. In all too many parts of the world, this has led to ferocious wars, usually characterized by a very high level of atrocity on both sides. By contrast, the number of cases in which a state has let a constituent part of its territory (rather than an overseas colony) secede peacefully is extremely few.

Wars have been especially characteristic of the end of empires: in the form of both rebellions against the imperial power in the name of independence, and post-imperial rebellions against the successor states. The Chechen wars since 1994 (like the Kurdish revolts against post-Ottoman Turkey) are relatively unusual, however, in that they combine features of both such struggles. The reason for this difference is of course that the Russian and Ottoman empires were not classical West European overseas empires, but land empires in which the "imperial" people were heavily mixed up with minority ethnic groups. This makes it extremely difficult for

Russia simply to pull out from Chechnya, as the West European colonial powers eventually did from most of their colonies, or to insulate itself from "postcolonial" developments in the area.

Nonetheless, for the Chechen problem of the 1990s to have reached its present disastrous state, five additional elements were needed:

- Calculations of dominant groups in Moscow concerning their own political advancement;

- Extreme demoralization and corruption of the Russian armed forces, which have contributed greatly to the brutality of their behavior;

- Striking and chronic inability of the Chechens to create a modern political nationalism and basic state institutions and habits;

- Strong historical tendencies in the Chechen social and cultural tradition toward behavior now generally dubbed criminal; and

- Entry into Chechnya—as into Afghanistan in the 1980s—of international Muslim radicals whose agendas stretched beyond Chechnya's borders.

None of these factors in itself is unique to the Chechen case, but taken together, the result is a conflict that has been especially resistant to solution, either by the victory of one side or by peaceful settlement. Chechnya looks as if it has become yet another long-running, bitter, intractable struggle similar to those in Kashmir and elsewhere. Like many such wars, the one in Chechnya has the potential to cause instability in the surrounding region through terrorism, refugees, and Russian pressure on neighboring countries to deny rebels "safe havens."

The deeper historical, cultural, and economic roots of the Chechen disaster of the past decade are beyond the scope of this essay. When it comes to shorter-term causes, however, two events were critical. The first was the Chechen national revolution of 1991. Chechnya was unique among the autonomous republics of the Russian Federation—and rare in the Soviet Union as a whole—in that armed nationalist protestors succeeded in overthrowing the local Communist Party authorities and introducing a nationalist government, headed in Chechnya by former Soviet major general Djokhar Dudayev. Everywhere else in Russia's regions, the existing communist leaderships simply renamed themselves, made certain tactical adjustments, and continued in power. Outside Russia, in Georgia, Azerbaijan, and Tajikistan, the communist authorities were overthrown, but nationalist groups failed to consolidate power, and former communist bosses later returned to rule based on old communist structures and patronage networks.

In Chechnya, this did not occur. Instead, power was seized and retained by a mixture of armed nationalist radicals and gangsters released from jail, over whom Dudayev exercised a form of shaky hegemony. The structures of the modern state, and even of modern life, crumbled and were not replaced. To a greater extent even than in the rest of Russia, wages and pensions went unpaid, state funding for public services collapsed, and the formal economy largely vanished. Public misery was diminished only by organized crime and a vast smuggling trade that distributed benefits through family and personal links as well as through Islamic charities. The effects of growing criminality on the Chechen population were at this time still checked by extremely strong social traditions inhibiting attacks on other Chechens. However, these traditions did not protect the local Russian population, most of which fled during this period.

The Dudayev regime was able to fight off challenges to its rule, first from the Chechen parliament in the first half of 1993 and then from the Russian-backed opposition in the north in the summer and autumn of 1994. The defeat of the opposition forces (and Russian "volunteers") in Grozny on November 26, 1994, precipitated the direct Russian military intervention the following month.

This intervention, and the war from 1994 to 1996 that followed, was the second critical event of the 1990s. It must be stressed that although the situation in Chechnya between 1991 and 1994 was certainly atrocious by contemporary European standards, it did not justify the launching of a brutal war. Although the economy was highly criminalized, and four armed hijacks of bus passengers in southern Russia by Chechen gangs took place from 1993 to 1994, nothing compared with the explosion of banditry that took place from 1996 to 1999. Chechen tradition certainly contributed, but the brutality and destruction of the war from 1994 to 1996 were chiefly responsible.

The inability of General Maskhadov to control this banditry after Russia withdrew its forces in 1996 was a central reason for Moscow's loss of faith in the Chechen president. Exasperation with the Chechen administration was understandable: Victims included two senior Russian envoys who were supposedly under Maskhadov's personal protection; and according to Western diplomats involved in negotiations for the release of Western hostages, the kidnapping gang of Arbi Barayev was under the protection of his relative, Maskhadov's then deputy, Vice President Vaqa Arsanov. Many Chechen kidnappings were accompanied by appalling cruelty, including torture, mutilation, and gang rape, with videos of these scenes sent to the victims' families and employers to increase the pressure for ransom. Among the victims were Russian journalists and human rights activists who from 1994 to 1996 had played a key role in mobilizing Russian sympathy for the suffering of the Chechens and undermining Russian public support for the war.

A second phenomenon from the first Chechen war was the appearance in Chechnya of a group of international Muslim radicals (so-called Wahabis, although use of this term is highly inexact) headed by Habib Abdurrahman Khattab, an Arab who like many of his soldiers had fought against the Soviets in Afghanistan (and was later poisoned to death in 2002, apparently by Russian intelligence). As in Afghanistan, Bosnia, and elsewhere, the idea of fighting a war of resistance against enemies of Islam, and creating a safe haven for their wider international activities, drew these men into the fray.

This force has received support from Osama bin Laden's al Qaeda and radical networks in the Middle East. Abu Daud, a senior aide to Osama bin Laden, confirmed this support to Associated Press, and these links were also published openly on the English-language web site of the Chechen Mujahedin, Qoqaz.net. [1] It was also confirmed by Egyptian security forces, who in July 2001 carried out a major operation against Egyptian Islamist radicals who were raising funds and recruits from Chechnya.[2] Khattab and his allies also received support from the Taliban in Afghanistan, the only state to have recognized Chechnya's independence.

Connections between parts of the Chechen separatist forces and the terrorist groups operating in the wider Muslim world were therefore anything but secret. U.S. official recognition of this in the wake of the September 11 attacks had the air of a major concession to Russia and was widely portrayed as a reversal of previous U.S. policy—a sad comment on the balance and honesty of previous U.S. official and unofficial positions.

The importance of Khattab's force is unclear. Russian claims of "6,000 Islamic mercenaries" in Chechnya and Georgia are a ludicrous exaggeration. To judge by the casualties (*Shaheeds*, or martyrs) reported on the Mujahedin web site, Qoqaz.net, a closer estimate might be in the low hundreds (more sober Russian reports speak of some two hundred "Arabs" having participated in the invasion of Dagestan in August 1999, and Shamil Basayev said afterwards that five Arabs and three Turks were killed).[3] Abu Daud claimed that bin Laden's group had sent 400 men to Chechnya, but there has been no independent confirmation of this. Supplies of money are probably of considerably greater importance—to buy arms on the post-Soviet black market, most of which are from the Russian military itself.

The growth of this group's power in Chechnya played a key part in precipitating the second war and in making any solution to it so extremely difficult. In 1998, Khattab's group forged an alliance with the Chechen warlord Shamil Basayev and with Dagestani Islamist radicals dedicated to the "liberation" of the Russian autonomous republic of Dagestan and its union with Chechnya in a single Islamic state. Toward this end, they launched a series of attacks that culminated in a large-scale incursion into Dagestan in August 1999 (on April 17, 1999, in Grozny at the Second Congress of the Peoples of Ichkeria and Dagestan, Basayev announced the formation of units to fight for this goal).

The Russian government has accused them of complicity in a series of bombings in Dagestan, Moscow, and elsewhere. Responsibility for these acts is in fact very unclear (and has been widely attributed to the Russian secret services themselves), but Khattab's links to Osama and his group lend these Russian accusations a certain plausibility.[4] A group of Dagestanis and Chechens has been brought to trial for the first of the bomb attacks in Buinaksk, Dagestan, that killed sixty-four people. Some of the accused have supposedly confessed to planting the bomb on the orders of Khattab, but this by no means constitutes conclusive proof. At the time, Shamil Basayev indicated that those responsible were Dagestanis taking revenge for the destruction of their villages by the Russians, although since then he has also accused the Russians themselves of responsibility.[5]

It is impossible therefore to imagine any Russian government agreeing to a settlement that does not involve the destruction or expulsion of Mujahedin fighters and their Chechen allies from Chechnya. In principle, this should be possible, given that the Wahabis are hated by the great majority of Chechens, and especially by Maskhadov and his followers, against whom they fought from 1998 to 1999. However, Maskhadov never managed to expel the Wahabis during those years. Their alliance with Basayev and other Chechen warlords gives them considerable local strength, as does their recruitment of young Chechen fighters impressed by their courage, their fighting spirit, their ideology, and—if Afghan experience is anything to go by—their access to money.

Conduct of the War

Prior to September 11, 2001, the prospects for meaningful negotiations, let alone peace, seemed very slight. There was little talk of such negotiations in either the Russian government or Maskhadov's camp, let alone among the more radical fighters. The war had settled down to a brutal stalemate with no end in sight. According to the Russian magazine *Itogi* in April 2000 (when it was still fully independent of the Putin administration),

> serious, constructive negotiations are now simply impossible. The main distinction between the current Chechen war and the last one is that there is nothing on which to come to any agreement. That time, inscribed on the militants' banners was the slogan of independence, and Moscow was fighting for territorial integrity. In such a case, the object of the bargaining was clear: the level of autonomy. Now the question of independence—of status in general—may be considered to have been taken off the agenda.
>
> Not a single responsible politician today views seriously the possibility of a state existence of Chechnya. Even Sergei Kovalev says that his "hair stirs on his head" at the very thought of "a free and independent Ichkeria." Russian troops this time went into Chechnya under the banner of destroying the gangster formations and returning Ichkeria to Russia's legal sphere. This phrasing of the question from the beginning does not presuppose negotiations: What is there to bargain about here? The peaceful Chechen population would be entirely ready to agree with the goals, but not with the reality of the military operation. Now, having tasted in full measure both the delights of "independence" and the monstrousness of more "constitutional order," the majority of Chechens are disoriented and reiterate one thing: "Let the Russians get out of here and take their Wahabi pawns with them." This formula likewise cannot be the subject of negotiations.[6]

My own interviews with Chechen refugees in Ingushetia and Georgia confirm these sentiments as an accurate picture of the opinion of most ordinary Chechens. The problem is that it is founded on a self-deception. There is no serious evidence whatsoever that the international Mujahedin and their local allies are in fact "Russian pawns"; and given the experience from 1996 to 1999, there can be no guarantee that in the absence of Russian troops, President Maskhadov and the mass of the Chechen people could expel these forces.

Nonetheless, from the beginning of 2001 there were certain signs on the Russian side that the top leadership at least had come to understand the counterproductive nature of much of the Russian strategy—and Russian crimes—to date and was searching for new approaches. Thus in January 2001, President Putin announced a new strategy involving the scaling down of military operations and a shift of responsibility for combating the "terrorists" to the Russian domestic intelligence service (FSB) and the pro-Russian Chechen police and paramilitaries.[7] In March 2002 the Russian commander in Chechnya, General Moltenskoy, issued an order setting down strict rules for the conduct of search and arrest operations by Russian troops—though there were well-based doubts about how much effect this order would have in practice.

The reason for this change in approach appears to have combined both domestic political calculation and military reality on the ground. In the first months of the war, the Russian army achieved a series of considerable successes, capturing Grozny and the other main population centers of Chechnya, and killing as many as 2,000 separatist fighters in the battle for Grozny and the Chechen retreat that followed.[8] These victories were especially striking of course when contrasted with the shambolic conduct of operations from 1994 to 1996, ensuring that Russian public support for the war would remain high for some time.

In the second half of 2000, however, as the war dragged on with no end in sight and casualties began to mount, Russian opinion polls began to show a significant drop in public support for the war (though thanks to Chechen behavior from 1996 to 1999, as of the spring of 2002, public support remained considerably higher than it had been at any time in the first war).[9] The Putin administration thus appears to have been anxious to do something to give the Russian public the impression of at least a qualified victory and a promise of a reduction in Russian casualties.

More important, however, was a growing recognition that the antipartisan strategy to date was not merely failing but was in many ways actively counterproductive—as the head of the pro-Russian Chechen administration, Ahmed Kadyrov, argued forcefully to Putin. Sweeps involving large numbers of troops gave the rebel forces ample warning time to elude the intended net. The acute demoralization of most of the Russian forces and their unwillingness to risk their lives by attacking the Chechens on the ground are also key reasons for the rebels' repeated escapes.

As was the case with the U.S. force in Vietnam, the tendency of units under even light fire from rebels has been to stop and call for air and artillery strikes, at which point the rebels scatter and escape to fight another day. In addition, the marked unwillingness of the Russian forces to carry out foot patrols by small units—especially at night—has allowed small groups of rebels to move around virtually at will in many areas. As a result, while the Russian forces have scored some successes in destroying rebel groups and killing or capturing their leaders, as of the spring of 2002, low-level attacks on the Russian forces and assassinations of pro-Russian Chechens continued on a daily basis. On April 12, 2001, in a stroke that underlined the extreme vulnerability of such figures, Kadyrov's chief deputy, Adam Deniyev, was assassinated while on television.

In the spring of 2002, the Russians were losing around ten men a week to low-intensity attacks, and the total Russian dead in the war by summer 2001 was approaching 4,000.[10] The Russian command issued continual statements about its success in capturing weapons and capturing and killing "terrorists," but as with U.S. "body counts" in Vietnam, there is good reason to suspect both that these claims have been considerably inflated and that many of the Chechen "fighters" killed or arrested have in fact been wholly or mostly innocent Chechen civilians.

The same appears true of those arrested at Russian military checkpoints in Chechnya. There is ample evidence to suggest that as the war has progressed, more and more of those detained were not even seriously suspected of any crime by the Russian soldiers involved. The real motive was sometimes to force local communities to hand over weapons, but more often simply to make money by extorting ransoms from the detainees' families (the reported sums demanded have ranged up to $5,000 per detainee).[11] The lower ranks are no doubt encouraged to engage in such behavior by the corruption of many of their superiors.[12]

This brings out an important distinction to be made in Chechnya and all wars of this kind. There is a difference between war crimes that are the direct responsibility of the state and the rebel movement concerned, and crimes that are the work of individual soldiers or groups of soldiers acting on their own initiative and for their own pleasure or profit. Apart from numerous individual testimonies, the discovery in March 2001 of a mass grave near a major Russian detention center ("filtration camp") strongly suggested that widespread abuses have occurred. The Russian military Procuracy has opened some forty criminal cases against soldiers accused of such abuses, but there can be no doubt that this only scratched the surface of the crimes and atrocities that have been committed.[13]

It is important to note, however, that the brutality of the Russian armed forces has been reflected not only in appalling behavior against Chechen civilians but also in atrocious bullying of younger Russian conscripts (*dyedovshchina*, or granddadism). Demoralization among the troops is reflected in Russia's increasing difficulty in recruiting contract soldiers to fight in Chechnya. In 2000, contract soldiers made up 38 percent of all defense ministry soldiers in Chechnya, but by the spring of 2001, they were being hired for three-month contracts or even, it is reported, for specific operations—more like "free companies" of the Hundred Years War, or Italian *condottiere,* than soldiers of a modern state.

Unwillingness to serve doubtless stems partly from concern about whether their wages will actually be paid.[14] As General Vladislav Putilin admitted in April 2001, after a determined effort in the first year of the war to pay generous wages and bonuses on time, compensation is paid late, at a reduced level, or not at all.[15] In the words of a leading Kadyrov supporter, Khalid Yamadayev, in April 2001:

> A year ago, bandit groups were active here, but the troops were fighting with them. Today, the gangs are still here, but the troops aren't fighting with them anymore. The bandits [that is, the separatist fighters] terrorize anyone who co-operates with the Federals. The Federals, for their part, arrest people on the slightest suspicion—and then their dead bodies turn up, or they don't turn up at all. If people once trusted the Federals, they don't trust them any more. They fear them, even hate them. The people are tired, discontent is growing. Therefore they have turned again to the fighters [*boyeviki*]....
>
> I sometimes ask people why they feel the way they do, and you know what they say? They say that after the fighters return they will at least be able to find the dead bodies [of people killed by the Russians]. The fighters are biding their time. They know that given time, the people will rebel. And that must not be allowed to happen! If it does, everything will go back to what it was, and all the blood spilled will have been in vain.

And I'll tell you something else. Sometimes, when new heads of [Kadyrov's] administration are appointed, they immediately send their emissaries to Shamil [Basayev] to find out whether it's OK to take the job. They know that if they don't get permission, they'll be killed sooner or later.[16]

As so often in antipartisan campaigns, these Russian tactics may have actually strengthened the rebels. Against the backdrop of a society whose ancient traditions demand revenge for the death of family members as a fundamental moral obligation, young Chechen men who have seen their homes destroyed and relatives killed or humiliated have sought the revenge their traditions demanded.

Russian Side

Even assuming that the Putin administration's intention in early 2001 to withdraw a large number of Russian troops was genuine, it was short lived. Around 5,000 Russian soldiers were indeed withdrawn (as opposed to being merely rotated out and replaced by new units), but by April 2001 this movement had come to an end. Officials announced that no further withdrawals were contemplated in the near future.

Urgent representations from Russian generals seem to account for the failure to implement further withdrawals. They warned that if Russia severely scaled down its forces while major rebel groups remained at large, it would risk a repeat of the catastrophic defeats suffered by the Russian forces in Chechnya in 1996.

In particular, critics pointed to the extreme unreliability of the "pro-Russian" Chechen forces who were supposed to take on the weight of the struggle against the rebels. These forces have always shown a marked disinclination for serious fighting against the separatists. This is partly because of continuing deep inhibitions against Chechens killing Chechens (although this has been eroded somewhat by the presence of international radical Muslim Mujahedin on the separatist side), and partly because of close kinship links between the two sides. Thus, during the first Chechen war, I was told of frequent cases where even leading allies of the Russians would shelter and protect relatives from the other side.

Moreover, the Russian-backed Chechen camp is divided into three mutually hostile groupings, each with its own rival backers among the Russian authorities. The head of the pro-Russian administration, Ahmed Kadyrov (formerly chief mufti or religious leader of Chechnya under President Dudayev), is opposed by two other forces: those of the former mayor of Grozny, Beslan Gantemirov, and those of Aslanbek Aslakhanov, a retired Soviet interior ministry lieutenant general.[17]

Given these splits in its own camp, it is highly unlikely that Russia can successfully pacify Chechnya in the foreseeable future. Indeed, by 2002 Russian officials such as presidential spokesman Sergei Yastrzhembsky were no longer even talking of this as a goal. Instead, they said that they were aiming only at reducing the conflict to the level of that in Northern Ireland from the 1960s to the 1990s; they also stressed that, like the British, they were prepared to go on fighting against "the terrorists" for decades if necessary. On the other hand, it also seems highly unlikely that the Russians will suffer defeats on the scale of 1996, and even if they do, they are unlikely to withdraw from Chechnya. The three cease-fires reached with the Russian forces from 1995 to 1996, effected by the Yeltsin administration's desire to conciliate Russian public opinion in the run-up to the June 1996 Russian presidential elections, played a key role in the Chechen separatists' ability to build and resupply their forces. With this memory in mind, the Russian generals are implacably opposed to any general cease-fire with the Chechen separatist fighters and the Mujahedin.

Equally important, it will be almost impossible for an administration in Moscow to admit defeat in this war—especially the administration headed by Putin, who launched the Russian counterinvasion of October 1999. There is a widespread and justified belief among Russians that when Russian forces withdrew in 1996, far from leading to peace, the withdrawal only ushered in worse dangers. Maskhadov has far less military power and less moral authority among his own people than he did in 1996. He is estimated to control only a small proportion of the Chechens doing the actual fighting and is therefore in no position to enforce any settlement that he makes with Russia. As for the Chechen and international radicals, they have repeatedly stated that they will accept no settlement short of unconditional and complete Russian military withdrawal.

In these circumstances, the war seems almost certain to continue for a long time to come, and even in the unlikely event that Russia suffers defeats, it will respond not with retreat as in 1996 but with reinforcement and counterattack. As in any war of this kind, if the political costs and the national risks of withdrawal vastly outweigh both the casualties being suffered and the political gains, then states will continue to fight. That has been the pattern with Turkey in Kurdestan; India in Kashmir; Nagaland, Indonesia, in Aceh and West Irian; and a good many other such conflicts around the world.

As the Indian example shows, democracy or the lack of it is of very little relevance when it comes to state behavior in partisan warfare over territorial or ethnic-based secessionist movements. Democracies are capable of fighting just as hard and just as ruthlessly for territorial sovereignty as any other kind of state, especially if—as in Kashmir and Chechnya—the separatist forces can be credibly linked to wider territorial, geopolitical, and ideological threats, and if those forces lack structures and leaders capable of enforcing discipline on their own followers and guaranteeing a settlement. By no means, however, are such wars good for democracies: They strengthen both authoritarian institutions of state and authoritarian and chauvinist tendencies in the general population.

Chances of Peace

If even limited peace is to come to Chechnya, it is likely to be only after a good many years and mainly the result of exhaustion. It is possible that in the long run the separatist fighters will be worn down to such an extent by years of warfare that most will stop fighting, and the war will be reduced to a limited terrorist struggle by small groups of diehards rather than the present guerrilla war. As of the spring of 2002 there were signs that this was happening. The chief leader of the international Mujahedin, Khattab, had been killed, as had a number of leading Chechen commanders; attacks on Russian forces and their Chechen allies had been reduced to terrorist actions and hit-and-run raids rather than the full-scale assaults of 1994–1996 and 1999–2000.

For any lasting peace, three processes have to take place in parallel. First, Russians must recognize that the long-term goal should be independence for Chechnya—though only after a long period in which the Chechen people have developed a peaceful society and demonstrated a capacity for modern state building. After the suffering of the Chechen people at Russian hands from 1994 to 1996 and 1999 to the present, it is highly unlikely that a majority of Chechens will ever willingly accept the prospect of permanent Russian rule, even at a distance. Second, Chechens must recognize that when they were given a chance at de facto independence from 1991 to 1994 and from 1996 to 1999, they made an appalling mess of things and created a nightmare for the entire region. Third, international Muslim support for the radicals in Chechnya must be greatly reduced, and the Mujahedin and their Chechen allies must be destroyed or driven from Chechnya. Here, the U.S. war against terrorism is already playing an important role by reducing international financing of Muslim radical groups and by hindering their ability to supply Chechnya through neighboring Georgia.

Before it can become a stable independent state, Chechnya needs to develop the social, cultural, and political foundations for such a state, including an organized political nationalist movement capable of mobilizing the population behind a state-building program. These foundations were lacking from 1991 to 1994, and wholly lacking from 1996 to 1999, with disastrous consequences. Even in the best circumstances, they will take years to develop.

Aslan Maskhadov is the legitimate president of Chechnya, elected in 1997 by an overwhelming majority (65 percent) in a vote certified by both international and Russian observers as free and fair. Although a majority of ordinary Chechens are deeply disillusioned with Maskhadov—judging by interviews with refugees in Ingushetia and Georgia—they still recognize him as the legitimate president. For the foreseeable future, any stable peace settlement in Chechnya probably needs to involve renewed Russian recognition of Maskhadov not as a "terrorist" but as a legitimate Chechen political figure. Among the greatest crimes of Shamil Basayev, Khattab, and other warlords from 1996 to 1999 was their contempt for the democratic will of the Chechen people and for the authority of their own elected president (who was also the chief architect of victory in the first war). Their defiance of legitimate state authority laid the basis for the subsequent disasters.

One possible ground for a settlement might be a formal, public Russian promise to grant Chechen independence in perhaps ten years, if a clear majority of the Chechen people vote for this in an internationally observed plebiscite and if in the meantime a number of conditions are met. Chief among these would be the departure from Chechnya of international Mujahedin together with those Chechen leaders who rebelled against Maskhadov's authority, attacked Russia, and participated in criminal activities

from 1996 to 1999. Their followers should be amnestied in return for the surrender of their weapons. A cease-fire (with a definite time limit and international guarantees) should be put in place to allow them to do so. If they
refuse, the war against them would have to continue, with the full backing
of Maskhadov and indeed of the United States. If he agreed to these terms,
Maskhadov could be restored as Chechen president and leader of a government of national unity.

As of the spring of 2002, however, there were very few signs indeed of
progress in this direction by either side. The Russian government appeared
to be observing a de facto, unadmitted truce with Maskhadov's men (which,
among other things, allows Maskhadov's wife Kusama to travel freely and
openly through Russia) and has made private offers of talks to Maskhadov.
However, the terms offered only amounted to surrender, with the possibility of future office as a Russian puppet in a Chechnya with limited autonomy. On the other hand, Maskhadov's representatives continued to demand
full and early Russian military withdrawal, coupled with empty promises
that Maskhadov will then control the situation in Chechnya and prevent a
takeover by Basayev and/or the international Mujahedin.

If after September 11, 2001, the United States has come to see Russia as
an important potential partner in the struggle against terrorism and still
wishes to play a positive role in this miserable conflict, then its approach
must be very different from that pursued before. It should in fact be mod-
eled closely on U.S. approaches to Turkey, another state with whose domestic record the United States is often unhappy, but which it sees as an
important strategic partner.

Thus pressure on Russia to reduce atrocities should be continued; not just
because this is morally right, but because such atrocities are not in Russia's
own interest. However, as in the case of past U.S. policy toward Turkey's war
against the Kurdestan Workers' Party (PKK) rebels in Kurdestan, this U.S.
pressure should be exerted within a framework of sympathy for the overall
goals of Russia's operation, help with intelligence and other means, and cat-
egorical support for Russian territorial integrity. In this context, moves such
as the U.S. Congress setting up Chechen, Avar, and Kabardin services of
Radio Liberty look utterly wrongheaded and unhelpful. In the case of
Turkey, for example, such a move would never have been considered. The
double or even triple standards that govern U.S. treatment of atrocities by
other countries have had a terrible effect on U.S. prestige in Russia and
need to be sharply modified.

One area where the West, and the United States in particular, can play a useful role is in helping to prevent the war from spreading, above all to neighboring Georgia. Since the war began, Russia has demanded on a number of occasions that Georgia allow Russian troops to operate on Georgian soil against Chechen fighters based there. This the Georgian government has rightly refused, backed by the great majority of Georgian public opinion and by the United States.

Russian statements about some 6,000 Chechen fighters based in Georgia are gross exaggerations. There are only 7,000 refugees in all in Georgia. However, Western diplomats in Tbilisi estimate the number of fighters based in Georgia's Pankisi Gorge to be between 200 and 300—and that is in itself a rather significant number in Caucasian terms. At least one leading Chechen commander, Ruslan Gelayev, has been based in Georgia at the head of a large force of Chechen fighters.

In November 2000, Georgian border guards intercepted a group of Gelayev's men who had come from Chechnya via Ingushetia carrying wounded. Subsequently they let the fighters go, and the wounded also later vanished. Russian anger at this helped produce greatly intensified Russian economic pressure against Georgia in the winter of 2000–2001. If Georgia repeats such behavior, the Russians are bound to react as the Turks did by repeatedly attacking PKK bases in Iraq and later by putting heavy pressure on Syria to expel the PKK.[18] In the fall of 2001, Gelayev's group was transported (apparently by the Georgian interior ministry) from the Pankisi Gorge across Georgia to the Kodori Valley on the borders of the separatist Georgian republic of Abkhazia, which they attacked before being driven back by Abkhaz forces supported by Russian airpower.

The U.S. "red line" against unilateral Russian military intervention in Georgia should nonetheless continue, because Russian action would do little good while creating a strong danger that the war would spread even deeper into Georgia itself. However, this U.S. stance should be accompanied by strong U.S. pressure on the Georgians to take real action to control their side of the Georgian–Russian border and to disarm the Chechen refugees within Georgia and expel the militants among them.

This must involve the creation of a strong Georgian military and police presence in the Pankisi Gorge in Georgia's northeastern mountains, where most of the Chechen refugees are situated, and which has been a "no-go area" outside Georgian government control. Future U.S. aid to Georgia should be made conditional on this—not so much for the sake of relations with Russia, but because the existence of such actual or potential safe havens for international terrorists is clearly against the vital interests of the United States. A strong step in this direction was taken in the spring of 2002 with the dispatch of 200 U.S. soldiers to train the Georgian army, together with more than $60 million in U.S. military aid. However, at the time of writing, it remains to be seen whether this effort will be successful in improving the lamentable Georgian forces, and also what use Georgia will make of any additional military strength.

If the United States demonstrates that it is genuinely sympathetic to Russia, it is possible that Russia might at some point welcome a U.S. role in mediating between Moscow and President Maskhadov. In the past, any contacts between Maskhadov representatives and U.S. officials have drawn a furious response from Moscow, but they could actually become useful.

U.S. financial aid could also contribute to a peace process by ameliorating human suffering and helping reconstruct Chechnya. Of course, one must not underestimate the deep corruption of the Russian and Chechen authorities, so often manifested in the past, nor indeed the perennial failure of the U.S. Congress in most of the world to match its grandiose moral rhetoric with real commitments of U.S. money. However, the massive atrocity of September 11, 2001, and the threat of even worse terrorist atrocities in the future have focused Western attention on the issue of failed and failing states in the Muslim world, and how such states can become havens for pathological activities that stretch far beyond their borders. Chechnya is a prime example of this danger and should therefore be a prime target of serious U.S. attention.

Notes

1. Kathy Gannon, "Aide Says Bin Laden Sent Troops to Chechnya," Associated Press, *Seattle Times*, August 30, 2000.

2. See Al-Sharq al-Awsat, London (in Arabic), as reported on the BBC Monitoring Service, August 6, 2001.

3. See Oleg Petrovsky, "The Chechen Field Commanders," in *Utro,* December 27, 2000; and the interview with Shamil Basayev in *Lidove Noviny*, Prague, September 9, 1999.

4. On the one hand, the bombings clearly helped Putin politically, and a curious "antiterrorism exercise" in the town of Ryazan in September 1999 increased suspicions of Federal Security Service (FSB) involvement. On the other hand, Western suggestions that Khattab's group would have lacked the expertise or the motive for such attacks are simply silly.

5. Basayev, *Lidove Noviny.*

6. Galina Kovalskaya, *Itogi,* April 25, 2000. It should be noted that the idea that Khattab and his group are Russian agents, endlessly reiterated by ordinary Chechens, has no basis in evidence or logic.

7. See Alexander Goltz, "Military Halted by Infighting," *The Russia Journal*, vol. 4, no. 3 (January 27, 2001).

8. See Pavel Felgenhauer, "The Warlords' Next Move," *Moscow Times*, February 1, 2001.

9. See, for example, the poll of the All-Russia Public Opinion Center reported by Interfax, January 29, 2001.

10. See Maura Reynolds, "Death Is the Only Victor as Chechen War Drags On," *Los Angeles Times*, December 31, 2000.

11. See Mayerbek Nunayev and Maura Reynolds, "Chechens Falling Prey to Russian Soldiers of Fortune," *Los Angeles Times*, October 25, 2000.

12. On the fight against military corruption, see the interview with Lieutenant General Valery Falunin, *Krasnaya Zvezda*, December 19, 2000. Ruslan Khasbulatov gave details of military corruption in Chechnya in *Nezavisimaya gazeta*, December 29, 2000.

13. This includes the rape and mutilation of Russian kidnap victims and the murder of Russian prisoners of war. Thus, in June 2000 Qoqaz.net (the web site of the international Mujahedin in Chechnya) announced the execution of nine Russian prisoners of war in response to Russia's refusal to hand over Colonel Budanov for execution.

14. NTV report, April 10, 2001, recorded by the BBC Monitoring Service on the same day.

15. Simon Saradzhyan, "Contract Soldiers Flee Army," *Moscow Times*, April 17, 2001.

16. Interviewed in *Kommersant*, April 2, 2001. I am indebted to Joan Beecher Eichrodt for this striking passage.

17. See the interview with Aslakhanov in *Kommersant*, March 26, 2001.

18. Russian leaders are already claiming that fighting is only continuing in Chechnya thanks to aid from abroad and that therefore "the crucial goal of the federal forces is the final closure of the channels of the arrival of mercenaries, armaments and money from abroad." General Valery Manilov, Deputy Chief of the General Staff, on *Ria Novosti*, May 11, 2001.

14

New Shape of the East–West Nuclear Relationship

Rose Gottemoeller

The East–West nuclear relationship has changed in the past decade, despite the failure of both countries to dismantle the Cold War nuclear legacy with its mutual emphasis on large numbers of weapons deployed on hair-trigger alert. This residual Cold War approach has not inhibited the two countries from developing a fundamentally new relationship that both implements older policy goals such as strategic arms reductions and addresses the problems that emerged following the dissolution of the Soviet Union.

This new relationship is the product of a quiet revolution that has occurred in the way that the two countries relate to each other in nuclear matters. Considerable distance and secrecy characterized the two nuclear arsenals during the Cold War era, but in the years since the breakup of the Soviet Union, the United States and Russia have built a multifaceted working relationship while maintaining safeguards to protect secrets from unauthorized leaks. Features of this new relationship range from formal measures arrived at in the arms control negotiating process to new types of cooperation that have sprung from efforts to solve post–Cold War problems such as the breakup of the Soviet nuclear arsenal. The U.S.–Russian effort to address the threat of nuclear weapons and materials falling into the hands of terrorists, often called cooperative threat reduction, is one important example of this new cooperation.

This revolution comprises elements of both the old-style formal arms control negotiation process as well as the more ad hoc approach to problem solving that arose in the 1990s. Although the Bush administration has sharply criticized the formal arms control process, the president did agree to negotiate a new agreement, the Treaty of Moscow, which he and Putin signed in May 2002. Bush thus seemed to acknowledge that the experience gained in negotiating and implementing arms control treaties is no less valuable than that gained in working on the new nuclear threat reduction agenda. The two are intertwined and thus form the new relationship.

This strategic relationship in turn forms a strong foundation for the development of a new framework for strategic cooperation that President Bush first proposed in May 2001, the need for which was embraced afterwards by Russian President Putin. President Bush has offered some general requirements for the framework, one of which—missile defense—is controversial among both the Russians and U.S. allies. Other requirements, however, are widely seen as timely and important, including further deep reductions in strategic nuclear forces and vigorous efforts to de-alert the strategic weapons that remain on operational deployment. The new strategic relationship that has emerged will speed the implementation of these elements that already enjoy broad consensus. Also, it may ease the emergence of compromise and eventual consensus in the controversial area of missile defense.

This chapter will explore how the new strategic nuclear relationship has emerged over the past ten years and will examine how it might contribute to the development of a new framework for strategic cooperation. The new relationship is a practical basis for progress in strategic arms control, but it has often evolved in response to necessity rather than through deliberative planning and the clear development of new strategic concepts. As a result, it has important limitations and problems that will also be described, for they tend to put roadblocks in the way of developing a new and comprehensive nuclear strategy. Finally, the chapter will conclude by describing how the new relationship can contribute to the emergence of a new strategic framework. It may be that the United States and Russia are not so far away from dismantling the Cold War nuclear structures as we thought.

Emergence of Strategic Consensus

For the bulk of the Cold War, the United States and the Soviet Union emphasized different strategic concepts. The United States relied on deterring its opponents through threat of unacceptable retaliation, an approach that stresses sustaining the capability to launch a devastating second strike even in the face of a powerful and unanticipated first strike. The Soviet Union, by contrast, maintained a strategy that emphasized warfighting—building the capability to fight a nuclear campaign that might contain a number of strikes, some massive (for example, preempting the opponent's first strike), some less so. The strategy was rooted in the premise that the opponent had to be denied his war aims, and had to know as much.

The two strategies were sometimes counterposed as "deterrence by denial" (the Soviet strategy) versus "deterrence by threat of retaliation" (the U.S. strategy). However, often during the Cold War, Western analysts argued that the Soviets did not recognize deterrence in their own strategic concept. Indeed, the Russian language seemed to convey this difference: *sderzhivanie* (restraining or holding someone back) described the U.S. deterrence concept in Soviet literature; *ugrozhnenie* (threatening or menacing someone) described the Soviet concept.

The greatest difference between these two concepts was their different answers to the question: How much is enough? The U.S. concept implied a short nuclear phase in any war, with enough capability needed to assure a second strike, but no more. Then, it was assumed, the war would stop. The Soviet concept implied that the nuclear phase might go on for days, weeks, or even longer, fought more or less as a conventional campaign. This drove a requirement for many warheads and launch vehicles, and an infrastructure that could perform even in a nuclear environment. The reason that the Soviets buried their plutonium production reactors in a mountain in Siberia, for example, was because they believed that they might have to continue producing plutonium for new warheads even at the height of a nuclear war. They believed that they could fight and prevail in a nuclear war.

Of course, the two approaches did not remain divorced from each other. The Soviet drive for higher numbers—underpinned by the new technology for multiple, independently targetable warhead reentry vehicles (MIRVs)—drove U.S. numbers higher. As long as parity was maintained, the argument in the 1970s went, the situation would remain stable, even if warhead numbers were very high. Higher numbers in turn enabled a somewhat hybrid approach in U.S. deterrence strategy. "Unacceptable retaliation," which could amount to going after cities alone, was adjusted to focus on targets that the Soviets would value most in their warfighting strategy. Instead of targeting cities and civilians outright, which, it was argued, would be an inhumane and immoral approach, the United States would target military capabilities, especially those serving the nuclear forces.

The drive for higher numbers eventually produced deployments of approximately 12,000 strategic nuclear warheads in each of the arsenals of the United States and Soviet Union. At this point, in the 1980s, the two countries embarked on a strategic arms reduction process that was predicated on the notion that stability could not be maintained indefinitely at steadily rising numbers, even if parity were.

There are probably many reasons why the Soviet Union decided to abandon the excesses of its warfighting strategy by the 1980s. Prominent among them were economic problems, because even before the Reagan administration embarked on its major military buildup, the Soviet economy had begun to flag. Reagan's policies drove home to Moscow the reality that the Soviet Union would lose in an economic competition for military superiority.

A second reason is that the two countries made an active effort to seek strategic consensus. The Strategic Arms Reduction Treaty (START) negotiations were accompanied, beginning in the late 1980s, with a high-level dialogue on strategic stability that was conducted under the chairmanship of Dennis Ross and Georgiy Mamedov. Ross was then chief of policy planning in the U.S. State Department, and Mamedov was chief of the Arms Control Directorate in the Soviet Ministry of Foreign Affairs.

It was this dialogue, accompanied by the strategic arms reduction process, that led for the first time to a confluence of U.S. and Soviet views on strategic offensive nuclear doctrine. That confluence produced results, especially a consensus that the strategic offensive forces of each country had to be protected from a preemptive first strike to assure the capability to retaliate. Continuing limits on missile defenses were one aspect of this consensus. Another was the ban on MIRVed intercontinental ballistic missiles (ICBMs) that appears in START II signed by Presidents Bush (senior) and Yeltsin in January 1993.

The consensus remained in force throughout the 1990s, in part because the economic crisis that followed the breakup of the Soviet Union did not allow the Russians to maintain their nuclear warfighting strategy. Moreover, the overall focus in U.S.–Russian relations was on establishing broader

economic and political links, beyond the nuclear and military preoccupation of the Cold War. Therefore, the strategic consensus remained in place
not because the United States and Russia tended it carefully, but because
each focused on other issues.

President Bush's call for a new framework for strategic cooperation, therefore, came at a time when the two countries were in accord on general
nuclear strategy, but in many ways because of neglect and not conviction.
The accord was fragile and did not rely on long and stable historic precedent. And Bush, in the first year of his administration, introduced three
shock waves. Even during his campaign, he had indicated that the START
process was over. This view was reaffirmed once he entered office. From that
point forward, Bush stressed, the United States and Russia should reduce
their strategic offensive forces quickly, through cooperative unilateral action,
without waiting for long, drawn-out treaty negotiations.[1] Then, in December 2001, he announced that the United States would abrogate the Anti-
Ballistic Missile (ABM) Treaty within six months.[2] President Putin's reply to
abrogation of the ABM Treaty was muted, but he reacted sharply to the
notion that the United States and Russia would no longer work together to
develop and implement legally binding arms reduction regimes. In this, he
seemed most concerned with a situation in which his force planners had lost
the means, through negotiations, to predict the future direction of U.S.
strategic forces. Like Bush, he affirmed unilateral reductions in Russian
strategic offensive forces, but insisted that they be backed up by a legally
binding agreement.[3]

The third shock wave that the Bush administration introduced was the
Nuclear Posture Review (NPR). This document, which was first announced
to the public in January 2002, placed a high premium on flexibility for the
U.S. strategic nuclear arsenal, regardless of previous arms control commitments. In particular, the United States asserted the right to return warheads
and launchers that had been put in storage to operational deployment if the
strategic situation warranted it.

Although it was highly critical of both the decision to withdraw from the
ABM Treaty and the NPR, the Moscow community enthusiastically
embraced the return of systems with first strike potential. When Bush
announced that he planned to abrogate the ABM Treaty, within hours
experts in Moscow were declaring that START II was dead, and with it, the
ban on MIRVed ICBMs.[4] If deployment of national missile defenses by the
United States was permitted, then so should be deployment of a small num-

ber of multiple warheads on the new Russian ICBM, known as the SS-27. With the end of total abstinence from these systems, the doctrinal consensus of the early 1990s was altered.

It is important to stress, however, that limits on first strike potential continue to operate. The Russians have talked of a "light MIRVing" of the SS-27, to involve perhaps three warheads. By comparison, the heavy missiles of the earlier era, such as the SS-18, carried ten warheads each and were capable of carrying more. The Russian arguments for light MIRVing revolve around the need for cost-effective ways to ensure that the Russian arsenal remains viable in the face of U.S. missile defenses, not around nuclear warfighting and denying the United States the ability to retaliate.

On the U.S. side, limits are also being placed on first strike potential, in the context of national missile defense. The new concept is a limited defense against rogue states and accidental launches, not a comprehensive defense system designed to deny Russia the ability to retaliate. This concept is one that the Bush administration is willing to back up by sharply reducing strategic offensive forces and thereby (in theory) removing the possibility of an offense-defense arms race. The Russians, on the face of it, should be comfortable with this approach, because they have maintained a limited defense of Moscow for nearly three decades.[5] However, their discomfort with current U.S. missile defense plans is evident, because they do not believe that the concept will remain limited. They are particularly concerned about the extension of U.S. missile defense capabilities into space.

In embarking on the search for a new framework for strategic cooperation, therefore, the United States and Russia will have to look beyond the general agreement on nuclear doctrine that existed in the 1990s. They will have to find new sources of consensus for the nuclear relationship, and in particular ensure that limitations remain in place on the first strike potential of strategic offensive and defensive systems.

New sources of consensus have in fact been developing quietly in the past decade, in response to acute problems that arose in the effort to deal with nuclear weapons after the Cold War. The solutions that have been worked out between the two countries tended to validate and strengthen the consensus on strategic nuclear doctrine, but in a way that often is not recognized.

Today, the question is whether or not such measures will continue to strengthen the consensus between the United States and Russia on strategic nuclear doctrine. The situation is trickier, because we are entering a more complex environment in which we are limiting systems with first strike potential rather than banning them. The following discussion describes the foundation that has been established but also considers whether it will be strong enough to handle the new challenge.

Quiet Revolution

Up to this point, implementation of strategic nuclear arms control agreements has gone forward on the basis of the strategic consensus arrived at in the late 1980s. Under the START I and START II processes, emphasis has continually been on eliminating the large multiple-warhead missiles that were specifically designed for the warfighting strategy (the Soviet-built SS-18 with its ten warheads is the quintessential example of this type). At the same time, new Russian missiles as of early 2001 have been limited to single-warhead designs in their testing and production, including the SS-27 single-warhead ICBM.

Some Russian commentators have talked about maintaining deployments of the SS-18 and its multiple-warheaded sister the SS-19 to counter U.S. missile defenses, but these missiles are nearly thirty years old and cannot be retained indefinitely. The Russians do not talk about restarting SS-18, SS-19, or SS-24 production lines to produce new copies of these missiles. (The SS-24 is the other large Soviet-era ICBM that is solid-fueled and designed to be mobile and launched from trains; most, however, have been deployed in silos.) One reason why the Russians do not talk about new production, of course, is the fact that the breakup of the Soviet Union left two of their main plants for the manufacture of ICBMs in the independent state of Ukraine. However, they also seem to remain convinced that they do not need to return to large, multiple-warhead missiles to address the U.S. threat, even if it includes missile defenses.

The implementation of START I and the negotiation of START II seemed to reinforce the consensus on a strategic concept that the two countries had arrived at when the Soviet Union dissolved. This is not to say that all has proceeded smoothly. The START implementation body, the Joint Compliance and Inspection Commission (JCIC), is the scene of many rancorous disputes over elimination, deployment, and maintenance practices on the two sides. The arguments continue to be made, however, with reference to the necessity of moving away from the old nuclear capabilities of the Cold War years.

An interesting development that has reinforced this phenomenon has been the emergence over the past decade of cooperative threat reduction (CTR). This joint U.S.–Russian effort is commonly known as the Nunn-Lugar program, after the two senators who established it. It is financed by the U.S. government and has enabled the Russian Federation to maintain the pace of START I eliminations, and even accelerate them, in the face of a considerable crumbling of the Russian nuclear weapons establishment. The overall enthusiasm of the Russian government for cooperation in this area thus underscores the continuing Russian commitment to the goals that underlay START I.

The institutional interactions that have grown up as a result of this and related programs have tended to reinforce this continuing commitment. The U.S. Department of Defense and the Russian Ministry of Defense have had a long-standing relationship in the arms control verification and monitoring arena. As noted above, it has involved efforts to resolve questions about deployment and testing practices in the JCIC, but it has also involved extensive on-the-ground interactions during monitoring and inspection visits. Out of this experience, the two countries have developed a more extensive mutual understanding of the inner workings of their nuclear forces than had been the case in the past. This is not new in that arms control monitoring and inspections pre-dated by some years the breakup of the Soviet Union.

But these activities have become significantly routinized in recent years, wherein it has become more "normal" for U.S. and Russian nationals to be working together at nuclear sites. Threat reduction cooperation has accelerated this process, at least at Russian nuclear sites.[6] The result has been an improved potential for joint problem solving on nuclear matters, either to address policy challenges that have arisen or to respond to new requirements. The solutions have been consistent with the existing consensus on nuclear strategy and have tended to reinforce it.

For example, a major policy challenge that arose in the aftermath of the Soviet breakup was the continuing presence in Ukraine, Kazakhstan, and Belarus of deployed nuclear warheads and launch systems. In Ukraine alone there were some 1,900 such weapons, with some 1,400 in Kazakhstan. Belarus had a small deployment of mobile ICBMs, representing fewer than 100 warheads, but still a very capable force. Had these weapons remained in these countries, Ukraine and Kazakhstan would have become the third and fourth largest nuclear weapons states, after Russia and the United States, with little capability to maintain and control them.

In response to this challenge, the United States and Russia, working together with Ukraine, Kazakhstan, and Belarus, engaged in a series of negotiations to bring about the removal of nuclear weapons from these countries. START I was the mechanism used. Essentially, eliminations of nuclear weapons systems under the treaty were carried out early in Ukraine and Kazakhstan in implementation of START I, while the systems in Belarus were sent back to Russia for redeployment.

The process was not straightforward, however. In the first instance, the treaty had to be adapted to facilitate the early eliminations in Ukraine and Kazakhstan—a step that took place through negotiation of the so-called Lisbon Protocol. Second, new procedures had to be worked out, some of which occurred as a result of enhanced monitoring requirements. The Ukrainians insisted, for example, that they have inspectors present at Russian warhead elimination facilities to ensure that the warheads leaving Ukraine were actually eliminated and not simply redeployed. Others emerged as a result of Russian concerns about the continued viability of their remaining nuclear weapons. In Kazakhstan, for example, U.S. contractors and government officials engaged in Nunn-Lugar projects could not gain access to SS-18 silos that were to be destroyed until the Russians had essentially stripped them of equipment that would enable the U.S. side to understand operational details of the missile. Nevertheless, the experience of working through these complicated problems continued to develop a U.S.–Russian community of experts, one that was committed to accelerating the elimination of heavy missiles and encouraging the deployment of small mobile ICBMs.

New requirements, it should be stressed, have emerged not only in the context of START I but also because of wholly new programs not related to that treaty. For example, the cooperative threat reduction program has undertaken a project to build a large plutonium storage facility at Mayak in the southern Urals, near the city of Ozersk. The U.S. Congress, in authorizing and appropriating funds for the construction of this facility, made a requirement that any material going into it be of "weapons origin," rather than material from the Russian civilian nuclear power program.

Devising a way to determine that material is weapons origin without disclosing its exact characteristics, which is information that would be invaluable to other weapons designers, was the challenge laid before U.S. and Russian experts. The result has been joint collaboration on information barrier technologies that has begun to address this new challenge laid down under the Nunn-Lugar program. However, the technologies will also have possible downstream applications to new arms control transparency issues, such as monitoring the storage or elimination of nuclear warheads. Again, the degree of consensus between the United States and Russia on the need to work on this problem has been considerable, even if the results have been incomplete thus far.

The examples cited have been in areas of strictly government-to-government cooperation, where there has been an interest in mutual national security goals, particularly accelerated implementation of the START I nuclear arms reduction treaty. Cooperation has also emerged in high-technology areas where government requirements coincide with particular commercial interests. For example, the United States has encouraged Lockheed-Martin to enter into a joint venture with Russian aerospace companies to develop a new space-launch vehicle for commercial purposes. It has also worked with the Boeing Corporation to develop the Sea-Launch Project, a U.S.–Russian–Ukrainian–Norwegian consortium for commercial space launches.

Although they cannot be linked directly to the strategic consensus that emerged at the end of the Cold War, these large joint aerospace projects illustrate how the urge toward cooperation has moved into the commercial arena as well as being present in the government-to-government sphere. Here again, the extent of institutional interaction has been significant. Whatever the difficulties, this process ensures that the U.S. and Russian aerospace industries that worked in isolation from each other during the Cold War will not easily be returned to such isolation in the future.

Limitations and Problems

While thus far we have emphasized areas where the fragile post–Cold War consensus on strategic matters has been borne out in practical ways on the ground, we also need to take note of the areas that have not been successful. They help to underscore the preexisting limits of the consensus and show problems that will require work if the United States and the Russian Federation are to devise a new framework for strategic cooperation.

The United States and Russia, for example, have achieved high-level agreement that bringing nuclear weapons down from the hair-trigger level of the Cold War is an important priority. In January 1994, President Clinton and

President Yeltsin, in agreeing on this priority, took a simple first step, de-targeting the nuclear weapons that are aimed at each other's territory on a day-to-day basis. De-targeting is inadequate to the task of de-alerting, because the missiles and their warheads can be re-targeted within seconds. Nevertheless, the summit agreement to de-target was an important initial step, because it conveyed high-level U.S.–Russian consensus about the importance of de-alerting.

Carrying this consensus to a higher and more effective level has been very difficult, however. President Clinton and President Putin agreed in June 2000 to establish a joint center in Moscow for sharing early warning data. Like de-targeting, cooperation on early warning is another important priority in the direction of de-alerting. In fact, early warning cooperation has more significance, because it will help ensure that a false warning will not trip a hair-trigger response and result in an accidental launch of nuclear missiles.

Implementing this presidential decision has been difficult because negotiations to establish the Moscow early warning center have stalled over issues that have dogged other cooperative efforts in recent years. These issues revolve around uncertainties and gaps in the Russian legal system that the Russians have not thus far been able to remedy through internal legislative or procedural changes. In the case of the early warning center, the issue of legal liability when an accident or mishap occurs has apparently been preeminent. In other joint projects, intellectual property protection and access procedures for military and nuclear facilities have been the major issues.

These legal and procedural questions are not at the level of major conceptual differences—both countries continue to stress that cooperation on early warning is an important, indeed a presidential, priority. However, they are real barriers to implementation of a high-level consensus. Indeed, one suspects in the midst of negotiating with the Russians that such issues are being used as proxies for strong and continuing bureaucratic opposition to the presidential decision, and indeed to the concept of cooperating with the Americans on important nuclear matters.

Such suspicions are unlikely to tell the whole story. The legal system in Russia is highly uncertain and prone to whimsical interpretation by individuals at various levels of power, as the Russian and foreign business communities have been complaining for years. When President Putin came to office, the corridors of power in Moscow became peopled by his old colleagues from the security services—individuals known less for whimsy than for punitive tendencies. This phenomenon has bred caution in the Russian ministerial bureaucracies. Those who might have been willing to negotiate a work-around to a legal issue to permit a U.S.–Russian program to go forward are no longer so willing to take the risks inherent in such an action. Inability to resolve differences over international property rights, liability protection, and access to facilities are symptoms of this phenomenon and remain strong barriers to cooperation.

The long-term solution to this problem, just as the business communities have been arguing, is for Russia to put in place reasonable and predictable laws and procedures that correspond to accepted international practice. President Putin has seemingly supported this goal by pressing a package of more business-friendly laws through the Duma in the 2001 legislative season. This positive pressure from the Russian president is welcome, because it shows his recognition that the Russian system will have to be reformed before it will be friendly to risk-takers, whether bureaucratic or commercial.

However, it is uncertain whether the package of laws will address the issues of most concern to U.S.–Russian nuclear cooperation, such as the matter of access by foreigners to Russian military and nuclear installations. Until such issues are addressed and resolved, implementation of U.S.–Russian programs will remain in doubt, no matter the number of presidential summits that occur.

Interestingly, Russian specialists and bureaucratic players emphasize that international treaties and agreements, especially if signed by the presidents and ratified by the legislatures, override certain Russian law and practice. In this way, START I and its accompanying Verification Protocol could be used to enable the access of U.S. inspectors to Russian nuclear missile bases and other sensitive sites. In the same way, they note, presidential declarations such as the 1990 Presidential Nuclear Initiatives launched by Presidents Bush and Gorbachev do not have the force of law and cannot be used to impel action—either changes in government practice or cooperative efforts that contradict Russian law.

Absent a treaty or agreement, legal shortcuts are still possible, given the considerable precedent that has been established in U.S.–Russian cooperation over the past ten years. The existence of a government-to-government agreement governing the Nunn-Lugar program, for example, has provided a stable umbrella for a number of U.S.–Russian implementing agreements, including a wide-ranging effort to improve the material protection, control, and accounting of weapons-usable nuclear materials at Russian naval bases and nuclear weapons facilities.[7] The Nunn-Lugar umbrella agreement is being provisionally applied pending future ratification by the Russian Duma. The mechanism of provisional application of an agreement has been a useful and highly effective, legal shortcut in the Russian system.

Thus, the barriers to cooperation that form around issues such as liability and access are legal and procedural. There is a possibility that they are also proxies for internal Russian opposition to cooperation with the United States on strategic matters, but this is difficult to ascertain.

The set of substantive issues that revolve around the offense-defense relationship are obviously the most important to be resolved in establishing a new framework for strategic cooperation and a common nuclear strategy. There are other substantive issues, however, that are not related to the offense-defense mix but have the potential to constrain future strategic cooperation. Differences over the maintenance of the nuclear weapons stockpiles are a case in point.

Over the past five years, the United States and Russian Federation have engaged in a running battle over the maintenance of their nuclear weapons stockpiles and how much cooperation should be engaged in this area. The United States has been expending over $4.5 billion per year in the maintenance of its stockpile—the so-called stockpile stewardship program that is designed to maintain the long-term operational effectiveness of U.S. nuclear warheads absent a nuclear testing program. The effort is highly dependent on technology such as high-speed computers and the National Ignition Facility (NIF), which will be used to simulate certain aspects of a nuclear test without requiring a nuclear explosion.

Russia at various times has complained that it is being left behind, not only because of its budget crisis, but also because the United States exercises controls on exports of high technology such as computers. In this way, the argument goes, the United States is willfully preventing Russia from pursuing stewardship of its nuclear weapons stockpile in a nontesting environment. This complaint has produced some extraordinary Russian behavior, including illegal acquisition of U.S. computer systems in the mid-1990s and the public celebration of this fact by then minister of atomic energy Victor Mikhailov.[8]

For the most part, however, the Russians have been emphasizing experimental activities at their nuclear weapons testing site on Novaya Zemlya. Some specialists in the United States believe that these activities have included nuclear test explosions in contravention of both Russia's unilateral moratorium on testing and the Comprehensive Test Ban Treaty (CTBT), which Russia has ratified. To build confidence about activities at the test sites, the United States has proposed reciprocal visits to Novaya Zemlya and the U.S. Nevada test site. The Russians have so far refused, asserting that if the United States requires transparency into test site activities, then the Russian Federation requires transparency into the rest of the U.S. stockpile stewardship program, including high-speed computer operations.

It is worth noting that many Russian nuclear weapons specialists say that they do not need to pursue stewardship of their stockpile in the same way that the United States is undertaking it. Indeed, they like to boast that the calculations that U.S. specialists do on computers they can do very nicely on the back of envelopes. The program that they portray is a kind of "stockpile stewardship on the cheap"—but one that relies on considerable work at the test site.

Although this issue is not in the mainstream of the offense-defense debate, it is a substantive matter over which the United States and Russia have had considerable differences in the past half decade. If the two countries do engage in further radical reductions in deployed nuclear weapons, as seems likely, the manner in which remaining warheads are cared for, whether on operational deployment or in the reserve, will if anything grow in importance. This trend will be regardless of future U.S. action, or inaction, on the CTBT, which the Bush administration has indicated it has no plans to ratify.

Therefore, to engage in successful cooperation, the United States and Russia must concern themselves with a mixture of procedural matters, substantive issues in the strategic deterrence relationship, and substantive issues outside that relationship but still touching on the future provenance and status of nuclear weapons. These are the limitations and problems that must be overcome as the two countries develop a new framework for strategic cooperation.

Conclusions

The issue areas that the United States and Russia must confront on the way to a new strategic framework are by no means intractable, but they each require attention. Some of this work must be conducted in capitals, as is the case with the effort to develop new laws in the Russian executive branch and the Duma. Other work is bilateral and near term; Moscow and Washington must continue to seek ways to develop legal shortcuts for cooperation already under way—for example, new procedural arrangements on access or new implementing agreements under the Nunn-Lugar umbrella agreement. Facilitating existing cooperation will contribute precedents to enable long-term resolution of the particular legal questions surrounding access, liability, and related issues. To be most effective, there should be a feedback loop between the unilateral development of new Russian laws and the bilateral practice that has been successful in the assistance programs over the years. If this process is successful, it will strengthen the environment in which the new strategic framework develops.

Other issues, however, are linked to policy that will have to be worked out at a high level and with considerable effort. The offense-defense debate will require considerable dialogue in a venue similar to the type that existed in the late 1980s—the so-called strategic stability, or Ross–Mamedov, talks. The creation at the May 2002 summit of a "Consultative Group for Strategic Security," chaired by the foreign and defense ministers, was a positive step in this direction. The success of this group will be linked to the willingness of both sides to step back from the conclusions reached in the earlier set of discussions, to examine assumptions and determine if it is possible to marry a limited missile defense with continued viability of strategic offensive forces on each side. Indeed, confidence that the strategic forces will remain capable of performing their deterrence function will likely require a considerable array of confidence-building measures regarding the new strategic defenses.

This realm of building confidence in a new missile defense environment is essentially unknown and can be created out of whole cloth to suit both parties if the United States and Russia engage each other in good faith. This effort will, however, require a great deal of energy, intellectual involvement, and attention to the engagement process.

Other nuclear issues, such as the dispute over stockpile stewardship, are preexisting. They have proven to be if not intractable then at least persistent in the relationship. Here the two capitals will also have to apply energy, intelligence, and attention, but they should also consider whether there is any value in renewing attention to what has already been tried. The United States and Russia have already had an effort under way to engage in cooperation, on an unclassified basis, relevant to stockpile stewardship issues.

The working groups have focused on such matters as improving the monitoring systems that would be available under the CTBT and on research to improve the safety of nuclear weapons during their long-term storage. Such cooperation, carried out under the aegis of the U.S. Department of Energy and the Russian Ministry of Atomic Energy, has developed a community of specialists on both sides who understand the issues well, both at a political and at a technical level.

In other words, solutions might be found through further attention to existing efforts, recognizing certain sensitivities on the U.S. part regarding the CTBT. The process does not have to be created out of thin air. It will, however, have to be invigorated to produce a more positive exchange on stockpile stewardship issues.

But despite these difficulties, the United States and Russian Federation may not be so far away from dismantling the Cold War strategic relationship as has been implied by their failure to radically reduce nuclear forces and remove them from their hair-trigger alert status. The two countries have a solid foundation to move forward, assuming that high-level political will and attention remain in place.

First, the United States and Russia continue to rely, although with alterations, on a conceptual consensus ensuring that both sides have the capability to conduct a retaliatory strike should a surprise first strike with nuclear weapons occur. There is now no longer a total ban on capabilities that contribute to first-strike potential, such as MIRVed ICBMs or ballistic missile defenses. However, both countries seem to be willing to place limitations on such systems. At the same time, the warfighting artifacts of the Cold War, such as SS-18 ICBMs, continue to be eliminated. In effect, nothing so far has disturbed the consensus, although its maintenance has become more complicated with the demise of the ABM Treaty and the ban on MIRVed ICBMs in START II.

The second element of the foundation is the considerable practical experience that the two countries have gained in their nuclear cooperation in the past ten years. Beginning with the arms control implementation, the United States and Russia have gone on to actually cooperate in the elimination of weapon systems under the Nunn-Lugar program and to address difficult technical issues, such as checking the warhead origin of nuclear materials. These efforts have produced much greater interinstitutional involvement than would have been possible through the arms control implementation process alone. The two countries have something of a community of experts in their defense and nuclear institutions who are accustomed to working closely together—although not, it should be stressed, at the cost of government secrets.

A related element is the considerable commercial cooperation that has developed, particularly in the aerospace industries. Here too, a community of experts has emerged, but if anything it has become even more intermingled because of the necessity of day-to-day interaction on high-intensity engineering and industrial projects. The mutual understanding about engineering and industrial practices encourages the notion of cooperative problem solving in even the most difficult of environments.

This well-established technical cooperation in the aerospace sector may help to launch cooperative projects to develop missile defense technologies, should the United States and Russia decide to proceed in that direction. In fact, the extent of existing joint experience may help to facilitate consensus between the two countries as projects develop, enabling a faster buildup of mutual confidence than would otherwise have been possible. This greater mutual understanding may in fact lead to the early development of confidence-building measures for emerging defensive systems, which would in turn give greater confidence in the systems to political leaders on both sides.

Thus, the potential developed over the past decade enables the United States and Russia to create a new framework for strategic cooperation in a short time—with considerable groundwork being laid within the current administrations of Presidents Bush and Putin. The two countries are nowhere near the weak starting point that they would have confronted had they begun such an effort ten years ago. They can begin from the practical foundation of a different, more deeply engaged relationship on nuclear matters and from considerable consensus regarding the purpose of strategic nuclear weapons.

Notes

1. A clear campaign statement of this position appeared in Bush's speech to the National Press Club in May 2000. The position was reaffirmed in remarks to the press in February 2001, after Bush assumed office. See "Bush Outlines Arms Control and Missile Defense Plans," *Arms Control Today*, June 2000; online at http://www.armscontrol.org/act/2000_06/bushjun.asp.

2. See Sharon LaFraniere, "Putin Calls ABM Move Mistaken," *Washington Post,* December 14, 2001.

3. For a clear statement of Putin's view on this issue, see Andrew Gowers, Robert Cottrell, and Andrew Jack, "Putin under Pressure," *Financial Times*, December 17, 2001.

4. Shortly after George W. Bush announced the intent of the United States to withdraw from the ABM Treaty, Alexei Arbatov, deputy chairman of the Duma Defense Committee, urged Russia to announce that it would no longer abide by START II. See LaFraniere, "Putin Calls ABM Move Mistaken."

5. Under the 1972 ABM Treaty signed by the United States and the Soviet Union, each country was permitted to build two ABM sites, one to defend its capital and one to defend an ICBM field. In 1974, both sides signed a protocol limiting each country to just one site. The United States chose to deploy a system around its Grand Forks missile base, but it never entered operational status. The Soviet Union built ABM defenses around Moscow that are still in use today.

6. U.S. contractors and government auditors have been present at Russian nuclear weapons sites in the course of carrying out threat reduction projects, such as eliminating old Soviet strategic strike submarines. Because Nunn-Lugar is an assistance program financed by U.S. government funds, however, there is no reciprocal arrangement for Russians to be present at U.S. sites, as there is in the case of START I.

7. The Material Protection, Control, and Accounting Program provides Russian nuclear facilities with modern material accounting and physical protection systems; training for nuclear personnel in proper techniques; assistance in developing a comprehensive and enduring regulatory basis for nuclear material security in Russia; and assistance in improving the physical protection of nuclear weapons–usable materials in transit.

8. The incident was reported by Michael Gordon in "Russia Atom Aides Buy IBM Supercomputer Despite U.S. Curbs," *New York Times*, February 25, 1997. Russia's nuclear weapons establishment obtained an IBM RS/6000 SP through a European middleman for $7 million. The head of public affairs for the ministry was quoted as saying, "If we see something we can buy on the European Market, we buy it."

15

Prospects for U.S.–Russian Cooperation

James M. Goldgeier

In August 1991, watching Russian President Boris Yeltsin standing on the tank in defiance of the last ditch effort of the old Soviet elite to hang onto power and empire, the West was euphoric. The old guard was finished, and within months, the Soviet Union, our main adversary of forty-five years, was finally placed on the ash heap of history. After the cooperation between U.S. President George H.W. Bush and Soviet leader Mikhail Gorbachev during German unification and then in the Gulf War, it seemed at the beginning of 1992 that a future partnership between Russia and the United States in a post-Soviet era would be relatively easy to achieve.

Ten years later, it was not partnership that defined the 1990s, but rather growing suspicions and finger pointing. In the 2000 U.S. presidential campaign, the talk was not about what had been achieved with Russia, it was about "Who Lost Russia?" With Russian President Vladimir Putin's government clamping down at home and U.S. President George W. Bush's top advisers initially calling Russia a threat to U.S. interests, the start of the second decade of America's relations with post-Soviet Russia began on a far different note than during the heady days of 1992.

There were several reasons for the difficulties of the past ten years. One problem was simply the overblown expectations after the collapse of Soviet

An earlier version of this chapter was published in the October/November 2001 issue of *Policy Review*.

communism about what Russia might achieve politically and economically. By all accounts, the last ten years should be seen as a major victory for freedom when one compares political and economic life to the odious nature of the Soviet period, and yet instead it seems to be woefully inadequate. Second was an underestimation in Moscow of how quickly Russian power would decline, leaving the Russian government outside the agenda-setting process, especially in Europe, which was not what Gorbachev and Yeltsin had envisioned. After all, they had assumed that Russia would be part of any major decision-making forums on the continent, as it had been, for example, during the nineteenth-century concert of Europe.

But these were not the fundamental obstacles to greater U.S.–Russian cooperation. To understand the crux of the problem in U.S.–Russian relations, one needs to remember what factors led to cooperation in previous eras, because none of these underlying dynamics is as powerful today as it was in the past. The real questions now are whether the September 11, 2001, terrorist attacks on America will provide sufficient long-term impetus for serious cooperation and whether Russia will become securely part of the new Europe.

Past Cooperation

Three basic reasons brought the United States and Russia closer together at different points during the twentieth century: (1) the fear of growing German and Japanese power in the decades after 1905 that culminated in the creation of the Grand Alliance of World War II; (2) U.S.–Soviet parity in strategic nuclear forces and a mutual fear that a Cold War crisis might escalate to nuclear war that led to the cooperative competition known as détente in the early 1970s; and (3) the domestic political needs of leaders on both sides that produced the Clinton–Yeltsin partnership in the 1990s.

Prior to the twentieth century, neither country had had much to do with each other because there was no real need, except for isolated incidents such as the U.S. purchase of Alaska.[1] But early in the twentieth century, changes in the European and Asian balance of power and the growing U.S. presence on the world stage led to a greater coincidence of strategic interests despite the political and ideological gulf that existed. Revolution in 1917 brought to power a regime in Russia that sought to undermine the capitalist order, and the United States did not even recognize the Soviet government until after Franklin Delano Roosevelt became president in 1933. By that time, both countries were concerned about rising German power in Europe and Japan's invasion of the Asian mainland. Even so, the Soviets shocked the world with their secret pact with the Nazi government in 1939, forestalling any cooperation with the West for two more years. But once the Soviet Union and then the United States had been attacked in 1941, a Grand Alliance was virtually inevitable, regardless of the ideological opposition to each other's regime.

President Roosevelt had gone out of his way to try to placate Soviet leader Josef Stalin during the war, culminating in the agreement at Yalta in early 1945 that became a symbol of perceived Western acquiescence to Red Army dominance in Eastern Europe. Much has been written about missed opportunities from 1945 to 1947 to forge some type of cooperation before the blocs truly hardened in Europe. And yet, as classic balance-of-power theorists of international affairs would expect, once a common threat had been defeated in 1945, it was difficult to avoid major power rivalry between the two greatest world powers, even if misperceptions and miscalculations perhaps hastened, deepened, and lengthened the Cold War hostilities between them.

The Cold War's most dramatic moment occurred over Cuba in October 1962. Following Moscow's humiliation—which the United States, Soviet Union, China, and Cuba each attributed to U.S. military superiority—the Soviet Union embarked on a dramatic military buildup, closing the missile gap and achieving parity in strategic nuclear forces by the onset of Richard Nixon's administration in 1969. With the United States looking for help withdrawing from its costly war in Vietnam, and with both sides looking to regulate their Cold War competition by trying to prevent crises from escalating into nuclear war, Nixon and Soviet General Secretary Leonid Brezhnev pursued détente. Détente did not mean that the sides would stop competing; it was an effort to place some reasonable boundary on that competition. And the two leaders pursued détente not simply as a desirable foreign policy in and of itself; rather, each used détente and the rhetoric of cooperation for domestic political purposes.

Détente had a brief heyday in 1972–1973, marked by the agreement to limit strategic offensive nuclear launchers under the Strategic Arms Limitation Talks (SALT I), the Anti-Ballistic Missile (ABM) Treaty, and rules of the road embodied by the Basic Principles Agreement and the Agreement on the Prevention of Nuclear War. But the perceptions on both sides of what détente meant were fundamentally at odds. The United States viewed détente as a means of preserving American superiority for as long as possible; the Soviet Union saw détente as a means to keep a competition it thought it was winning from escalating to nuclear war. With the United States embroiled in Vietnam and facing economic challenges from a rebuilt Europe and Japan on the one hand, and the Soviets outpacing the United States in building nuclear weapons on the other, there was a general perception that the U.S. position was weakening, and the Soviet position was strengthening.[2]

War between Arabs and Israelis in October 1973, civil war in Angola from 1975 to 1976, and finally the Soviet invasion of Afghanistan in December 1979 killed détente. The Cold War resumed at the end of the Carter presidency and particularly after the onset of the Reagan presidency in 1981. By then, Soviet hopes that the United States was in retreat had been dashed, as the United States had begun a new military buildup and the Soviet economy was clearly stagnating. Mikhail Gorbachev's rise to power in March 1985 swung the pendulum dramatically back again toward cooperation. Gorbachev quickly realized that to have any hope of achieving his goal of restructuring the Soviet economy, he needed a more benign international environment. A less hostile world would mean that he could shift money out of the defense sector to raise the standard of living in an economy that had slipped from second to third, behind that of Japan.[3]

To forge this new world, Gorbachev agreed to reductions in intermediate-range nuclear weapons as well as conventional weapons in Europe, ended support for Eastern European communist rulers and other anti-Western regimes, and withdrew Soviet troops from Afghanistan. His unwillingness to use 300,000 Soviet troops in Germany as a tool to prevent German unification and then his support for the coalition against Iraq in 1990–1991 signaled that there were apparently no limits to Soviet acquiescence to the U.S. global agenda.

Remarkably, from 1991 to 1993, Boris Yeltsin sought even *deeper* partnership with the United States. Yeltsin wanted Western assistance not only for his domestic reform programs but also because he was trying first to outflank Gorbachev and then to defeat the remnants of the Communist Party of the Soviet Union who dominated the Russian parliament. To outflank Gorbachev, he had to show that he was the real democrat, the real reformer, which meant going even further than the Soviet hero of the West in satisfying the demands of the United States and its allies. As he worked to consolidate his power in Russia from 1992 to 1993, Yeltsin wanted to destroy the Communist Party. In that process, he and his foreign minister, Andrei Kozyrev, were eager to develop the most pro-Western foreign policy platform imaginable for a Russian government. [4]

After Clinton assumed the presidency in January 1993, Yeltsin had a partner whose domestic political need for good relations was equal to his own. Clinton's agenda (like Gorbachev's after March 1985) was focused on the domestic economy. Given his spending priorities in education and health care, he could not afford any renewed threat from Moscow that might lead to higher defense budgets. Even more, it seemed to many in the West that with Boris Yeltsin in power, a new world order could be forged—with a democratic, market-oriented Russia finally integrated with the rest of Europe. Assisting Russian political and economic reform became President Clinton's top foreign security policy priority at the start of his presidency, as he and his top advisers often proclaimed in the first half of 1993. Signaling this, his first trip outside the country was to meet Yeltsin in April 1993 in Vancouver, where he unveiled a huge assistance package for his new friend.

The Clinton administration's philosophy of engagement was fairly simple. First, despite the rhetoric about supporting a process, U.S. officials saw Boris Yeltsin as the embodiment of reform; they did not believe reform would continue without him (which was no different from the view held by the Bush administration regarding Yeltsin in 1992 or about Gorbachev before that). Second, the United States should and could work closely with the reformers working for Yeltsin who shared Western objectives. If the United States wanted to pursue reductions in nuclear weapons, it could identify Russian officials who did as well. If the United States wanted to promote democracy and market reform, it could find Russian officials who spoke the same language. Efforts like the oft-maligned commission established between U.S. Vice President Al Gore and Russian Prime Minister Viktor Chernomyrdin were developed precisely to create these channels of engagement between U.S. and Russian officials across the board—from the foreign and defense ministries to commerce and agriculture and space agencies—to make this engagement process regular and institutionalized.

Critical for U.S.–Russian engagement was the "Bill–Boris" relationship. Yeltsin desperately looked for ways to make Russia appear as if it belonged on the world stage with the other great powers, and Clinton was more than eager to help him. Clinton made sure Russia had a place in the Implementation Force (IFOR) in Bosnia after the 1995 Dayton accords. He made sure there was a North Atlantic Treaty Organization (NATO)–Russia ceremony in Paris in May 1997 prior to NATO's July summit in Madrid that issued invitations to new members. And he let Yeltsin pretend that the Group of Seven advanced industrialized democracies was really a Group of Eight. In return for the symbolic bolstering, Yeltsin went along with most of the U.S. diplomatic agenda, especially in Europe. Clinton always seemed to want Russia to "feel good" about itself to help bring it into the West. And Yeltsin in return always tried to deliver for his U.S. counterpart.

The dynamics of this relationship, built on the domestic political needs and ideological leanings of both leaders, must not be underestimated. Sticking points arose throughout their time in office—over Bosnia, NATO enlargement, Kosovo, Iraq, Iran, and others. Each time the bureaucrats on both sides failed to close a gap between the two nations, Clinton asked the Russian leader directly to "do the right thing." He would appeal to Yeltsin's desire for Russia to be firmly part of the club of major Western powers. And Yeltsin would almost always deliver, at least in terms of committing himself to trying to fix the problem, even though economic, military, or parliamentary forces beyond his control might have prevented the solution that the two leaders had worked out from coming to fruition. Clinton and Yeltsin felt that they needed each other; they looked for ways to help each other politically; and they were ideologically committed to good U.S.–Russian relations.

Current Situation

In each of the earlier periods—the 1940s, the 1970s, and the 1990s—international or domestic pressures forced cooperation. Even so, rivalry between the United States and Russia continued to exist. During World War II, the two raced to control territory in Europe and Asia as the war wound down; during détente, they continued their efforts to dislodge one another from various Third World outposts; and in the 1990s, they were at odds over U.S.-led efforts such as NATO enlargement, the war on Kosovo, and Russian exports of sensitive technologies to Iran and North Korea.

In addition, in both the 1970s and the 1990s, while leaders had domestic support for cooperation, there were also powerful domestic forces in both countries that opposed engagement and cooperation. U.S. opponents of détente believed that the United States was not forceful enough regarding Soviet human rights abuses and, indeed, about Soviet strategic ambitions. Led by Senator Henry M. Jackson (D-Wash.), they undermined Henry Kissinger's efforts to craft a subtle, nineteenth-century-style foreign policy in which the superpowers would accept each other's sphere of influence. Meanwhile, Soviet military and ideological hardliners pressured Brezhnev to continue the global competition even while the technocrats were trying to gain access to Western economic credits and technology. [5] In the 1990s, Clinton's foes in the U.S. Congress and Yeltsin's in the Russian Duma worked hard to deny the two presidents the opportunities to engage as fully as they wished. Republicans argued that Russia's cooperation with Iran's nuclear program merited sanctions and a suspension of aid. Communists in the Russian Duma refused to ratify START II as part of their domestic political strategy to stymie Yeltsin, even though they realized that Russia's nuclear arsenal was going to decline for financial reasons while the United States could afford to maintain as high a level as it wished.

Today, rivalry on various issues remains, as does strong political opposition to greater cooperation. Prior to September 11, 2001, there did not appear to be any pressing international or domestic forces that could induce either country to make a major effort to cooperate. The United States and Russia have for some time theoretically shared an interest in stopping nuclear weapons proliferation and keeping the territory of Afghanistan from being used as a staging ground for international terrorism but had done relatively little to cooperate in these areas. Even after the horrific attacks on the United States, the threats posed today are much vaguer and harder to pinpoint than were the threats of the 1940s, and thus by themselves are unlikely to produce sustained cooperation.

In addition, while there have been plenty of security specialists on both sides pressing the leaders to worry about nuclear holocaust and the vast number of missiles that remain on a high state of alert, it has been difficult to generate much enthusiasm for the problem among the broader population because there is little worry that either country might deliberately start a war or even that a crisis situation might develop that would have the potential for escalation. There are some concerns about accidents or unauthorized use of nuclear weapons, but these do not induce the same sense of urgency that existed during the Cold War.

Neither President Bush nor President Putin benefits as much politically from good relations as did his predecessor. Bush certainly does not strengthen his domestic political base with lower defense budgets as Clinton did, and in any case, security concerns about Russia are no longer a primary consideration in assessing threats or planning spending levels to meet them. Meanwhile, Putin did not gain power the way Yeltsin had; he won by portraying himself as a nationalist who could bring back the country's prestige, and not as a Westernizer looking for ways to accommodate Washington. Since September 11, he has been far out in front of his political and military elite in his accommodation of the United States on a number of issues during the war on terrorism.

George W. Bush's foreign policy agenda in the first months of his administration did not start, as Clinton's did, in Russia; rather, it started in Mexico, Europe, and Japan. George W. Bush made it clear during his campaign that before meeting with Russian and Chinese counterparts, he would meet first with his friends in Latin America, Europe, and Asia, and he followed through on that promise.

Meanwhile, Putin cannot continue to acquiesce to the U.S. agenda without getting something tangible in return. After all, Yeltsin in the end never got much for his accommodation. The Russians initially were pleased that Bush had won the election over Vice President Al Gore. They thought they had rid themselves of those annoying Democrats who were always telling them how to build a market democracy and complaining about Chechnya. And they saw in the new team an old realpolitik approach that to them meant the two countries would deal with each other on great-power security issues the way great powers do. It would not be cooperation 1990s style; it would be a return to cooperation 1970s style—some measure of détente on great-power concerns like arms control within a framework that had an underlying rivalry, particularly in the Caucasus and Central Asia if not in Ukraine and the Baltics. In this view, if the United States were feeling magnanimous, it might even implicitly consider ceding Russia a sphere of influence in its region the way traditional great powers do—as Nixon and Kissinger did.

Even in this vision, the relationship would be more disengaged than the 1970s interaction between two superpowers who engaged each other in every corner of the globe and on every major issue in world politics. Russia has little capacity to project conventional military power beyond the borders of the former Soviet Union. It has no serious diplomatic weight in major world bodies apart from its veto in the United Nations. And while it has good relations with countries like Iran, Iraq, India, and China, it has no major alliance partners. Worst of all from the Russian government's perspective, because conservative Republicans also care about human rights, even the Bush administration's realpolitik types initially had to show concern over Chechnya, although those criticisms were immediately muted after the terrorist attacks on American soil.

New Basis for Cooperation?

Yet as is even more apparent after September 11, Bush can neither ignore Russia nor afford conflict with Russia if he wants to redirect resources to deal with a terrorist threat and a rising China. And Putin needs the United States to pay attention to him so that he can look like a major world leader—after all, creating "bipolar moments" is a lot harder than it used to be. Ironically, Bush's Russia policy within months turned out to be not so different from where the Clinton administration left off after the Yeltsin era. During the course of the Clinton years, the United States developed an agenda in the Balkans, Iraq, and other places, and Russia's weakness meant that it could do little to stop the United States from pursuing what it deemed in its interests. Furthermore, Clinton never developed a relationship with Putin as he had with Yeltsin. The difference between where one administration left off and the other began is not so much in substance as in style. While a President Gore may well have pushed for some kind of missile defense, given political realities in the United States today that favor pursuit of at least a minimal shield against ballistic missiles, he would not have made it a top foreign policy priority. He also would have continued to press Moscow on its arms and technology sales to Iran, but his rhetoric and desire for engagement would have been noticeably different than Bush's was in the first six months of his presidency.

Russia's attempt to adjust to its change in status from a major global actor in the late 1980s to a large territory beset with enormous political and economic weaknesses in the early 2000s has been difficult. The former superpower has not adjusted as easily as Great Britain did in the years after World War II, for example. But just because Russia is weak does not mean it cannot hurt the United States. And just because Russia is weak does not mean that Russia cannot help the United States. Many of the threats that face both the United States and Russia are best dealt with together, and Russia can certainly make the threats that exist worse for U.S. interests. These include the proliferation of weapons of mass destruction, terrorism, and the flow of illegal drugs. Each country has much to offer the other in dealing with problems that affect both countries. But if the United States really wants something from Russia, it must offer something in return, and vice versa.

One possible source of cooperation would be the rise again of a threat that would loom so large to both countries that it does not even take far-sighted leadership to recognize the value in cooperation. At the moment, there are two such threats apparent to the leadership of both countries. The longer term threat could be an increasingly powerful China. A massive Chinese military buildup would threaten both the United States and Russia. Chinese threats to Russian territory as well as to Taiwan and other U.S. allies in Asia might lead to the kind of pressures for cooperation that existed in the first half of the twentieth century. But one should neither wish for this future nor develop policies to effect it.

The second common threat that now looms immediately is terrorism. The Russians have long argued that the United States should stop criticizing their behavior in Chechnya and recognize Osama bin Laden's role in supporting the rebellion. And while U.S. administration officials have been horrified at Russian tactics, there has been sympathy since 1994 for the problem Russia faced in dealing with a secessionist movement on its own territory.

The best hope the United States has for dealing with major threats to its core national interests lies with cooperation with its major allies, particularly in Europe. And it is the U.S.–Europe–Russia relationship that may prove the most important vehicle for promoting strong U.S.–Russian relations for combating terrorism and other common problems.

Cooperation in Europe

Europe is one area where each country truly needs the other to fulfill its wider agenda. The United States could enlarge NATO or fight a war over Kosovo even if Russia stands in opposition. But to advance the U.S. objective since 1989 to extend the Western zone of peace and prosperity and foster a Europe "whole and free" that will work together with the United States, Russia has to be integrated. Without an integrated Russia, there is too much potential for instability in the Baltics, Ukraine, and Caucasus. Instability in those regions then puts pressure on U.S. allies like Poland and Turkey. In general, the Europeans will worry if Russia is either unstable or menacing or both, and will object to U.S. policies that seem designed to bring this about.[6]

Putin also needs Russia to be part of Europe to fulfill his foreign and domestic agenda. Russia's European border is its most stable and remains the most promising source of foreign investment. Unrest to the south and particularly activities fostered by Iran and Afghanistan are only likely to become greater concerns for Russia as it worries about instability in the Caucasus and Central Asia. To the east, while a fruitful Russia–China relationship has developed, it will always be uneasy, especially as China gains so much economic and military power relative to Russia. Compared to these other areas, Europe is the natural place for Russian foreign policy makers to seek good relations. There is no threat of military incursion or fomenting religious strife as there is elsewhere.

Thus, despite it all, Russia would appear to have no choice but to try to be part of the West. And while U.S. critics of the West's Russia policy argued in the 1990s that Russia received bad economic advice from the International Monetary Fund or complained about young Western know-it-alls telling Russia how to run elections, there was someone on the other end who wanted the advice to be part of the club.

The rhetoric of Russia in Europe, however, is not the same as Russia being a significant force in major European institutions. It is not easy for the West to find a place for Russia as both the European Union (EU) and NATO enlarge, nor is it easy for Russia to find its place. The Europeans can help as they enlarge their union by minimizing problems for Russia in Kaliningrad or on the border with the three Baltic countries. This will require consideration of special economic zones and visa regimes in areas bordering the EU to minimize the effects of enlargement on the eastern part of Europe. Those worried about a new dividing line in Europe should focus on the EU, not NATO, given the EU's strict border regime.

But even if EU enlargement is potentially much more devastating to Russia's interests than NATO's forays, only NATO has been a "four-letter word" in Moscow. Over time, the alliance must find a way for a democratic Russia to have a place in European security decision making. It is understandable that NATO does not want to privilege Russia over those countries aspiring for membership. Nor does it want Russia to have a veto over NATO operations. But especially on issues such as proliferation and terrorism, real Russian participation in decision making should be welcomed if Russia lives up to its end of the bargain by working to combat these common threats rather than simply trying to find ways to weaken the alliance's ability to function. The Permanent Joint Council (PJC) established by the 1997 NATO–Russia Founding Act was a start but never really developed because of the suspicions that remained on both sides about the other. It met regularly, although it was interrupted for a year by the war in Kosovo and its aftermath. But because the NATO countries had to reach a consensus before meeting in the PJC to discuss issues with Russia, to the West it often appeared that Russia was merely there to undermine NATO, whereas to Russia it appeared that the West was merely looking for Russia to give it a green light to act. At a minimum, the new NATO–Russia Council will have to get beyond this structural problem to succeed.

Ever since Thucydides, we have known that states view growing power elsewhere as a matter of grave concern. And thus it is natural for Russia to look at the enlargement of the EU and NATO as threats. It is not, however, productive; Russia would seem to be better off looking at these institutions as providing opportunities for it to be part of the new Europe. But because of the mutual suspicions that have grown stronger, the effort to bring Russia into Europe is not as easy as it might have appeared in the early 1990s. Russians see the West as having taken advantage of the end of the Cold War in ways that highlighted Russia's diminished status. NATO's inclusion of Poland, Hungary, and the Czech Republic as new members started this process, and the war on Kosovo provided an even bigger shock. But for the West, the war was a shock as well, because Russia was siding not with a military campaign on behalf of a victimized population but rather with Slobodan Milosevic, whom the West considered the greatest threat to post–Cold War European security and stability.

No discussion of Europe is complete without mentioning missile defense and the ABM Treaty. Given that the technologies do not yet work, we do not know where the Bush administration's efforts to field a missile shield will lead. We do know that the United States will try to develop some kind of defense against at least small-scale missile attacks. America's European allies will remain unhappy with this policy if Russia is not accommodated in some way. Russia has every incentive to seek a deal with the United States to develop a new framework—after all, a joint declaration would be a "bipolar moment," however fleeting. The Bush administration is in the driver's seat, having been able to withdraw from the treaty without eliciting a firestorm of protest. It should, however, be wary of overplaying its hand, for example, by not agreeing to actual reductions on the offensive side (and the

United States does not need all of those thousands of warheads in storage to deter future adversaries).[7] Given that any U.S. missile defense effort will likely have no effect on the Russian nuclear deterrent, both sides should welcome some new understanding of the rules of the road that allows the United States to proceed but that helps the Russian government with its domestic political fallout. It is quite possible, however, that domestic political forces in both countries—Republicans who do not like constraints on U.S. action and Russian hardliners who do not want to make missile defense easier for the United States to pursue—will prevent real cooperation in this area. A failure to cooperate will affect the process by which the United States and its allies work together in Europe, and thus how they in turn work together with Russia on the other big issues of the day.

Final Thoughts

The U.S.–Russian relationship ended the 1990s on a highly suspicious note. U.S. critics of the Clinton administration's Russia policy believed that the United States does not really need to work with Russia, that Russia's behavior in Chechnya should provoke U.S. disengagement, that Russia really cannot be trusted, especially regarding sales of sensitive technologies to states of concern, or all of the above. Russian critics of the Yeltsin administration's policy believed that Russia was taken for a ride in the 1990s by Western governments and financial institutions that were determined to ruin Russia in order to eliminate it as a threat once and for all.

These kinds of perceptions on both sides existed in the 1930s, and they were only temporarily put aside when Germany and Japan became the larger threat. Will the terrorist threat provide this same kind of impetus? In the aftermath of the September 11 attacks, Putin immediately signaled greater willingness to cooperate with the United States and its allies in the war on terrorism, particularly in intelligence. Putin has also expressed flexibility on Russian arms sales to Iran if properly compensated. The United States has long sought to buy out Russia in exchange for halting sales of sensitive technology and equipment to Iran but had not previously been able to offer enough to push Russian domestic interests fully in this direction. (In 1995, for example, Secretary of State Warren Christopher offered $100 million to help Russia build new nuclear reactors if Russia halted its sales to Iran, but this paled in comparison to the $1 billion that Russia's Ministry of

Atomic Energy was securing in its deal to help Iran build a nuclear reactor at Bushehr.) Putin can be confident that Western criticism of Russian behavior in Chechnya will stop, even though the United States will continue to condemn tactics that result in indiscriminate civilian deaths. Putin will not want Russia isolated in the U.S.-led war on terrorism and will want to use it to settle his own scores. The major constraint is the concern of the Russian military that the United States will develop bases in Central Asia that will become permanent U.S. military staging grounds in the region.

As with earlier periods, even if there is significant cooperation today in the war on terrorism, underlying rivalries will remain, certainly unless and until Russia is truly integrated into Europe. Since the end of the Cold War, the United States—in seeking to extend the European zone of peace and stability eastward or to promote independence for the states of the Caucasus and Central Asia—has pursued objectives such as enlarging NATO or promoting multiple pipelines to export oil from the Caspian. The United States will not abandon these objectives even if it seeks more cooperation from Russia to combat terrorism. Russia meanwhile has pursued economic interests in Iran and China that raise concerns in Washington. What each country has to keep in mind is that the two nations are no longer enemies, and while we may never again see a period like the one that existed in 1992–1993, we can certainly seek something more rewarding than the relationship as it existed at the start of the Bush presidency. In the longer term, only if Russia stays on the democratic path and integrates more fully into Europe will a true partnership between the two countries become a sustained possibility.

Notes

1. For a good overview of the earlier history, see John Lewis Gaddis, *Russia, the Soviet Union, and the United States: An Interpretive History*, 2nd edition (New York: McGraw-Hill, 1990).

2. The best concise discussion of Soviet views remains Coit D. Blacker, "The Kremlin and Détente: Soviet Conceptions, Hopes, and Expectations," in *Managing U.S.-Soviet Rivalry*, ed. Alexander L. George (Boulder, Colo.: Westview Press, 1983), pp. 119–37.

3. A good discussion is Leon V. Sigal, *Hang Separately: Cooperative Security between the United States and Russia, 1985–1994* (New York: Century Foundation, 2000), ch. 2.

4. For more, see James M. Goldgeier and Michael McFaul, "The Liberal Core and the Realist Periphery in Europe," *Perspectives on European Politics and Society*, vol. 2 (June 2001), pp. 1–26.

5. For a further discussion of Kissinger's difficulties, see James M. Goldgeier, "The United States and the Soviet Union: Lessons of Détente," in *Honey and Vinegar: Incentives, Sanctions, and Foreign Policy*, ed. Richard N. Haass and Meghan L. O'Sullivan (Washington, D.C.: Brookings Institution Press, 2000), pp. 120–36; on politics within the Soviet Politburo, see Jack Snyder, "The Gorbachev Revolution: A Waning of Soviet Expansionism?" *International Security*, vol. 12 (Winter 1987/88), pp. 93–131.

6. See Ivo H. Daalder and James M. Goldgeier, "Putting Europe First," *Survival*, vol. 43 (Spring 2001), p. 83.

7. See Derek H. Chollet and James M. Goldgeier, "Missile Defense in Perspective," *Washington Times*, May 22, 2001, p. A19.

Conclusion

16

Russia Rising?

Andrew C. Kuchins

Agreat deal has changed in Russia for the better in the past ten years. Political authority is determined by competitive elections at virtually every level. More than 70 percent of Russia's gross domestic product (GDP) is produced in the private sector. The economy and the society of Russia have been demilitarized to a greater extent than at any time in modern history. Several hundred thousand nongovernmental organizations have emerged to form the core of a growing civil society. The transformation that is taking place in Russian politics, economics, and society has been accompanied by a revolution in foreign and security policy as well. After more than forty years of opposition to the West during the Cold War, Russia has worked with the North Atlantic Treaty Organization (NATO) to bring peace to Yugoslavia and has supported the United States in the war against the Taliban in Afghanistan. Russia has acquiesced to a U.S. military presence in Central Asia as well as in the Caucasus. Russia is actively seeking membership in the World Trade Organization and seeks to integrate more deeply with NATO and the European Union (EU).

Of course there are many dark spots in the picture as well. The war in Chechnya grinds on with no end in sight. Arbitrary arrest and imprisonment of some activists and scholars and the curtailment of media freedom impinge on human and civil rights. Political life has acquired more of a stage-managed quality, and political parties have been stunted in their development. Social services for most of the population have continued their decline and poverty has grown. The overall health of the Russian population has worsened and is a major contributing factor to a deepening demographic crisis. Despite protestations to the contrary, Russian enterprises continue to proliferate nuclear and ballistic missile technologies.

The chapters in this volume address many of the core issues that have shaped Russia's development over the past ten years and suggest possible short-term scenarios along with key factors that will shape the future. This concluding chapter looks further into Russia's future. What will we be saying about Russia twenty or thirty years after the collapse of the Soviet Union? What are the forces that will shape Russia in the next decade or two? Can one make a plausible argument that Russia is rising after an undeniably precipitous fall? Let us stretch our imaginations and get beyond what may or may not be the inscrutable Putin's true intentions, the implications of NATO expansion, and other issues of the day. I should say at the outset that one embarks on such an exercise with much trepidation and humility; after all, in 1982 virtually nobody predicted the Russia that exists today.

The future economic development of Russia is a reasonable place to begin, as success in this area could provide the foundation for increasing the size of both the middle class that is essential to Russia's democratic development as well as the resources that would be allocated to foreign and security policy. Fortunately, the egregious miscalculations that marred estimates of the size of the Soviet economy twenty years ago are most certainly a thing of the past. It is unlikely that present estimates of the Russian economy are nearly as far off the mark and, as such, they provide a more reasonable basis for speculation on the future of Russia's economic performance. For example, in *The Rise and Fall of Great Powers*, Paul Kennedy cited World Bank figures that show the Soviet GDP in 1980 as a little less than 50 percent of the U.S. GDP ($1.2 and $2.6 trillion, respectively). Nineteen years later, in 1999, the World Bank estimated the U.S. GDP at $9.1 trillion and the Russian GDP at $401 billion. Taking into account that Russia is not as large as the Soviet Union, which skews the comparison some, it is hard to believe that even Russia fell that far that fast. It is certain that Russia will not be able to rapidly recover such relative economic power, if indeed it ever had it.

To help us think about how large the Russian economy could be in ten or twenty years, tables 16.1 and 16.2 illustrate World Bank calculations of Russia's GDP and relative position in 1999, as well as projections of possible growth along with comparisons of growth in selected countries.[1] These

Table 16.1 Gross Domestic Products of Russia and Selected Countries, 1999

Rank[a]	Country	GDP	GDP, PPP	Rank in PPP terms
1	United States	9152.1	8867.7	1
2	Japan	4346.9	3151.3	3
3	Germany	2111.9	1949.2	5
4	France	1441.8	1342.2	6
5	United Kingdom	1432.3	1314.6	7
6	Italy	1171.0	1278.1	8
7	China	989.5	4534.9	2
8	Brazil	751.5	1182.0	9
9	Canada	634.9	800.4	12
10	Spain	595.9	712.5	14
11	Mexico	483.7	801.3	11
12	India	447.3	2242.0	4
13	Korea, Rep.	406.9	736.3	13
14	Australia	404.0	466.1	16
15	Russia	401.4	1092.6	10
16	Netherlands	393.7	382.7	19
17	Argentina	283.2	449.1	17
18	Switzerland	258.6	193.9	33
19	Belgium	248.4	260.2	26
20	Sweden	238.7	200.5	32
21	Austria	208.2	203.0	31
22	Turkey	185.7	410.8	18
23	Denmark	174.3	137.8	42

a. Countries listed in order of gross domestic product, not adjusted for purchasing power parity (PPP).
Source: World Bank, *World Development Indicators 2001,* CD-rom (Washington, D.C.: World Bank, 2001).

projections show average growth rates over ten and twenty years for Russia and other leading countries at 3, 5, and 7 percent using 1999 figures at fixed exchange rates.

In the next twenty years, the best-case scenario is for Russia to boast an economy about the size of Brazil or India, depending on their own growth rates. Instead of being less than 5 percent of the U.S. economy, perhaps Russia could grow to 10 percent of the U.S. economy; obviously a far cry from where we thought the Soviet Union was twenty years ago.[2] It will almost certainly not be possible for Russia to catch up with China, although its per capita income will remain substantially higher. Instead of being one-fifth of the size of the German economy, Russia may be one-quarter or one-third, and it may be more than half the size of the economy of France or Great Britain.

Table 16.2 Projected Growth Rates for Selected Countries (GDP in current U.S. $billions)

	10 years[a]			20 years[b]		
	3 percent	5 percent	7 percent	3 percent	5 percent	7 percent
United States	12299.7	14907.8	18003.6	16529.7	24283.2	35415.7
Japan	5841.9	7080.6	8551.0	7851.0	11533.6	16821.1
Germany	2838.2	3440.1	4154.4	3814.3	5603.5	8172.4
China	1329.8	1611.8	1946.5	1787.1	2625.4	3829.1
Brazil	1010.0	1224.1	1478.3	1357.3	1994.0	2908.1
India	601.1	728.6	879.9	807.9	1186.8	1730.9
Russian Federation	539.4	653.8	789.6	725.0	1065.0	1553.3
Turkey	249.6	302.5	365.3	335.4	492.7	718.6
Korea, Rep.	546.8	662.8	800.4	734.9	1079.6	1574.6
Mexico	650.1	787.9	951.5	873.6	1283.4	1871.8

a. Calculated assuming growth of 3, 5, or 7 percent every year for 10 years.
b. Calculated assuming growth of 3, 5, or 7 percent every year for 20 years.
Source: World Bank, *World Development Indicators 2001*, CD-rom (Washington, D.C.: World Bank, 2001).

Rather than languishing in fifteenth place in the world, Russia has a reasonable chance of cracking the top ten world economies in twenty years, but it will be nearly impossible to advance beyond eighth place in that time.

Because military power is derived from economic and technological strength, we can also conclude that it is impossible for Russia to mount the kind of superpower military capacity that it did during the Cold War, even if it so desired. Military expenditures beyond 5 percent of GDP would have a detrimental effect on long-term economic growth, let alone the astronomical level of more than 20 percent allocated for the military during the Soviet period. Thus, Russia will be in no position to balance U.S. power but will likely instead choose to bandwagon with the United States, a strategy that proved extraordinarily successful for Western Europe and Japan during the Cold War and after. Because of its long shared border with China, Russia's relations with China will remain important, but an alliance with China (or any other state) against the United States is unlikely, as it would conflict with Russia's developmental needs. The combination of the need for internal development and the nature of Russia's external security environment will push Russia to further advance a foreign policy orientation of "leaning to one side" (the West), while simultaneously continuing to develop constructive relations with key partners on its periphery, including China, Japan, India, and Iran.

Russia has been extraordinarily sensitive about developments in Central Asia and the Caucasus. This southern periphery is composed of former Soviet republics and has been jealously viewed by Moscow as within its sphere of influence. It would be premature at this point to suggest that Russian acquiescence to the U.S. military presence in Central Asia and Georgia in the wake of September 11 amounts to a real partnership. However, there are a number of indications—including Russia's more flexible position on the legal demarcation of the Caspian Sea and its interest in resolving conflict between Armenia and Azerbaijan—that Russia's zero-sum approach to the Commonwealth of Independent States (CIS) is gradually dissipating. First there is the recognition that Russia does not have the capacity alone to address potential security threats such as terrorism, Islamic extremism, and drug trafficking. The failed state of Afghanistan under the Taliban epitomized the worst-case scenario, but a number of other states in Central Asia and the Caucasus suffer from some of the same pathologies. Moscow views unstable and weak regimes in the region less as an opportunity to exert influence and more as a danger to Russia's interests. This marks a significant shift in Russian foreign policy under Putin. In part this shift can also be traced to the increased importance that Putin gives to economic factors in prioritizing regional interests.

To the east, although many Russians are nervous about the growing power of China, for the next twenty years the greatest danger to Russia would be instability in China. China's diminished capacity to govern effectively could make border management more difficult. We should expect that Russia and Japan will resolve the dispute over the Kuril Islands and sign a peace treaty well before twenty more years pass, closing the book on World War II. This long-awaited agreement would enhance Russia's geopolitical position in Asia as well as encourage more Japanese economic engagement with Russia. It is, of course, not only the dispute over the islands that discourages Japanese investment, but more so the underdeveloped legal and financial infrastructure to protect foreign investors. In the coming years, Russia's greatest challenge in Asia will be to reinvigorate the depressed Russian Far East by creating a more attractive investment climate for Asian business interests. Russia's initial ticket to greater economic integration into Northeast Asia should be energy exports, and the investment required to develop the extraction and pipeline infrastructure will involve multiple partners.

The expansion of the EU eastward will result in greater interaction with Russia whether Europe likes it or not. Europe already is and will continue to be Russia's largest trade partner. Even more so than in Asia, Russia will be an essential energy supplier to Europe. Increased trade with Europe based to a considerable extent on Russian exports of oil and gas, however, does not ensure that Russia will become a fully democratic polity. It is possible that Russia could evolve more as a necessary evil for Europe, much like Saudi Arabia is for the United States. It is possible that Putin's avowed European vocation for Russia may be ephemeral. I am more optimistic on this score, however. Because of Russia's discomfort with overweening U.S. power, concern about its southern periphery, and uncertainty about the durability of partnership with China, Russia will have strong geopolitical as well as economic incentives to solidify ties with Europe. And because of geographic proximity, Europe will have a strong interest in a stable Russia that is more integrated into European economic and political institutions. This logic will encourage steady pressure on Russia to strengthen its market and legal institutions as well as abide by human rights norms.

The prospects that Russia will become a full member of the EU by 2022 are difficult to assess; how effectively integration of the ten future members now on the waiting list proceeds will shed some light on Russia's chances. But we can certainly anticipate that Russia's affiliation with the EU will become much tighter and increasingly institutionalized over time. Russia's future relationship with the main Euro-Atlantic security institution, NATO, is perhaps even harder to predict, since it will depend to a great degree on what role and mission this institution plays in international security issues in the future. It seems that NATO now is evolving more into a political institution with less operational military significance—something the Russians have long advocated. NATO may no longer exist twenty years from now, but if it does, I would venture that Russia will be a full member. A more tantalizing question outside the scope of this study concerns the future of U.S.–European relations. Already on a wide variety of important foreign policy issues such as the Kyoto Protocol, missile defense, Iran and Iraq, and others, the Europeans are in greater agreement with Russia than with the United States.

Over the course of the coming years there will be ample opportunity to turn the rhetoric of U.S.–Russian strategic partnership into reality. The status of the United States as sole superpower is unlikely to change, and it is possible that the distance between the United States and the rest of the world in military capabilities could be even greater. Simply by virtue of its enormous Eurasian geography, Russia will have interests, as it does today, in Europe, the Middle East, the Caspian, Central Asia, South Asia, and East Asia. What appears to be changing now is Russia's inclination and capacity to act positively to enhance regional security. For the past ten years the U.S. security agenda with Russia has been principally defined by negatives: do not proliferate nuclear and ballistic missile technologies; do not compromise the independence of CIS neighbors; do not support international rogues like Milosevic, Saddam Hussein, or others. The terrorist attacks of September 11, 2001, and President Putin's subsequent support for the U.S. military action in Afghanistan have helped us to break this negative paradigm. Certainly our interests will not always coincide, and there will be ups and downs. For example, it will be difficult but important in the near term for Washington and Moscow to resolve long-standing differences over Iran and Iraq. Failure to reach a creative consensus on these countries will imperil any future partnership to constrain proliferation of weapons of mass destruction. But broadly speaking, Russia desires peace and stability to focus attention on domestic recovery, and the United States has the greatest capacity to supply security in the regions most important to Russia on its vast periphery, from East Asia to Central Asia to the Caucasus.

Generational change will greatly influence the Russia of twenty years hence. Recall that both Gorbachev and Yeltsin represented a new generation of Soviet leadership that finished their education and started their professional lives after the death of Stalin. The current Russian leadership is now dominated by "baby-boomers" who were educated and began to work during the decades of stagnation. In twenty years, Russia's political and business elites will be increasingly drawn from those who completed their higher education after the collapse of the Soviet Union. Increasing numbers will have studied in the West, and far larger numbers will travel internationally on a regular basis. They will be computer literate and able to surf the Internet for a cornucopia of information. They will not have personal experience with the literal and figurative walls that separated their parents and grandparents from the rest of the world. The Cold War will only be a topic of history. And with any luck, they will mature in a world in which Russia is recovering and on the rise rather than stagnating or worse. Their career prospects and opportunities for self-fulfillment will be expanding rather than contracting. Since this generation's formative experiences will so differ from those of their predecessors, there will be enormous consequences for Russia that I hope will be broadly positive.

It is too early, however, to draw conclusions about the outlook of the generation that will rule Russia twenty years hence, and it is possible that Russia's equivalent of "generation X" (those born after 1964) will look more like a "lost generation." Much of this generation will have reached the formative years of adolescence during the 1990s, a decade of traumatic societal dislocations. We already know that increasing numbers of people are retreating to drugs and alcohol to assuage psychic pain and despair. The sharing of needles among drug users and the failure of so many to practice safe sex in the face of an HIV epidemic speak not only to ignorance but perhaps more to a profoundly pessimistic view of the future. And while some of the walls of the Soviet period have broken down, new walls have arisen to constrain one's socioeconomic status. In comparison with the Soviet period, students' access to the elite institutions of higher learning is now based more on financial means than on academic merit. There are fewer students from the provinces enrolling in the top institutions in Moscow and St. Petersburg.

Russia remains mired in a demographic crisis. Since it is very difficult to turn around deeply embedded demographic trends, it is virtually certain that the Russian population of 145 million today will be no higher than 135 million, and possibly substantially less, in twenty years. The generation of Russian children and youths of the 1990s is probably more sickly than any since World War II. Most worrisome is the explosion in the number of HIV infections in Russia that, if left unchecked, could approach proportions comparable to those in some parts of Sub-Saharan Africa in a few years. Drug addiction continues to rise and alcohol consumption remains high. Not only will the size of the labor force likely be smaller than today, but also its quality may be further diminished by chronic health problems.

Migration policy may alleviate demographic decline, but growing Asian and Muslim populations may give rise to aggravated social and ethnic tensions. U.S., European, and other international experience of recent decades suggests that growing minority populations can contribute significantly to economic, intellectual, and cultural dynamism. Russia's geography makes it a natural candidate for being a sort of "Eurasian melting pot," and if managed effectively this could be a great help in aiding Russia's recovery. But for Russia to become a net importer rather than exporter of human capital, local conditions must provide for greater prosperity and opportunity. In the Tsarist period, for example, Russia attracted thousands of Germans who contributed a great deal to the prerevolutionary development of Russia. It is certain that in the future, Russia will be more ethnically diverse than it is today, and if it manages to sustain economic growth over the next twenty years it could be an attractive land of opportunity for those on its periphery with less means but plenty of ambition.

One of the most positive developments of the past ten years has been the emergence of a growing middle class. Judyth Twigg in her contribution to this volume estimates that between 10 and 15 percent of the Russian population can qualify as "middle class," and between 5 and 7 percent enjoy Western middle-class standards of living. And despite the dip after the 1998 financial crisis, this number has been growing fairly steadily. Barring another long downturn in the Russian economy, the growth of the middle class will continue. These are the people now buying cars and cell phones and building dachas at record rates, and this is the sector that will be the backbone of any Russian liberal market democracy in the future. Once private property rights are resolved and a real banking sector emerges—developments we can expect long before 2021—these will be the people taking out mortgages, making house payments, and investing retirement funds in domestic and international equities.

The development of a business climate less hostile to small businesses and start-ups will provide more opportunity for a growing middle class and offer greater opportunities for innovation and technological breakthroughs to emerge from Russia in the future. The Russian economy today suffers from endemic corruption, legal deficiencies, and an underdeveloped banking sector. Progress in rectifying these problems would be especially beneficial for small businesses and start-ups. The current Russian economy is dominated by fifteen to twenty large conglomerates that have very close ties to the state as well as, in most cases, large interests in the development of natural resources. Huge *chaebol*-like firms involved in natural resource extraction will certainly be an important feature of Russia's economic landscape in twenty years' time. But Russia's ability to foster a climate more welcoming to small businesses and start-ups would probably make better use of the comparative advantages Russia has in some areas of science, mathematics, and technology. Russia possesses some of the human capital prerequisites to become a significant player in the ongoing high-tech revolution in the coming decades, but it will require breaking from Soviet- and Tsarist-

era economic cultural traditions of state-directed management to fully realize this potential.

The start of a new century holds special significance for Russia since the
twentieth century was in so many ways such a disaster. It was not only the
decade of the 1990s, although the last ten years or so may be likened to a
modern-day "Time of Troubles." Russia began the twentieth century with
status and power comparable to that of other great European powers of the
times, as well as the young United States. We know where Russia finished
the century. Decisions that Russians made during much of the last century
had a tremendous impact not only for Russians but also for Americans and
much of the rest of the world. It has been fashionable in recent years to dismiss Russia as a dysfunctional has-been, a country that does not matter a
great deal anymore. Looking over the thousand-year history of Russia, I
can only conclude that such a view is shortsighted and premature. Decisions
made by this and the next generation of Russians will be highly consequential for all of us, and I hope that this volume has made a modest contribution to our understanding of the scope and significance of the
challenges that were undertaken only slightly more than ten years ago.

Notes

1. The projections use 1999 baseline numbers from the World Bank, *World Development
Indicators 2001* (Washington, D.C.: World Bank, 2001).

2. Three percent is a reasonable average growth rate for the United States because it has been
the average for the last fifty years. Note that prolonged U.S. flat growth would likely mean a
global recession that would constrain the growth of all.

Abbreviations and Acronyms

ABM	Anti-ballistic missile
AIDS	Acquired immune deficiency syndrome
APEC	Asia Pacific Economic Cooperation forum
BEEPS	Business Environment and Enterprise Performance Survey
CFE	Conventional Armed Forces in Europe Treaty
CIS	Commonwealth of Independent States
CPSU	Communist Party of the Soviet Union
CTBT	Comprehensive Test Ban Treaty
CTR	Cooperative threat reduction
CVD	Cardiovascular disease
EAU	Euro–Asian Union
EBRD	European Bank for Reconstruction and Development
EU	European Union
FDI	Foreign direct investment
FSB	Federal Security Service
GDP	Gross domestic product
GKChP	State Committee for the State of Emergency
GNP	Gross national product
HIV	Human immunodeficiency virus
ICBM	Intercontinental ballistic missile
IFOR	Implementation Force
IMF	International Monetary Fund
JCIC	Joint Compliance and Inspection Commission
KGB	Committee for State Security
LDPR	Liberal Democratic Party of Russia
MIRV	Multiple, independently targetable warhead reentry vehicle
NATO	North Atlantic Treaty Organization

NGO	Nongovernmental organization
NIF	National Ignition Facility
NIMBY	Not in my back yard
NMD	National missile defense
NPR	Nuclear posture review
NPT	Nuclear Non-Proliferation Treaty
NTV	Russian television station
PfP	Partnership for Peace
PJC	Permanent Joint Council (of NATO)
PKK	Kurdistan Workers' Party
PLA	People's Liberation Army
PPP	Purchasing power parity
RPPK	Republican People's Party of Kazakhstan
RSFSR	Russian Soviet Federative Socialist Republic
SALT	Strategic Arms Limitation Talks
START	Strategic Arms Reduction Treaty
STD	Sexually transmitted disease
TMD	Theater missile defense
TPC	Temperature per capita
UES	United Energy Systems of Russia
UN	United Nations
USAID	United States Agency for International Development
USSR	Union of Soviet Socialist Republics
WMD	Weapons of mass destruction
WTO	World Trade Organization

Tables and Figures

Tables

Figures

Index

Contributors

Anders Åslund is a senior associate at the Carnegie Endowment for International Peace. He is the author of numerous books and articles on communist economies and post-communist economic transition, including *Building Capitalism: The Transformation of the Former Soviet Bloc* (Cambridge University Press, 2002). He has served as an economic advisor to the Russian government, to the Ukrainian government, and to President Askar Akaev of Kyrgyzstan. He holds a doctorate from Oxford University.

Harley Balzer is associate professor of government and foreign service at Georgetown University, where from 1987 to 2001 he directed the Center for Eurasian, Russian and East European Studies. He has been a fellow at Harvard's Russian Research Center, the MIT Program in Science, Technology and Society, and the U.S. Institute of Peace. Dr. Balzer's research focuses on Russian politics and society in nineteenth- and twentieth-century Russia. His most recent book is *Russia's Missing Middle Class: The Professions in Russian History* (M. E. Sharpe, 1996). He received his Ph.D. in history from the University of Pennsylvania.

Clifford Gaddy is a fellow at the Brookings Institution. He specializes in Russia and its post-Soviet transition economy. He is the author of numerous books and articles on Russia's economic development and recently co-authored with Barry Ickes *Russia's Virtual Economy* (Brookings Institution Press, 2002). Dr. Gaddy received his Ph.D. from Duke University in 1991.

James Goldgeier is an adjunct senior fellow at the Council on Foreign Relations and an associate professor of political science at George Washington University, where he serves as the director of the Institute for European, Russian, and Eurasian Studies. His most recent book is *Not Whether but When: The U.S. Decision to Enlarge NATO* (Brookings Institution, 1999). He received his Ph.D. from the University of California at Berkeley in 1990.

Rose Gottemoeller is a senior associate at the Endowment and holds a joint appointment with the Russian and Eurasian Program and the Global Policy Program. A specialist in arms control issues in Russia and the other former Soviet states, Gottemoeller's research at the Endowment focuses on issues of nuclear security and stability, nonproliferation, and arms control. Before joining the Endowment in October 2000, Ms. Gottemoeller was deputy undersecretary for defense nuclear nonproliferation in the U.S. Department of Energy.

Thomas E. Graham, Jr., is the director for Russian affairs on the U.S. National Security Council, where he moved after serving as associate director of the State Department's Policy Planning Staff. From 1998 to 2001, he was a senior associate in the Russian and Eurasian Program at the Carnegie Endowment for International Peace. Prior to that, Mr. Graham had a long career in the U.S. Foreign Service, in which he had several assignments in the U.S. Embassy in Moscow, including head of the Political/Internal Unit and acting political counselor. Between tours in Moscow, he worked on Russian/Soviet affairs in the State Department and Defense Department. Mr. Graham has a Ph.D. in political science from Harvard University.

Joel Hellman is lead specialist on governance for the Europe and Central Asia region at the World Bank and senior adjunct fellow at the Council on Foreign Relations. Previously he was senior political counselor in the Office of the Chief Economist at the European Bank for Reconstruction and Development (EBRD) and an editor of the EBRD's *Transition Report*. He has also been an assistant professor of political science at Harvard University and Columbia University, and has lectured and published widely on the politics of economic reform, corruption, and governance. Dr. Hellman received his Ph.D. from Columbia University in 1993 and an M.Phil. from Oxford University in 1986.

Stephen Holmes is a professor at New York University School of Law and a nonresident senior associate with the Carnegie Endowment's Democracy and Rule of Law Project. A specialist on constitutional law and legal reform in the former Soviet Union and Eastern Europe, he is researching issues relating to rule-of-law reform in Russia and other post-communist states. His distinguished teaching career includes appointments at Yale University, Harvard University, Princeton University, and the University of Chicago.

Andrew Kuchins has been director of the Carnegie Endowment's Russian and Eurasian Program since May 2000. He came to the Endowment from the Center for International Security and Cooperation at Stanford University, and, from 1993 to 1997, he worked at the John D. and Catherine T. MacArthur Foundation as a senior program officer. He is the co-editor of *Russia and Japan: An Unresolved Dilemma Between Distant Neighbors*. Dr. Kuchins received his Ph.D. in international relations from Johns Hopkins University's Nitze School of Advanced International Studies.

Anatol Lieven, a British journalist, writer, and historian, joined the Carnegie Endowment in March 2000 as senior associate for foreign and security policy in the Russian and Eurasian Program. He was previously editor of *Strategic Comments* and an expert on the former Soviet Union and on aspects of contemporary warfare at the International Institute for Strategic Studies (IISS) in London. Anatol Lieven is author of three books: *Chechnya: Tombstone of Russian Power* (Yale University Press, 1998); *The Baltic Revolution: Estonia, Latvia, Lithuania, and the Path to Independence* (Yale University Press, 1998); and *Ukraine and Russia: A Fraternal Rivalry* (U.S. Institute of Peace, 1999).

Michael McFaul is a senior associate at the Carnegie Endowment for International Peace, the Peter and Helen Bing Research Fellow at the Hoover Institution, and an associate professor of political science at Stanford University. He is a frequent commentator and author on U.S.–Russian relations and domestic politics in Russia. His latest book is *Russia's Unfinished Revolution: From Gorbachev to Putin* (Cornell University Press, 2001). Professor McFaul received his doctorate from Oxford in 1991.

Martha Brill Olcott is a senior associate at the Carnegie Endowment for International Peace. She is also professor of political science emerita at Colgate University. She has written numerous studies on Central Asia and the Caucasus and on ethnic relations in the post-Soviet states, including *Kazakhstan: Unfulfilled Promise* (Carnegie Endowment for International Peace, 2002). She received her doctorate in political science at the University of Chicago.

Lilia Shevtsova is a senior associate at the Carnegie Endowment for International Peace. She is author of a forthcoming book on Putin (Carnegie Endowment for International Peace, 2003), *Gorbachev, Yeltsin, Putin: Political Leadership in Yeltsin's Russia* (Carnegie Endowment for International Peace, 2001), and *Yeltsin's Russia: Myths and Reality* (Carnegie Endowment for International Peace, 1999). She holds a doctorate from the Institute of International Relations and the Academy of Sciences in Moscow.

Dmitri Trenin is deputy director of the Carnegie Moscow Center. He is an expert in military and security issues in the countries of the former Soviet Union and writes frequently on foreign policy issues in Eurasia and between the United States and Russia. His most recent book is *The End of Eurasia* (Carnegie Endowment for International Peace, 2002). From 1972 to 1993, he held various positions in the Soviet and Russian armed forces. Dr. Trenin received his Ph.D. from the Institute of the USA and Canada in Moscow in 1984.

Judyth Twigg is associate professor of political science at Virginia Commonwealth University. She has written numerous articles on Russian health and social policy and co-edited *Russia's Torn Safety Nets: Health and Social Welfare during the Transition* (St. Martin's, 2000). She received her Ph.D. in 1994 from the Massachusetts Institute of Technology.

Carnegie Endowment for International Peace

The Carnegie Endowment is a private, nonprofit organization dedicated to advancing cooperation between nations and promoting active international engagement by the United States. Founded in 1910, its work is nonpartisan and dedicated to achieving practical results.

Through research, publishing, convening, and, on occasion, creating new institutions and international networks, Endowment associates shape fresh policy approaches. Their interests span geographic regions and the relations between governments, business, international organizations, and civil society, focusing on the economic, political, and technological forces driving global change. Through its Carnegie Moscow Center, the Endowment helps to develop a tradition of public policy analysis in the states of the former Soviet Union and to improve relations between Russia and the United States. The Endowment publishes *Foreign Policy*, one of the world's leading magazines of international politics and economics.